# I $EE THE BENEFIT

# AN HR TREASURE CHEST

# I $EE

# THE

# BENEFIT

## AN HR TREASURE CHEST

BY

**James J. McSweeney**

**Comprehensive Benefit Services, Inc.**

USA

# I $ee The Benefit

## An HR Treasure Chest

### Copyright © 2012

### by James J. McSweeney

I See The Benefit was developed in conjunction with Jay Lumbert.

This book may be ordered through booksellers everywhere, or by contacting:

Comprehensive Benefit Services, Inc.

www.askcip.com    admin@askcip.com

ISBN -13:978-0-9848683-0-8 (pbk)

ISBN - 13:978-0-9848683-1-5 (ebk)

Printed in the United States of America

I would like to dedicate this book to my family:

To my wife Debbie. Thank you for all your love and support. None of this would have been possible without you. I hope you see the benefit.

To my children, Shannon, Bobby and Olivia. Thank you for filling my heart with pride and joy.

To my parents, Joe and Susan. Thank you for constantly showing me the importance of hard work and commitment.

To my in-laws, Bob and Judy. Thank you for being so supportive and selfless.

## Author's Note:

With 25 years of experience in the employee benefits arena, I have had the opportunity to work with some amazing entrepreneurs. I wanted to be able to share some of the insights and experiences I have gained from these individuals on how they have built successful companies by investing in human resources. My experience has been that the companies that have solid HR practices are usually the ones that are the most successful. Despite this, the human resource department in many companies is often underutilized and undervalued. The analogy that comes to mind is that you can have a beautiful house, but if it doesn't have a solid foundation, it will inevitably collapse. This holds true for any company that doesn't have a commitment to their most valuable resource: their employees.

I See the Benefit covers a wide range of HR protocols that are essential at different life stages of a business. I hope that this book provides a guide to help you understand and be aware of the core and peripheral HR issues that are critical in making your business an ongoing success.

I have had the privilege of working with some amazing and committed professionals. Without the following people, I don't know if we would have had the success that we have experienced: Bob McGowan, Danielle Harrington, Sandy McQuade, Cheryl Guiry, Kelly Holland, Gregg Semprucci, Jim Toohey, Andy Ross, Larry Ragland, Kathryn Monteiro, Cheryl Cote, Stacy Constantino, Jim Gordon, Jay Lumbert, Karin Brosnahan and many others over the years that have supported and guided me. Thank you for caring.

# CONTENTS

## PART ONE

## THE BIG PICTURE

# PART TWO

# PEOPLE

# Part Three

# Attract & Retain

# Part Four

# Performance Management

# PART FIVE

# BENEFITS MANAGEMENT

# PART SIX

# THE BENEFITS LANDSCAPE

# PART SEVEN

# RETIREMENT PLANS

# PART EIGHT

# NON-QUALIFIED PLANS

# PART NINE

# QUALIFIED & NON-QUALIFIED SUMMARY

# PART TEN

# BUSINESS OWNER PLANNING

- Death

    o   Buy-Sell Agreement

## PART ELEVEN

# COMPLIANCE & REPORTING

# SUMMARY

Form 5500
Group Term Life Insurance Imputed Income
Taxability Of Disability Benefits
Domestic Partner / Same Sex Marriage (Income Tax Treatment)

# CONTENTS

87 ## SECTION TWO
## STATE COMPLIANCE REQUIREMENTS (MASSACHUSETTS)

## 88 SECTION THREE      361
## RETIREMENT PLANS & DEFERRED COMPENSATION

# PART THIRTEEN

# SAFETY & LOSS CONTROL

# PART FOURTEEN

# HR RESOURCES

- Associations & Organizations

- Websites

- Publications

# PART FIFTEEN

# SUMMARY

# I $EE the BENEFIT

## PLEASE NOTE:

YOU CAN FIND MORE DETAILED IN-
FORMATION, INCLUDING REGULATORY
UPDATES AT THE FOLLOWING WEBSITE
ADDRESS:

WWW.ASKCIP.COM

# INTRODUCTION

If you are like most small to medium sized business managers you want to:

- Save Time
- Save Money
- Make Money
- Get Things Done

I am going to try to help you do that.

I understand that you are overwhelmed with your HR duties. Unlike large companies, you can't assign specialists to handle each of the critical functions — hiring, training, firing, health and retirement benefits, COBRA, payroll, tax structuring, etc. You can't attend seminar after seminar to learn how to do things most effectively. You don't have time to earn a Master's Degree in Human Resources. You don't have a team to deal with all of the government regulations that can cause problems for a business — sexual harassment training, OSHA regulations, ERISA filings, etc. You do all this yourself, or with just a small group of key employees.

What you *do* have is experience. Experience is far more important than anything learned from a book or a seminar. It is a well-worn path that leads to your HR destination.

Unfortunately, a path may not be the most direct way to get there. Sometimes a road works better.

The purpose of this book is to be your road. Stay on your path, but use the road where your path gets too rough and slow.

This book will not teach you how to do your job; you do it better than I ever could. You helped build the company. You are the one fighting the competition. You know your product or service better than anyone else. You know the marketplace and you know your people. This book will teach you how to do your job more effectively.

## A TEMPLATE

The purpose of this book is to give you an easy-to-follow HR template, a reference manual that will save you time and make more money. It is designed to give quick access to important information that will help you conduct your business more effectively. It hits the highlights, the key factors to improve your performance in the shortest time, with the least amount of effort. You can read it from cover-to-cover, or you can pinpoint specific areas of opportunity and focus your attention there.

## THE 80/20 ZONE

The Pareto Principal tells us that we can accomplish 80% of our goals in 20% of our time. Some argue that this ratio has grown to 90/10. Incremental gains beyond the efficient point come at a steep cost, in both time and resources.

Small to mid-sized company managers are forced to live within the boundaries of the Pareto Principal. They wear so many hats that they must achieve maximum efficiency in everything they do. As a result, most of what gets accomplished must take place within this 80/20 Zone. We are forced to do more with less.

With this in mind, I will try to give you the most useful information in a manner that allows you to minimize the time it takes to accomplish your most important HR functions. If you have critical needs in any one area, you can drill down and learn more.

I have included an *Employer Checklist* — to outline the areas where a little bit of your effort can bring about the most results.

## BUSINESS DARWINISM

Herbert Spencer coined the phrase, "survival of the fittest," after reading Charles Darwin's book, *On the Origin of Species.* Using this quote, Spencer drew parallels between his own *economic* theories and Darwin's *biological* ones.

Darwin focused upon animals. Spencer focused on business and economics. Both centered their studies on the power of adaptation and evolution. *If we don't evolve, we become extinct.*

Welcome to the jungle. My goal is to help you manage your business evolution and thrive in today's ultra-competitive world.

### Embrace Evolution

Virtually every business sector is evolving rapidly. Some of this evolution comes from within — innovation. If we innovate, we thrive.

Most business evolution is out of our control; it is literally forced upon us. Some evolution occurs through the innovation of competitors within our own industry. Some occurs though innovation in other business areas. Some comes through economic conditions. Still more is thrust upon us by regulations and other outside forces.

Technology is moving at an increasingly rapid pace. Laws keep changing, usually not for the better. Regulations and restrictions appear without warning. Social trends are dramatically altering where and how we work. Some costs are growing faster than revenues. Many of these challenging issues fall squarely upon the shoulders of the HR manager.

An HR manager must develop a business framework that reacts positively to change, but also maximizes profitability in every area possible.

## HR: THE FRONT LINE OF PROFITABILITY

For many years, human resources managers were second-tier players at the executive conference table. Hiring employees was considered a mere numbers game. Employee benefits were easy to manage. Training needs were minimal. Federal laws wouldn't send us to court, jail, or kill our business.

The changing workplace and the soaring cost of benefits have now put human resources near the head of the executive table. Decisions made at the HR level have a dramatic impact on the profitability and the viability of every company. This presents a challenge to many small to mid-sized businesses, because smaller companies don't have the manpower of larger corporations, or specific, concentrated training in most of these areas.

I hope that his book will give you the tools you need to manage your HR duties most efficiently.

## COMPANY CULTURE

Every company has a personality, a dominant corporate culture. A technology firm develops an entirely different culture than a law firm, a government organization or a factory. Even companies within the same industry can be very different from one another.

**Reason 1.** A big determinant of corporate culture is the set of skills required to accomplish company goals. An artist may not thrive as a factory worker. A factory line worker might not enjoy working at a literary magazine.

**When you hire and train your employees, you must be keenly aware of the demands and requirements of your industry, as well as your specific company.** We will spend some time working on how to determine the skill sets most appropriate for your company a little bit later in this book.

**Reason 2.** The other area that affects corporate culture is the environment that management creates. If a company builds an on-site daycare center, it may find more young mothers in its workforce. If a company requires suits and ties, certain people may opt out. If you monitor every phone conversation and email transmission, or test for drugs, certain employee types may choose to work elsewhere. If you encourage daily prayer meetings or *rah rah* cheering sessions, some people may just not fit in.

Management-created *personality* starts with the CEO and works down to the basic rank and file. Large companies develop mini-cultures within departments or locations. They are able to support a diverse corporate culture with relative ease.

With smaller companies, diversity tends to bend at the edges, with employees conforming to the dominant culture, as set by its leaders. The smaller the company, the more personalities tend to mirror that of its CEO.

**If you are the one person who can bend a company, you must look at yourself in the mirror and determine if the personality *you* are setting for *your* company is the right one, or if it can be improved.**

If you answer to the CEO, you probably adjust your behavior to become more in line with him or her.

As the HR director, you may actually need to help your CEO change (evolve) for the good of the company. You may have to evolve yourself.

### Diversity

Too much conformity to a CEO's viewpoint, too many "yes men" and "yes women," can prevent the constant innovation and evolution that is often essential in business today.

If you are the CEO, or work in a company where the CEO is a dominant personality, you must remain hyper-vigilant to make sure that the CEO's shadow does not stunt the growth of your organization.

Diversity is important and it should be encouraged. Large companies use it to enormous advantage, building mini-cultures within their various departments.

Small to mid-sized businesses usually don't have the luxury of creating diverse corporate cultures. This can become a problem if not managed properly.

With fewer employees, too much diversity can create conflict and inefficiencies.

Small businesses must cultivate team members that work *together* toward common goals.

**The challenge for small business HR is to hire (and train) team members who fit the physical and emotional criteria that are critical to thriving in specific jobs.**

You must hire people who will enjoy the culture created by management. Employees must be diverse enough, and independent enough, to allow innovation to thrive, without creating corporate conflict and disharmony.

You must determine the best people to employ, what you want to teach them, and the behaviors you want to encourage and reward. To do this most effectively, you must fully understand your corporate culture. You must determine the specific skill sets needed to accomplish each job. You must then find people that fill these requirements and also work well within your unique company culture.

My goal is to help you do that.

# EMPLOYER CHECKLIST

In order to maximize the value of your time, I have included an employer checklist for you to use with this book. As you read through each chapter, refer to the checklist and complete as many items as you can.

No one person can do everything. Few private companies have the resources to employ every HR concept to its fullest potential.

If you spend your time addressing the issues that make the most impact, you can accomplish 80% of your needs with 20% of your time.

This list outlines the key concepts that HR professionals have found most effective for improving business productivity, as well as tools that can help you implement your HR practice efficiently.

Some of the items on this list are covered in detail. Others receive less attention. I had to make concessions, using my own80/20, as I tried to manage the size of this book. If you need further help, there are resources available. Some are noted throughout the book.

The checklist begins by addressing the fundamentals that should provide the foundation for *every* business. If you master the fundamentals, you are on your way toward excellence. Don't ignore them.

Keep your checklist in a three-ring binder, or its computer equivalent, so you can refer to it at any time. Each item on the list should have its own tab in this binder. As you address an issue, put your work in the binder. This will keep you focused and efficient.

## EMPLOYER CHECKLIST

Mission Statement
Darwinism – How Do You Compete?
Define Your Corporate Culture – What makes you great?
Organizational Hierarchy Chart – Position and Duties
Competency Models
Skills Inventory
Build Employee Templates
Job Descriptions
Creating a Hiring Framework

Make People Great
Training Plan
Your Communication Policy
Compliance Checklist
Interview Questions
Off-Limits Question Form
Blank Interview Evaluation Form
Candidate Evaluation
Candidate Rating
Reference Check Letter
Employment Inquiry Release
Consent to Criminal Background Check
Background Check Permission
Consumer Report Disclosure
Fair Credit Reporting Act Rights
Receipt Confirmation For Fair Credit Reporting Act
Disclosure Of Adverse Action Based Upon Fair Credit
Offer Letter
Rejection Letter
Employment Agreement
Employee Review Sheet (After Orientation)
Policy & Procedures Manual
Team Checklist
Sample Training Program
Employee Survey For Training
Employee Training Assessment Form
Compensation Philosophy Form
Wage & Salary Data As Percentage Of Revenues By Industry
Job Rating Checklist
Performance Evaluation Meeting.

List Every Job:
- Relate job to Mission
- Indispensable?
- Difficulty?
- Generate Revenue?
- Other factors?

# Chapter One
## HR
## The Big Picture

## MISSION STATEMENT

**Every company should have a mission statement.** This is your company's reason for being. It outlines the fundamental goals of your organization — in a way that all employees can understand.

Every employee should know your mission statement by heart, because it is the prime directive of employment with your company.

A mission statement shouldn't be long. It should be concise and to the point. For example, my company's mission statement reads as follows: "To provide innovative HR and benefit solutions with the highest quality service."

If you do not have a mission statement for your company, then you need to put it at the top of your priorities list. It is that important.

Here are a few examples of concise mission statements for major companies:

- 3M - "To solve unsolved problems innovatively."
- Mary Kay Cosmetics - "To give unlimited opportunity to women."
- Merck - "To preserve and improve human life."
- Wal-Mart - "To give ordinary folk the chance to buy the same thing as rich people."
- Walt Disney - "To make people happy."
- CIP - "To provide innovative HR and benefit solutions with the highest quality service."

## CORE VALUES & PRINCIPLES

Mission statements should be followed by a list of core values & principles which further refine the mission. For example, Walt Disney includes the following:

- No cynicism
- Nurturing and promulgation of "wholesome American values"
- Creativity, dreams and imagination
- Fanatical attention to consistency and detail
- Preservation and control of the Disney "magic"

Every employee at Disney understands that the prime directive of the company is to make people happy.

The mission for Starbucks Coffee is *to inspire and nurture the human spirit – one person, one cup and one neighborhood at a time.*

Starbuck's mission statement is followed by a set of core principles that are easy to understand and communicate to employees and deliver to customers. These can be found at

http://www.starbucks.com/about-us/company-information/mission-statement.

# REVIEW YOUR MISSION STATEMENT

What is your mission statement? Is it simple and powerful enough for every employee to understand and internalize? Does it help you drive the type of organization you wish to become? If not, you need to make one now. Get your top people in a room for lunch one day and discuss the most important goals and features of your company.

Once you have an appropriate mission statement, put it on a clear coated business card and make sure that each employee carries one at all times.

If you would like to learn more about mission statements, I recommend the following website: www.businessplans.org.

# Chapter Two
## HR
### The Big Picture

## BUILD AN EMPLOYEE TEMPLATE

It is not enough to hire good people. A business needs to hire the right people. This begins with understanding the specific needs of your company culture, as well as your own personal bias.

We often want to hire people "just like us." This creates problems. Unless you are hiring someone for *your* job, the people best for positions in your company probably won't be just like you.

Clones are copies. A copy is never as good as the original. Make sure that you hire people with the proper skill set, values and attitude for the position and your company.

### SKILL SET

Once you define your dominant corporate culture, you will have a better idea of what types of people will fit best within your organization, and how they will blend together to support each other.

### DEFINED ROLES

You must create clearly defined roles for each position. Each role will demand a specific skill-set, which should be built into the job description (discussed later) for each position. This begins with clear definitions of the **core competencies** needed for each role. In some cases, you will have a good idea what these might be. In others, you must rely on your employees or advisors to create the template for each key role within your company. Send out an email or letter.

Ask each employee to tell you the key functions of their job. You will be surprised by many of the responses. This also communicates to employees that you are listening to their needs.

The following is a simple employee template that might be used with a firm that sells insurance and investments on a retail level. It starts by listing the attributes that are important to the dominant corporate culture. It continues with the attributes that are important for the job itself.

# EMPLOYEE TEMPLATE EXAMPLE:
## *INSURANCE & INVESTMENTS*

### DOMINANT CORPORATE CULTURE PREFERENCES

- Honest
- Highly Ethical
- Friendly
- Embrace Improvement
- Willingness to Accept Constructive Criticism
- Comfortable in Business Attire
- Respectful of Traditions
- Family is Important
- Desire for Knowledge

### JOB SPECIFIC: SALES

- Tenacious
- Attention to Detail
- Customer is King
- Good Organizational Skills
- Experience Selling Insurance & Investments
- Core Competencies (PowerPoint, Contact Manager, Spreadsheets)
- Willingness to Learn (Our way)

Think about your own business and try to determine the elements that define your dominant corporate culture. These are the things that will keep the members of your organization working effectively. For each specific job, you must determine the attributes that lead to the successful fulfillment of its duties. Use these attributes to develop a useful template for every position in your company.

# Chapter Three
## HR
### The Big Picture

# RECRUIT EVERYWHERE

Recruiting is expensive — in both time and money. Most smaller businesses don't have the resources to maintain full-time human resources personnel, or hire outside consultants to execute this important function. The person doing the hiring may also be the CEO, the sales manager, or the CFO.

Hiring new personnel can be seen as an unwanted diversion from the "essential" duties of the recruiter's other jobs. Because of this, many executives take short-cuts. Executives interview a couple of candidates, and then hire one. They hire a friend's child or the friend of a friend. In doing so, they sacrifice one of the most powerful tools in business productivity — the right employees.

**Taking extra time to hire the right person at first can save enormous amounts of time (and money) in the future.**

Hiring well makes for a successful company. Think of it as laying a proper foundation before building a home. If a home's foundation is weak, the home can't be structurally sound. If the foundation is strong, the home can be made strong. The same holds true in business. If you hire correctly, your business your business foundation will be strong, and your business can be made strong.

When you have few choices while filling positions within your company, you will hire mediocrity. A large talent pool will give you a strong employee foundation. This is why it is important to recruit **everywhere**. Use every available outlet that you can find. Here are some (but not all) of the places you may find good potential employees:

- Recruit from within
- Employee referrals
- Classified ads
- Internet job boards (Monster, CareerBuilder, etc.)
- Recruiters
- On-campus recruiting
- Open houses
- Job fairs
- Professional associations
- Government employment services
- Your own website

# Chapter Four
## _____HR_____
## The Big Picture

# ATTRACT & RETAIN

With small and mid-sized businesses, every dollar counts. One of the most efficient uses of capital is to make sure that you **attract** the **right** people and **keep** them.

While this sounds very basic, putting this into practice is far from basic. Attracting and retain employees requires a good deal of conscious thought and continual attention to critical details.

## ATTRACT

Other than a salary, what is it that you offer to prospective employees?

- Have you taken as much time creating your "presentation" to prospective employees as you have with the presentation that you give to prospective customers?

- Have you framed your company in the best possible (but still accurate) light?

- Have you created a persuasive *value proposition* that will make the most desirable candidates want to give serious consideration to your company?

Unfortunately, many HR executives with private companies do

not understand the critical nature of "selling" their company to prospective employees, in the same way that they sell to prospective clients and customers.

You need to think of the hiring process as one where you:

- Attract enough prospective employees to consider working for your company.

- Evaluate appropriate and attractive candidates.

- Sell them on the idea that your company is the best place to fulfill their dreams.

Top candidates often have choices of where to work. You don't want to lose the best ones. You want the best candidates to work for you. This takes planning.

Take a look at the "careers" section on the website for any major company. On that site, you will see that company's value proposition on full display — with videos, brochures, testimonials and a list of benefits.

Big companies understand that efficiency and profitability begin with hiring the best employees. They sell the benefits of their company to prospective employees, long before they have entered the company door.

When you set out to hire someone, you must convince them that your company is a great place to work. This should be a well-thought-out process, not simply a statement like, "this is a great place to work" during an interview.

## RETAIN

Once you have hired good employees, you need to retain them. After all the expense of hiring and training, why would you want to lose a good employee? You don't. You can't afford it.

Paying competitive salaries is just the start of a good employee retention program. Many other factors should contribute to making sure that your employees remain productive members of your work-force. Some of these require significant expenditures, such as health insurance. Others, like making employees feel appreciated, can come at a far lower cost. Sometimes all it takes is a little praise or recognition to keep an employee happy and content with your company.

Make liberal use of the inexpensive ways to keep employee morale and productivity high. I explain the process in the Attract & Retain section of this book.

## Chapter Five
## _____HR_____
## The Big Picture

# CREATE JOB DESCRIPTIONS

Every company should have job descriptions for each role within the organization. Job descriptions keep employees on task. They prioritize functions. They allow for effective performance evaluation and set standards that must be met or exceeded.

Job descriptions should be **written** and **specific**. Every employee should know their own job description by heart.

Specific job descriptions help in other ways:

- They help with successful recruiting, because prospective employees want to know their roles.

- They increase productivity and profitability. Employees who understand their specific duties will perform more efficiently.

- They allow managers to hold employees accountable and provide a tool for improving performance.

- They avoid duplication of tasks, and keep employees focused on what they _need_ to do, not what they may _want_ to do.

## Chapter Six
## HR
### The Big Picture

# TRAIN TO BE GREAT

If you have ever worked for a large employer, you have been exposed to training programs. The bigger the company, the bigger they are on training.

Ask yourself this: Do large companies train because they are big? Or, are they big because they train?

Too many companies ignore the critical nature of ongoing training. Too many new employees only get only a quick lesson on the essential skills of their job. Too many existing employees are left alone, causing their skills to rust like tools left out in the rain.

Every company needs to train for greatness. This means having an internal training program for each job in your company. It means encouraging employees to utilize outside resources to improve their skills and learn new things.

There is an old business adage that you always need to "sharpen the saw." If you have ever cut wood, or a Thanksgiving turkey, you know what I mean. A dull blade doesn't cut very well. A sharpened blade makes the work easy. You want to make your employees' lives easy — not hard. Training will do that.

# Chapter Seven
## HR
## The Big Picture

# SUCCESSFUL CORPORATE CULTURE

Every successful organization has a dominant personality. IBM became famous for its blue suits. Apple employees work without ties, including their CEO. FBI field agents wear aviator sunglasses.

A company's culture is initially forged by its management team. This culture then takes on a life of its own, shaping employees in an ever-changing way.

Within large companies, there are many sub-cultures. Salespeople are different than the accounting staff, who are different than those in IT. Even so, successful organizations do maintain a dominant theme throughout the company. Just read their mission statements.

Managers in smaller, private businesses must give serious thought to the dominant culture they wish to have in their company.

What are the dominant traits that will make *your* company great?

Write your company's dominant traits out like the Ten Commandments. These traits help form the foundation of your company.

For example:

Technology companies must constantly innovate. Therefore, the dominant culture of a technology company must encourage creativity, not stifle it. Large technology companies are famous for their playrooms, where employees can go at any time to "clear their heads" and remain productive.

A contracting company does not have the same requirements as a technology company. If a plumber takes two hours to play video games in the middle of the day, money is lost.

Once you understand the corporate culture that gives your company its best chance to thrive, you need to do everything you can to nurture that culture. Make your company a great place to work, by catering to the needs of your culture. Advocate for your employees. Give them as many options as you can.

If you employ a lot of young working mothers, make accommodations that help them manage the challenges of work and motherhood. Flex hours or a daycare center (perhaps shared with other close-by employers) might help improve productivity.

If you employ a lot of single men and women, perhaps an after-hours bowling league or softball team can help maintain good communication, teamwork, and productivity within your company.

Think of what you can do to enhance the lives of your employees — making your company a great place to work.

## Chapter Eight
## _____HR_____
## The Big Picture

# ENCOURAGE EXCELLENCE AND HIGH PERFORMANCE

If you have ever stood at the counter of any McDonalds restaurant, you have seen a picture of the "Employee of the Month." The picture is never one of the franchise-owner, but one of a fry cook or a counter worker.

McDonalds' management is famous for understanding that the job is *not* the person. Great people often work in not-so-great jobs.

McDonalds' managers also understand that ***every job is important to the company***. McDonalds values excellence, regardless of where that excellence occurs.

Many a fry cook has graduated to "Hamburger U" and become a millionaire franchise owner. Many a Fortune 500 CEO once repeated the words, "Would you like fries with that?"

In your management role, you must learn to value people in a manner that is not based upon their job classification. You must view every employee as a valued person and encourage them to achieve to the best of *their* abilities.

Every person wants to feel appreciated. Every employee wants to feel needed. Every individual wants to improve their station in life, regardless of where they start.

Employees work harder and more efficiently when they feel that management appreciates what they do.

If you drive along the highway, you will see dozens of bumper stickers saying things like: *My child is Student of the Month*, or *Proud Parent of a Boy/Girl Scout*, or *I ♥ my Soccer/Football/Hockey Player*, or *Have You Hugged Your Child Today?* The list is endless, and changes with our stages in life. It graduates from honor student to college stickers and armed forces stickers.

Successful companies do the same for their employees. They make them feel appreciated. This makes them better workers, which makes for a better company.

Successful companies encourage excellence. They promote from within. Successful companies reward initiative — emotionally and financially. Employees who receive rewards for excellence will achieve it. Those who feel that their work goes unnoticed will perform poorly.

So, make your place of work one of excellence.

## Chapter Nine
## HR
_____
## The Big Picture

# KNOW THE LAWS

# BE PROACTIVE

Nothing can ruin your business faster than breaking the law.

Today's regulations are so complex that it is difficult to keep abreast of them. We routinely break the rules laid out by the regulating agencies without even knowing it.

Minor laws may be broken with relative impunity. Breaking major laws, like not paying your taxes, may send you to jail. Breaking others, like asking the wrong question in an interview, may cause embarrassment, get you fined, or result in a lawsuit.

The challenge for today's small or mid-sized business is to:

1. Understand all of the laws; and

2. Put a system into place that keeps the business in compliance and out of trouble.

Many regulations are a nuisance. But they exist for serious reasons, with big teeth to see that you obey them. In the compliance section, I will outline many of the major laws, and highlight the key regulations you need to understand about them.

Don't ignore regulations. They won't go away. Learn how to manage them on your own, or hire someone to do that for you.

**Chapter Ten**
## HR
**The Big Picture**

# HARNESS TECHNOLOGY

If you are going to thrive in today's business world, you should make technology into your new best friend. By embracing technology wisely, you will enhance productivity. It will save you time. It will make you money. This does *not* mean that you should routinely purchase all of the latest technology. Know *what* you are getting and *why* it makes good economic sense.

## EXPENSE

Executives in every business are challenged with the expense of new technology. These expenses come in two forms — money and time.

Implementing certain technologies requires significant *capital* outlay. Implementing others requires enormous amounts of *time* in retraining an organization. Some technologies take both. You will need to evaluate the costs versus the benefits of *every* technological decision.

Many productive technologies require little expense. Using all of the features of a Blackberry is a good example. Electronic email and texting is a no-brainer. Businesses integrate free technologies such as Twitter, YouTube or Facebook with their websites and advertising campaigns.

Too many small businesses fail to put these inexpensive technologies to good use, let alone the costly ones. This leads to lost opportunities, lower profits and ultimately shutting the doors.

## COMFORT ZONE

We have all had the experience of being with a group of people near the cold waters of the ocean, a lake or a pool. Some of us jump right in to get beyond the initial shock. Some of us wade slowly into the water, marshaling our nerve to take that final dive once the water reaches our waist. Some of us decide that the water is just too cold. We take a pass and remain outside; we take the safer, more comfortable route.

## JUMP IN

To be successful in business, we cannot always do what is safe and comfortable. Sometimes we must jump right into the water, whether we want to or not.

## EMBRACE TECHNOLOGY

Don't be afraid to step out of your technological shell. Embrace the new world of business. Try new things and demand them of others. Remember — business is survival of the fittest. You need to adapt to the changing technological world. It won't slow down for you.

# Chapter Eleven
## HR
## The Big Picture

# COMMUNICATE EFFECTIVELY

Information is the lifeblood of any business. Conveying important information requires effective communication.

Effective communication takes many forms. It can come in the form of individual face-to-face meetings, large or small meetings, emails, bulletins, your website, daily briefings, etc.

The more information you share with your employees, the more they will share your vision and embrace your culture.

Communication should include such items as:

- Your mission statement

- Your short and long-term business strategies

- Sales figures

- Competitor stats

- Challenges and opportunities in the marketplace

- Employee surveys

- An electronic (or manual) suggestion box

As you share information with your employees, they will share information with *you*. Make sure that you listen to what they say. Acknowledge good ideas and suggestions with regularity. You might even find your Employee of the Month in your suggestion box.

# Chapter Twelve
## HR
## The Big Picture

# EVOLVE CONSTANTLY
# MANAGE CHANGE

There is an old saying that goes like this: "As long as you're green, you're growing. As soon as you're ripe, you begin to rot."

To remain competitive, a business must evolve. Constantly. If you don't, you run the risk of being left behind on the business highway, fluttering into the wind like an old dandelion.

Some of your changes will be driven by the business marketplace — by what your competitors do, or what technologies evolve. Others will be driven socially. Some changes will radically affect the core of your business model, while others will evolve over time, just as the society slowly morphs around us.

It is critical that you build a corporate culture that accepts change as normal. You must embrace the natural evolution of business. You must think proactively, and learn to anticipate change, not simply react to it. This way, you won't waste time making changes that you must later undo.

## PLAN YOUR CHANGES

Don't make changes in a knee-jerk fashion, just because you read about something in an article, or an employee makes a demand. While you must continually evolve, you don't want to make changes that you must reverse a month later. Take your time. Think things through. Commit to the change and then do it.

# Chapter Thirteen
## _____HR_____
## The Big Picture

# ORGANIZE

This may seem like an odd topic to include in an HR book, but good organization is essential in all phases of business.

Potential employees will be turned off by an unorganized interview, just as they will be impressed by an orderly interview process. Existing employees will be more efficient when their tasks are clearly defined and an organizational infrastructure is in place to help them maximize their time.

Organizational consultants tell us that the average employee can lose up to one full week of productivity per year, simply by looking for things that are lost or out of place.

I have tried to structure this book in a way to help you organize your business around the key HR issues — with the least amount of time and effort on your part.

There may be topics you need to address in more depth than I cover in this book, or details I have skipped as I limited the scope of this book along the lines of 80/20. I give references to other sources, but you should always be on the lookout for ways to improve your organizational skills.

# Chapter Fourteen
## HR
### People

# BUILDING A STAFF

As a general rule of thumb, a productive employee represents $50,000 to $100,000 in value to a company. There are many exceptions to this rule, but a profitable business with fifty employees could be worth about $5,000,000. Five employees might be worth a quarter million; a hundred employees could be worth ten million.

What sort of attention would you give to a $100,000 piano? How well would you protect a piece of jewelry worth fifty or a hundred grand? This is the kind of value that you are managing with every employee in your company.

## EACH PIECE HAS VALUE

The effectiveness of your staff, and the value of your company, is entirely dependent upon how well you put the pieces together. Before you hire a staff, you must have a clear idea of the role each person must play within your organization.

Look at your hierarchy chart. If you don't have one, make one. Every essential function/position in your company should be listed on this chart. Put your company CEO (or chairman) at the top and work down from there. Executives that are under the direction of the CEO should be in the second tier of your chart, and so on. You should detail the personality traits and skill set needed for each position in your company. This information is derived from your competency models.

When you hire a new employee, that employee's traits and skills should match the attributes detailed in your chart. At times, you may need to adjust employee functions based upon the individual characteristics of your existing and prospective employees. In other words, you need to hire people based upon the specific needs of the company, not the specifications of each job. The specifications of each job must be modified based upon your personnel. Remember, you must continually adapt for your business to thrive.

Small employers often fudge this process. They hire each person in the same way. They don't adjust the job descriptions based upon their existing or prospective talent pool.

Imagine a professional football coach that keeps his offensive players on the field to play defense. Imagine Tom Brady trying to cover a wide receiver. Brady throws the ball better than anyone. If you ask him to run fast, only bad things will happen.

You need to manage the talent on your business roster in much the same way. Hiring all employees to the same criteria won't win you many games. You won't stay in business for long.

## COMPETENCY MODELS

The best way to become more efficient at hiring and managing is to build Competency Models. Your models should be based upon the specific skill set and personality traits that are needed for superior performance in each role within your company.

# HOW TO BUILD
# A COMPETENCY MODEL

Spend some time with your staff, particularly your top performers.

- Ask them what makes them successful.

- Have them detail the specific skill set they need to perform their job well.

- Make an inventory of each top performer's personality traits.

    o This includes their work ethic, their way of dealing with others and their value system.

Speak with your customers. Ask them about the service they are receiving from your company.

- What is it they like?

- What could be improved?

- Who do they like working with the most?

- Who do they dislike?

You will be amazed at the responses you receive, and it will help you with your staffing decisions.

You should create a current **SKILLS INVENTORY** for your company. This is a list of the combined attributes that exist within your organization. This includes the experience, credentials and the skill sets of each of your employees. You may have much of this information in your head, or within each individual personnel file. If you compile a combined skills inventory, you will have a good idea of what you've already *got*. This will help you determine what you *need*.

### Employee Skills Questionnaire

Employees know the skills that are required to accomplish each job in a company. Create a simple employee questionnaire and send it out to your employees. It might look like this:

We would like to improve your experience in working with our company. We are seeking to evaluate the skills that are required for each job. This will help us understand your needs and develop new training. It will also help us evaluate employees for evolving and expanding roles within the company. Would you please describe:

- Your role in the company.
- Your educational background.
- What tests you have taken.
- Your licenses & credentials.
- Your prior training.
- Your experience — within our company and with others.
- Your skills.
- Your areas of knowledge.

Please return this form to _____. Your responses will be helpful, as we strive to compete in today's challenging business climate.

Take this information and use it to help build a framework for every key role in your company.

# Chapter Fifteen
## HR
### People

# HOW TO HIRE

Private businesses cannot afford to hire the wrong people. It's that simple. One or two bad hires can hold a company back for years. Therefore, it is critical that you plan your hires well in advance, and give careful thought to far more than the "job" itself.

Look back to your Employer Checklist. By now, you should have addressed the following:

Mission Statement
Darwinism – How Do You Compete?
Define Your Corporate Culture – What makes you great?
Organizational Hierarchy Chart – Position and Duties
Competency Models
Skills Inventory
Build Employee Templates
Job Descriptions

You have focused your company's mission to a few short sentences. You understand what your company must do in order to compete, today and in the future. You have a better idea of your dominant corporate culture, and the culture that you are trying to create. You have created a hierarchy chart, which details the specific duties that each employee should be accomplishing. You have created competency models for your company and determined the specific skills inventory of your existing people. You have built employee templates and written out detailed job descriptions.

# CREATING A HIRING FRAMEWORK

Now it is time to create a hiring framework. In order to be most effective at hiring, you need to:

- Have a firm and detailed picture of your ideal candidate.
- Know how to find that person; and
- Evaluate him/her appropriately.

**Once you have found this person, you need to be able to make him or her want to work for *you*.**

This is all fairly simple, yet few private employers follow a systematic process that achieves optimum results. Too many companies "fly by the seat of their pants." They put a few ads in the paper, maybe post something on the Internet, ask a few friends. They conduct a few interviews, often as few as possible, because they are busy. Then they hire someone and hope things work out. Sound familiar?

**If you lack the right hiring framework, it could cost you tens of thousands of dollars (if not more) each year.**

Hiring should be a process that helps you find the best possible candidates for each job, and get them to want to work for you.

Here are the essential tasks that you must complete:

- **Review your mission statement:** Every employee should be advancing your company's mission. You will need to share this with your candidates, so *you* should know it by heart.
- **Review your corporate culture:** You need to have a good grasp of your company's culture, or the sub-culture of the department where your new hire will be working. If you hire outside far your culture, you are asking for trouble.
- **Review your hierarchy chart:** You should review your hierarchy chart and know where each new employee will fit on the chart. This may help you see any "holes" in your organization that can be filled by your new employee.
- **Review your company skills assessment:** Do

this as you review your hierarchy chart. Remember, you are not just looking for a salesman or a bookkeeper; you are looking for the *best possible candidate to enhance your overall company.* Sometimes, employees hired for one job end up performing in others within the company.

- **Review your job descriptions, particularly the one for each new hire:** You need to have a concise picture of the person you want to hire. You must be able to convey this vision to potential employees. Nobody wants to go work for a company that is disorganized, or commit to a position with nebulous duties. If you can't present a detailed job description, you may lose your best candidates. This wastes valuable time and money.

- **Interview your current employees:** Before making a new hire, you should take the time to speak to your current employees about the requirements of the job. In doing this, you will often learn valuable information that will enhance the hiring process.

- **Determine the specific needs & skill set required and desired:** Many private employers do not take the time to write out the specific qualities they are looking for in a candidate. Take a few minutes to write down the precise skills you are looking for in a candidate. This can help you set up a simple scoring system to use with potential employees. Set your standards high. You will always get enough candidates with lesser qualifications.

- **Determine the personal qualities desired:** Once you have determined the skill set that your new employee should possess, you should then make a list of the intangible qualities that you would like to see in your new employee. This might be as simple as jotting down a few characteristics like "team player," "detail oriented," or "sunny disposition."

- **Develop specific interview questions:** If you

are going to interview a number of candidates, you will need a scoring system. If you prepare a question track in advance, you will be able to categorize each candidate's answers in a way that will help you make a final decision. Also, an organized interview gives the right impression to the best candidates when they are deciding whether or not to work for you.

- **Prepare to present/sell your company:** Always remember; you want to hire the best people for your company. As discussed earlier, your most qualified candidates may be interviewing with several companies. You want to give them the most compelling reasons to work for *you*. You cannot simply present a job description, salary and benefits and expect the best candidates to begin lining up at your door. You need to present candidates with a compelling reason to work for you. This means sharing your company vision (mission statement) and letting them see what their role within this vision might be and become. This means delivering materials to your candidates that present your company in its best possible light. Give them a folder that highlights your company's mission. Include brochures, testimonials, and comments from your employees, anything that will make the candidate feel pride in working for your organization.

- **Recruit everywhere:** Once you are ready to begin your interview process…Once you know your ideal candidate…Once you have prepared for your interview and rehearsed selling candidates on your company, you are ready to begin looking for your new employee. As you do this, you should be prepared to recruit everywhere.

  - Get referrals from existing employees.
  - Use social media.
  - Use the print media and Internet in every capacity you can.

    o   Utilize job boards and association listings.

    o   Network with other businesses in the area, even your competitors.

- You have set your standards high, so you need to cast a wide net to make sure that every top candidate will hear about your company. Don't stop recruiting until you have a good number of qualified candidates. This may take a little extra time and money, but it will come back to you many times over.
- **Avoid the "same" syndrome:** We often like to hire people just like us. The ideal candidate won't be just like you. Beware of hiring someone because you like them, or because they share the same interests. Stick to the script. You know what you are looking for. Don't get distracted by less important criteria, like a great smile, attendance at the same high school, or nice shoes.
- **Share your ideas & candidates with current employees:** Before you make a new hire, you should have this person interview with others in your company, particularly the employees with whom this person will be working. Share your ideas and get lots of feedback. This can act as a failsafe against hiring for the wrong reasons.
- **Make your final decision and then *sell* it:** Remember; you want to hire the best candidate and pay them as little as possible at first. You can always increase someone's pay, give a bonus or a promotion. You do not want to be in the position of having to overpay someone, simply because you haven't invested the time to find enough good candidates. You also don't want to make your best prospects feel like they aren't wanted. Make candidates feel special, because they are.

## Chapter Sixteen
## _____HR_____
## People

# BEFORE THE INTERVIEW

There are many things that should be done before you begin to interview candidates to work with your company. Some of these tasks are critical, especially when they are meant to help you navigate the law. Others are designed to help you become more efficient in your hiring process.

## THE JOB APPLICATION & RESUME FORM

A job application is standard operating procedure for almost any company. You want to ask questions that help you screen candidates, so that you interview only those who meet the minimum requirements of the job. You should also ask for a cover letter.

Unfortunately, there are many seemingly innocuous questions that cannot be asked on a job application (or in an interview) without inviting litigation.

Many generic job applications are available to employers. Most of these will help you obtain the information that you need — and will keep you out of trouble. Type "generic job application" into a Google search and you will get some examples.

If you want to avoid litigation and fines, why not go to the source? The U.S. government has many useful websites to help educate employers about the law. The following site provides a compendium of employment law information:

http://www.dol.gov/compliance/guide/index.htm.

As you will see, the laws are daunting, with danger lurking everywhere.

## WHAT YOU *CANNOT* ASK

Here is a quick primer on what you cannot ask potential employees. You cannot inquire about a potential employee's:

- Sex

- Race

- Religion

- Age

- Marital Status (including maiden name or a spouse's maiden name)

- Height & Weight

- Military Service

- Political Affiliations

- Disabilities or Handicaps

- Criminal Records

- Home Ownership or Rental Status

This list has caused many a private employer to shake their head, wondering how they can make an informed determination regarding a candidate's fit for a job.

## PROTECTING RIGHTS

Answers to the above questions would provide you with useful information, particularly in regards to a candidate's character, and how they might mesh with your company culture. These questions are banned because employers are prone to discriminate, by making snap-judgments regarding this information, rather than examining the whole of a candidate. You will have to learn about your candidates in some other way.

## WHAT YOU *CAN* ASK

A job application can (and should) ask for the following information:

- Name & Address, including email address

- Personal Background Information

    o   This includes skill sets & core requirements

- Educational Background (except dates)

- Work History

## HOW TO ORGANIZE

You should use the job application to screen potential employees for the minimum qualifications of the job. I recommend setting up **three folders**.

- The first folder should hold the applications of those that exceed your minimum qualifications by a significant margin. This is your "A" list.

- The second folder should contain applications from those that meet the qualifications of the job, but don't stand out as high quality candidates. This is your "B" list. You will interview individuals from this grouping, only if you don't have success with your A list.

- Your "C" list folder will contain the names of those that do not meet the requirements of the position.

You should review your B and C candidates to see if they have qualifications that might be appropriate for some other position within your company.

You may wish to create additional, job specific folders, in which to keep these applications for the next time you are looking to fill a spot.

## WHAT TO DO WITH YOUR "A" LIST

Once you have narrowed your search to the top candidates, you should spend time drilling down through the applications/resumes for clues indicating the true *quality* of each candidate. Let's face it; every resume makes a candidate look like they could be your next CEO. Here is what you should do:

- Evaluate the cover letter for the communication skills of the candidate. Beware; many cover letters are prepared by professionals or taken from other sources. A good cover letter should be grammatically correct and well-conceived. A detailed letter also indicates that a candidate is interested in your company.

- Look for details. A good rule of thumb is: The more details you receive in the application or resume, the more valid the information.

- Give weight to a history of stability and advancement. Good employees are hard to find and expensive to train. Long tenures with prior employers bode well for a candidate's tenure with your company.

# RED FLAGS

You should always look for red flags; they are easy to spot. Look for areas of inconsistency, quality or lack of clarity. When you find red flags, you should place these candidates to the bottom of your A list, or even move them into your B or C folder.

The following are signs that a candidate may be misrepresenting themselves (which is obviously bad), or that they didn't write their own resume (which may or may not be a deal-breaker).

## CLARITY

- **Amorphous job descriptions.** If a candidate cannot be specific about what they've done, they probably didn't do it.

- **Participation trophies.** The words "participated in" or "helped with" are often clear signs that someone is riding the coat tails of others. Look for words like "headed" or "led" or "delivered."

## CONSISTENCY

- **Large gaps in employment chronology** are a definite red flag. Get them explained. "Unemployed" is not necessarily a bad thing. Many good candidates have been unemployed while looking for work. "Consultant" is a traditional code word for unemployed.

- **Short employment stints** are another area of concern. This may mean that an employee cannot get along with others, or that their job performance is not up to expectations.

- **Lack of advancement** is also a potential concern. It may represent a lack of motivation.

## QUALITY

If a candidate makes **mistakes** on a job application, such as errors in grammar or spelling, you should expect the same faults in their everyday work. With spell check software, careless mistakes like this are nearly unforgivable.

Once you have narrowed your stack of resumes to the chosen few, it is time to move on to the next phase of the employment process.

# Chapter Seventeen
## HR
## People

# INTERVIEW STRATEGIES

Unless you conduct employee interviews on a full-time basis, it is important that you structure them in a consistent manner. You want to ask each candidate the same questions. This will help you differentiate between candidates.

Do not conduct employee interviews until *you* are fully prepared. This means that you have done the following:

- Prepared your mission statement
- Completed your hierarchy chart
- Conducted your skills inventory
- Prepared a detailed job description
- Assembled the materials to "market" your company
- Prepared a complete set of questions to ask each candidate
- Thoroughly reviewed the resume of each candidate you will interview

# INTERVIEW GOALS

The initial job interview should be designed to address important key issues. You want this interview to provide answers to the following questions:

- Does the candidate fit your company culture?

- Does the candidate have the necessary skills to excel in the job and grow with your company? Is the candidate intelligent, enthusiastic and adaptable?

- Does the candidate's personality match that of his/her resume? Is this the type of person you would be proud to have working for your company?

You should not expect the initial job interview to produce a hiring decision. Although it may give you a feel about the candidate's ability to match your needs, it should not be the final meeting you have with any candidate before offering a job.

## THE WARM-UP

When the candidate enters your office or conference room, you should do your best to make this person feel welcome. The candidate may be nervous at first, so your initial goal should be to get beyond the awkwardness this creates.

No employee will be nervous when they are performing the tasks of their job, once you hire them. If you create an interview environment that is stressful, you will not get an accurate picture of the candidate's potential.

Give the candidate a smile. Shake your candidate's hand. Start with a little small talk. Once this is over, and the candidate is at ease, you can begin your interview.

## THE SET-UP

You want to be in **control** of the interview **without being controlling**. You want your candidate to open up and give you their best.

You should begin by telling the candidate how the interview will be conducted and how long it will take. Then you should use variations of the Socratic Method to learn what you can from the candidate. Ask questions, lots of questions — but only ones that matter.

## QUESTIONS

There are three main categories of questions — Closed-Ended, Hypothetical & Open-Ended. Each question form requires the candidate to respond differently. A good interviewer includes questions of each type, depending upon the information one is looking to obtain.

**Closed-Ended:** Closed-Ended questions require a "yes," or "no" answer, or a number. An example would be, "How many years have you been selling widgets?" or "Do you like travel?" You should use these questions to gather specific information that you need.

**Hypothetical:** Hypothetical questions are open-ended questions that require a candidate to imagine themselves in a new situation, perhaps the one for which they are being interviewed. You want to use these questions to determine how quickly a candidate can adapt to new situations, and how they might relate their personal skills and experience to the job.

You might ask something like, "If you were our sales manager, what steps might you take to increase sales?" or "If you were me conducting this interview, what questions would you be asking?"

**Open-Ended:** Open-ended, hypothetical questions are the best kind to use in any interview. Answering an open-ended question requires thought. A candidate must draw upon their **experience, attitudes, interests** and **opinions**. You may ask a question like, "In your last job...could you give me an example of a problem you faced and how you solved it?" or "Can you tell me what steps you took to become more productive at your last job?"

## WHAT *NOT* TO DO

The job interview performs two critical functions:

- It helps you evaluate each candidate and choose the best one for your company.

- It helps you sell your company to your best hiring prospects.

**Never make the candidate feel that you are not 100% invested in the interview.**

You must make your candidates feel important. Do not convey to them that you are too busy. Don't answer your phone, emails or texts while you are conducting the interview. Focus on the candidate.

**Be energetic and enthusiastic about the interview.**

You should always make the candidate feel like they are interesting and worthy. Don't let a candidate think you are bored, even if this is the tenth interview of your day.

**Don't talk. Ask.**

Dale Carnegie used to teach individuals how to make other people like them. It is a well-known fact that, if you make someone feel important, they will like you. If your top candidates like you, they will think more favorably about working for your company.

If you do most of the talking, rather than most of the listening, you are not conducting a good interview. Remember our 80/20? You should be talking only twenty percent of the time.

**Remove the halo.**

There is a common phenomenon among interviewers that causes them to focus on one or two things, rather than the whole of a candidate. This is known as the halo effect.

Just because a candidate likes shopping or fantasy football like you do, does not qualify the candidate for a job. Just because someone was a member of the same sorority, knows every baseball stat, grew up in the same neighborhood, drives the same type of car, or wears nice clothes…you get the picture. Don't let one or two things about a candidate color your judgment.

**Don't be a shrink.**

Never think that a one-hour meeting has allowed you to learn everything that is important about a candidate. Our **instincts** make us want to **categorize** people from the outset. That may have been fine 20,000 years ago, when we needed to flee from a saber-toothed tiger. It is not a good practice when interviewing a candidate for a job

# LISTEN

You should listen carefully to the words of each candidate. You should also watch for body language.

Make a note of areas that make your candidate nervous. These could be red flags for you to address later on. Don't focus on your next question (which is probably written down anyway). Pay attention to each response from your candidate.

Worry less about the impression you are making on a candidate than the impression they are making on you.

You should always give your candidates plenty of time to respond. Remember, you want them talking, not hearing a lot of your words.

# MAKE NOTES

As you listen, you should be **writing things down**. This will keep you focused on the candidate's answers. It will also convey to the candidate that you care about what they say. This helps candidates open up. It helps sell your company, by conveying the proper impression and gathering important data. You will want to refer to your notes in later interviews.

# PROBE

The first answers you receive from a candidate will be the ones the candidate thinks you want to hear. These answers may have been rehearsed. They have probably been given to other potential employers. They are usually not the ones that will give *you* the most important information.

You should follow each question with deeper, **probing** questions that delve further into the subject matter. Your probing questions don't need to be profound. They could be simple questions like, "Could you tell me more about that?" or "Could you go into a little more detail about that?"

## DON'T MAKE SNAP JUDGMENTS

Humans have a tendency to make prejudicial judgments about other people. Don't feel bad about this; it is part of our DNA. We categorize everyone as soon as we meet them. We all have our own rating system, whether we want to admit it or not — smart/not smart, attractive/not attractive, nice/not nice, rich/poor, tall/short, slim/fat… We do this with everyone we meet.

Computer programmers have taken this very human trait and integrated it into the digital world, creating "hashtags." These are digital markings (tags) that categorize virtually everything that is put online.

As an interviewer, you must actively seek to suspend any judgments you might make. Ignore the nose ring or the pink hair at first. Outer appearance is not necessarily the best gauge of a candidate's true qualifications for a job.

## WHAT QUESTIONS TO ASK

I recommend that you break your questions into **four distinct categories**:

- **The Opening**

- **Personal**

- **Work Experience**

- **This Job**

Begin your interviews with questions that allow the candidate to become comfortable while talking. Your first questions should be quite **general**, requiring little thought from the candidate, while giving them great leeway in crafting their answers. A few short questions can help determine the course for the remaining interview, and also allow you to establish a good path to follow.

Your second set of questions will focus on the candidate's personal qualities. These questions should reveal a good deal about the type of person he or she might be, and whether or not they are a good fit for your organization.

After you have a good idea about the personal qualities of your candidate, you will want to learn more about their specific qualifications for the job. You want to learn how a candidate's personality and skills might translate into success with your company.

Your line of questioning might look like this:

# OPENING QUESTIONS

- Could you please tell me a little bit about yourself?

- What brings you here today?

- How did you learn about us?

- Why are you interested in our company/this job?

- Why do you want to leave your current position?

Remember, what you are looking to do in the opening of your interview is to get your candidate talking. The more comfortable your candidate feels at this stage, the more information you will learn.

**Your first questions should be completely open-ended.** This will help reveal what qualities the *candidate* thinks you are looking for.

The next few questions should reveal the candidate's current employment status, and why the candidate feels like your company may be a good fit for their talents.

What you are looking for here is **feel**. Good opening questions will give you a good gut-check of your candidate. While we always want to be careful about making stereotypical judgments, we should also listen to the positive or negative feedback our subconscious gives us when we meet a new candidate.

A negative visceral reaction is often correct. If your body warns you about a candidate from the outset, this is a clear warning sign, and you should make a note of it. If your stomach churns, or your hair stands on end, take note and beware.

A positive reaction is also suspect. We often like people who are wrong for the job, and will find ways to rationalize around our feelings.

If you like someone, that is good. But pay careful attention to the qualifications the candidate actually possesses. Don't let the halo around a candidate color too much of your judgment.

## SCORE THE OPENING

### Initial Impression

When you have completed your opening set of questions, you should give your candidate a score of 1 through 10 regarding your initial impression. A high score means that your candidate is worth pursuing further. A low score (5 or below) means that there is no way that the candidate will fit within your organization.

Since time is money, if you are sure that a candidate is not right for your company, you will want to shorten your interview. Continue asking questions, but ask fewer of them. Be polite. Remember, you are also representing your organization. Even though someone is not right for your company, or the current position, all candidates deserve consideration and respect.

# PERSONAL QUESTIONS

Here is a list of effective questions that you may wish to ask your job candidates:

- If I were to ask your best friend to describe you what would he say? Follow up: Would you mind if I called him to ask him that same question?

- What are your two greatest strengths? Follow up: How have you developed these strengths? Could you give me some proof? Do you mind if I ask others about your strengths?

- What are your two greatest weaknesses? Follow up: What have you done to improve them?

- Can you tell me something negative that your current boss would say about you? Follow up: Why is that?

- What have you done to improve yourself?

- Can you give me some examples of things you have done to help others improve themselves?

- Where do you see yourself in the next five years? What are your short and long-term goals?

- How do you keep yourself organized?

- How do you deal with conflict in the workplace?

- What would you do if you witnessed another employee doing their job incorrectly?

- Please give me an example of an ethical dilemma you have had to face. Follow up: How did you deal with it? Why did you do it that way?

- How do you deal with stress? Follow up: What

do you do to reduce your stress?

- Would you please describe the perfect work environment?

- What are the last three books you have read?

With personal questions, you are looking to see if your candidate has the right work habits for your company. Does the candidate fit in with your corporate culture? Is she **morally and ethically sound**? Will your candidate be **supportive** of others and **represent** your company well? Will this person **build** others up, rather than tear them down? Can she manage the **stress** of the job, **balance** her life and not become overwhelmed?

### Personal Score

When you have completed your personal questions, you should give each candidate a grade of 1 through 10. Do it immediately after the interview, because this is the time when the candidate's answers will be clearest in your mind.

Make notes for future reference. Later, you may want to consolidate your top scorers for a second interview. Candidates with high personal scores, but lower work experience scores (covered next), may be good candidates for other positions within your company.

## WORK EXPERIENCE QUESTIONS

- Please tell me about your work style. (Or management style.)

- Can you give me an example where you succeeded beyond all expectations? Follow up: Any others?

- Tell me about a time when you had to overcome obstacles at work.

- Give me an example where your creativity was essential for a successful outcome.

- Can you give details about a time when you had to be highly analytical in order to succeed at a task?

- What was your greatest business achievement?

- Tell me about your worst business failure. Follow up: How did you resolve the issue?

- Where are you most competent? Follow up: Can you give me some examples?

- Could you give me an example where you have had to work with others?

- Give me an example where you have had to work alone.

- Do you prefer working alone or with others?

### Work Experience Rating

When you have completed this set of questions, you should give each candidate another grade of 1 through 10. Do the skills and experience of this candidate match those of the job? Has the candidate demonstrated the appropriate creativity and work ethic? Can the candidate work with others (at least as much as you want them to)? How does this candidate rank against employees already working for your company, as well as others you have interviewed for this position?

# QUESTIONS ABOUT THE JOB

- What can you do for us that others cannot?

- How would your skills and your past experience translate into success in this job?

- What is the first thing you would do if we hired you?

- What would you do in the first three months?

## Overall Impression

At this point you should rank your overall impression of each candidate. Again, you should give a score between 1 and 10. Here are a few of the criteria you should use to determine the rank of each candidate:

- You have a first (gut) impression.

- You know what is important to the candidate.

- You understand some of the candidate's strengths and weaknesses.

- You know how this candidate has functioned in previous jobs, and how the candidate might fill a role in your company.

- You have asked the candidate to wear the shoes of the job, and what he would do if he came to work for your company.

Now, give your candidate a *firm* score.

# CLOSING THE INTERVIEW

Once you are done with *your* questions, you will want to ask the candidate if he (or she) has any questions about the job and your organization. Pay close attention. The questions a candidate asks will give you a good idea about their interest in the position.

A good candidate will ask you questions about how they might fit in with your company. They will ask you about the work environment, what growth opportunities there are in the company, and where your organization is heading (including its stability).

Beware of the candidate who asks about salary, perks and vacation time. Be aware that a well-coached candidate knows to avoid these questions.

## To Finish:

- Give a short synopsis of your company and the position you are offering.

- Give the candidate a summary of what you perceive to be their strengths and weaknesses. Explain how the candidate might (or might not) fit with your company.

  o   You should then give your candidate a chance to add to you your summary or challenge your findings.

- Tell the candidate what comes next. Is this the end of the road? Will the candidate be asked for another interview session? Are there tests to complete, or background checks to be performed?

- Once the candidate is aware of your impressions and what comes next, you should end the interview. Stand, extend your hand, look the candidate in the eye and smile. "Thank you for coming today. It was a pleasure to meet you…"

# YOUR FINAL GRADE

You should schedule time after every interview, so you can review the session in your mind. Every candidate will have a different feel; they are as unique as snowflakes. Make notes on your impressions while they are still fresh in your mind. You will want to review these later. Once you are done, give the candidate a "**yes**" or a "**no**" beside their name.

### Final Score

At this point, you should give each candidate a final score. Your final score should be on a scale of 1 to 100. This is when the information is fresh in your mind, so don't procrastinate.

If you are doing things correctly, you will conduct further interviews with your top candidates. The initial interview score will not be the one that determines your ultimate choice, but it will be a big part of the final choice process. Make it count.

## DON'T DISCRIMINATE: FOLLOW THE LAW

### What You *Can't* Say

The antidiscrimination laws from the 1960s (and beyond) severely restrict the types of pre-employment questions you can ask. Asking the wrong interview questions can get you into serious legal trouble. That's why it is important that you understand what you can and cannot say. You can ask many of these questions once a candidate becomes an employee, but not before. Interview laws are designed to prevent you from discriminating against candidates based upon their:

- Age
- Race
- Gender
- Religious preferences
- Nationality
- Health
- Home ownership status
- Marital status
- Language

## AGE

Before hiring someone, you cannot ask how old they are. You may not ask them questions like, what year they graduated high school, or anything that would lead you to know their age. Once a candidate is hired, it is okay to know when they were born.

## RACE OR NATIONAL ORIGIN

You cannot ask where a candidate was born, where the candidate's parents were born, or what native language they speak. This includes asking questions that might give you clues regarding any of the above.

## GENDER

Employers cannot discriminate by gender when it comes to any aspect of employment, including hiring. There are laws against gender discrimination regarding firing, equal pay, job assignments, promotions, layoffs, training, fringe benefits and any other condition of employment.

## RELIGIOUS PREFERENCES

You are not allowed to ask *any* questions that would cause you to learn the religious preference of a candidate. Do not ask things like, "What holidays do you observe?" or, "What frat were you in while attending college?" Any question that would lead you to learn religious information could be deemed discriminatory.

## NATIONALITY OR CITIZENSHIP

You are not allowed to ask questions about any candidate's country of citizenship. While you can't ask if the candidate is a U.S. citizen, you are allowed to ask if they will be able to prove (once hired) that they can legally work in this country.

## HEALTH

Disability laws forbid potential employers from asking candidates about *any* health issues that are not directly connected to the requirements of a specific job. You may not ask questions that might lead her to reveal a current (or even previous) health condition. This includes whether the candidate has received disability payments or workers' compensation in the past.

## OWNERSHIP

Because home ownership may lead an employer to guess nationality or minority status, questions regarding home ownership are forbidden. It is okay to ask an address, just not whether a home is rented or owned.

## MARITAL STATUS

This one is particularly challenging. As an employer, you are not allowed to know (in advance) whether or not a candidate is married. Employers are not allowed to ask any questions that might lead to this information, such as, "What is your maiden name?" This sort of question also applies to questions regarding national origin.

## LANGUAGE

Language preference will often reveal a candidate's country of origin, and must therefore be off your question list. Any question that would lead an employer to learn the language of choice is against the law. Once employed, this type of question is okay. Not before.

## SUMMARY

Hiring should be an organized process that ensures that you find and recruit the most highly skilled candidates for your business.

Proper preparation is important. You must create an interview template that will help you effectively evaluate each candidate, so that you choose the proper one. You should ask the right questions and avoid the wrong ones.

If you follow this advice, the quality of your new employees will continually improve.

**Chapter Eighteen**
## HR
**People**

# EVALUATING CANDIDATES

## EVALUATION:

Okay. You have interviewed as many candidates as you can stand. It is now time to narrow the field.

If you have done an effective job in recruiting, you should have a number of promising candidates.

At this point, you should:

- Review and assess the **position** — again.

- Make sure that you know what your company needs — overall, including the specific requirements of the job in question.

- Review your job description for this position. Know what you are looking for.

- Rehearse your presentation, because you will not only be evaluating candidates, but *selling* the best ones on coming to work for your company.

Go through your stack of candidates and select those with the highest grades. If you have made careful notes, this should be easy.

You may find that you have two real grading systems. You have an objective grading system, based upon each candidate's job experience and skills. You probably also have a gut sense, a visceral rating for each candidate.

Your gut is just as important as your brain. But make sure that your gut likes someone for the proper reasons, not because of the halo effect.

# HOW THE PROS WORK —

# PAST PERFORMANCE

Hiring professionals know that the best indicator of a candidate's future performance is past performance. If a candidate has demonstrated the ability to work hard in the past, to advance, to learn new concepts and support the "team," they will usually do so again.

An employee who was a bust in their last position, regardless of their excuses, is less likely to thrive in their new job.

Of course, there are exceptions to any rule. Prior conditions may have been different. Circumstances may have dramatically affected a candidate's ability to perform. You should, however, always consider past experience as rule #1.

## REFERENCES

You should always take the time to check references. Make sure that your candidates know that you will be checking them. References will not always be reliable, but they can give you a good indication of the validity of a candidate's information.

Use references as a fact-checking device. Try to get a candidate's references to be as specific as possible. When Linda says, "Mary was a very good employee," you might ask, "Could you elaborate on that for me, Linda?"

# GUT CHECK

Pay attention to your overall impressions of each candidate. If you really can't warm to someone, despite their qualifications, try to figure out why. Liking someone is not necessarily a reliable indicator of good performance, but people often don't work well with people they dislike.

# AN OVERALL SCORING SYSTEM

You took time to assign scores to your candidates while you conducted your interviews. Now, it is important that you refine those scores so that you choose the absolute best candidates to work for your company.

## WEIGHTING

Let's face it; some qualities are just more critical than others.

The important requirements for every job should be listed in its job description. If you haven't done this, you are severely restricting the quality of your hiring process. Review your job description for each position, and break out the most important requirements. Give each of them a ranking of 1 to 10, with ten representing the highest importance.

**For example:** Let's say that you are hiring someone to provide support to your field salespeople. This person should have prior knowledge of the industry, as well as your product. Computer skills are essential, since this person will need to navigate quickly, as they support the field. Perhaps this person will need to deal with customers, so customer service experience is important. They must possess good people skills, the ability to speak well, perhaps have an empathetic nature. The candidate must also be able to multi-task and handle stress. The candidate must be intelligent and adaptable. They must have a good work ethic and a history of superior job performance.

Set up a grid, listing the requirements of each job, and the weighting you want to assign to each attribute of a candidate's score. Your grid might look like this:

## CANDIDATE # 1

| Performance Category | Weighting | Score | Weighted Score |
|---|---|---|---|
| Product Knowledge | 5 | 8 | 40 |
| Computer Skills | 8 | 4 | 32 |
| Customer Service Skills | 7 | 6 | 42 |
| Speaks Well | 7 | 8 | 56 |
| Shows Empathy | 6 | 8 | 48 |
| Multi-Task | 8 | 5 | 40 |
| Intelligent | 7 | 9 | 63 |
| Adaptable | 9 | 9 | 81 |
| Work-Ethic | 10 | 6 | 60 |
| History | 10 | 6 | 60 |
| | | Total Score | 522 |

You can construct a grid in any way you wish. You might even add items that create a negative score. A candidate's salary requirements might be used in this way. Paying a higher salary demands greater productivity. If you adjust for the higher salary in your scoring system (with a negative weighting), this may help you determine the most value for your money.

## DON'T RUSH

When a private business is looking to hire someone, the position is usually critical, and must be filled as soon as possible. It is very easy to rush the hiring process because you've got "more important things to do." Au contraire, mon ami.

If you rush the hiring process, the cost could be devastating to your business. If you hire the wrong person, you will have to fire your new employee (if you can) and start the entire process over again. *That* would really waste your time and money. So take your time. Get some feedback from others (but not too much) and check out the facts. Call references, cross-verify wherever you can, and look for inconsistencies as you gather data.

## THE SECOND INTERVIEW

The second interview is a good place to get other employees involved in your process.

Employees can act as goodwill ambassadors for your company, helping you sell attractive candidates on your company. Other employees may also be able to give valuable feedback on traits you may have missed or overlooked.

Once you have chosen your top candidates, invite them back to meet with you, along with a few of your company's employees.

This second session should be more heavily weighted toward the candidate's skills and experience, and how they will directly translate to success in their job with your company.

Give each candidate time to ask questions. They are evaluating *you* as well.

## FINAL SCORE

Once you have conducted your follow-up interviews, you should determine a final score for each candidate. Rank them, with #1 being your top choice. Huddle with your employee-interviewers and ask what they think. They will each have a favorite, although the favorite won't always be the same among your employees.

Once you have found your top candidate, you are ready to move to the next stages of your hiring process.

**Chapter Nineteen**
## HR
**People**

# USING THE INTERNET

Although the Internet is everywhere, many employers have not fully embraced it as a hiring tool.

The Internet can be used to post job listings on sites like Career-builder.com, Craigslist.com and Monster.com. Monster and Career-builder also have arrangements where employers can review hundreds of (hidden) resumes that are posted online.

Employers who are willing to put in some effort can review the resumes of many candidates who would not normally respond to their posted advertisement. You may find many of your best candidates in this manner. This could keep you from wasting time responding to the hundreds of nonqualified candidates (which will come to you like spam).

The Internet can also be used to learn more information about candidates. Through the Internet, information will come to you in a raw, far less filtered manner than in a resume.

More and more candidates are building Facebook or LinkedIn accounts. These can be used to verify information and achievements. Individuals are less prone to hyperbole (or flat-out lying) when they know that friends and co-workers will be reading what they say. These profiles, particularly on non-business sites, often reveal personality traits that will never show up on a resume or in an interview.

Many a candidate (and employee) has met his doom because of Internet postings.

Search engines like Google are another good source of information. Google a candidate's name and see what you get. You can often learn what they have done, in business and in the community — all without having to ask! This information is public. You may use it as best you can, even if it is information you could never ask for during an interview.

## Chapter Twenty
## HR
### People

# TESTING & PRE-EMPLOYMENT SCREENING

Pre-employment testing and screening (like background checks) treads on tricky legal ground, upon which you may or may not want to venture. When done before hiring, testing and screening can violate a candidate's civil rights.

Why do it then? *Effective* testing and screening can save you money and time.

Correctly administered tests can objectively measure skills, assess knowledge and qualifications, and determine personality characteristics that may be critical to top performance. Many tests can be conducted at reasonable costs. They can provide information that will help you make good hires, as well as help you manage new employees effectively.

## DO NOT USE A TEST UNLESS:

- Your test results produce a high correlation with job performance.

- Your tests assess the appropriate skill set required for the job.

## AVOID TESTS THAT:

- Discriminate.

- Produce data that is erroneous or irrelevant.

There are literally thousands of tests you can perform. If you are a member of an association, try checking with your association's executives to see which tests are most appropriate for your industry.

There are two books that review tests which may be helpful for your company. They are entitled, *Tests in Print* and *The Mental Measurement Yearbook*. You can learn more about these at:

http://www.unl.edu/buros/bimm/html/catalog.html

# USING TESTS EFFECTIVELY

## PERSONALITY TESTS

Personality tests can be enormously helpful in your hiring process, as well as in employee management. These tests can measure (and quantify) the key characteristics needed to perform well at certain tasks.

Wouldn't you like to know if a potential salesperson is naturally resilient? Wouldn't you like to know that a potential client service rep has empathy? Of course you would!

Tests like the Minnesota Multiphasic Personality Inventory (MMPI), the Thematic Apperception Test (TAT), the Birkman Method, or the Rorschach (Inkblot) test can be helpful in understanding the **dominant personality characteristics** of a candidate (or employee). These usually require the help of a trained psychologist.

There are many "four quadrant" models (such as Amiable, Analytical, Expressive, and Driver). These are easy for the layman to understand and utilize effectively. The Myers-Briggs Type Indicator is quite effective. It measures how people view the world and make decisions.

With today's computer power, most personality tests can be scored, evaluated and printed for you quickly, at very reasonable costs.

I suggest that you employ this type of testing only as a *final* criterion when evaluating a candidate.

**Caution:** Testing is a powerful tool if used properly, and dangerous if used incorrectly. You must be willing to take the time to understand the relevancy of this type of testing to your business. You must also be willing to cede some of the hiring power to others. Outside experts (who may or may not know your business) will become part of your critical hiring decisions.

## SKILLS TESTS

Many of us took Achievement Tests before applying to college. Achievement Tests are a fairly accurate measure of an individual's cumulative knowledge in a subject, and can be a tool to help predict one's future success in college.

There are tests that measure skills in virtually every business area. If it is important, you will find a specialized test to measure any skill set that you need in a candidate.

The reliability of skills testing is generally quite good, particularly if you have a baseline from current or former employees.

## ABILITY AND APTITUDE TESTS

Many of us took the SATs while in high school. These tests measure "scholastic aptitude," and have a fair correlation with academic success. There are exceptions. Many bright people with comparatively low SATs have been high academic achievers. Many with high SATs have flunked out of school. The same will hold true with any aptitude testing you may require. These tests can be quite helpful, but should be used only as one predictive indicator of future success.

Aptitude (achievement) tests can be helpful in identifying:

- Base Intelligence — such as verbal capabilities, the ability to reason, or perceptual speed.

- Mechanical Abilities — such as the ability to distinguish mechanical differences that are not apparent to others. People with high mechanical abilities understand how things "work."

- Mind/Body Abilities — such as the ability to learn new motor patterns.

The U.S. government makes their General Aptitude Test Battery available to employers at:

http://www.doleta.gov/.

**Beware of Rights**

Be very careful when using aptitude testing, as it is easy to violate the rights of disadvantaged groups under EEO law.

## HANDWRITING TESTS

Don't mess with them.

## INTEGRITY TESTING

Integrity testing is an area of great debate. Tests that measure honesty and integrity must be job-related, or they can be deemed discriminatory.

Companies that deal with customer finances, private data or trade secrets may have a need for this type of testing. Companies that run the risk of employee theft also have need for this type of testing.

Some tests can be very good indicators of a candidate's moral character.

## Polygraph Tests

The Employee Polygraph Protection Act of 1988 restricts the use of polygraphs within private companies. In many instances, it is illegal to ask an employee to take one. However, under certain circumstances, companies involved with money and security issues may be able to utilize lie detector tests.

The reliability of these tests is debatable, and highly dependent upon the skill of the test operator. Seek legal counsel before traveling down this road.

## TESTING SUMMARY

Testing can be a valuable tool in your employment arsenal, particularly if you narrow the scope and fully understand the testing methodology. In order to be most effective with your testing, you should:

- Learn about the entire testing landscape. There are many tests. Take care to find the right ones for your company.

- Have a clear understanding of what you are trying to measure.

- Be sure that the testing results are reliable.

- Check the credentials of any testing company and/or test professional.

- Understand the legal restrictions to any testing you may wish to utilize.

- Don't violate a candidate's (or employee's) civil rights.

# Chapter Twenty-One
# HR
## People

## THE JOB OFFER

Once you have decided upon a candidate, make an offer. You should do this quickly and professionally. Prepare a one-page sheet with your candidate's name along the top. This sheet should give a brief job description, along with your proposed salary, bonus arrangement, perks and other benefits.

You should give your candidate time to respond, but you should also set an acceptance deadline. This may be a week or so for senior management positions. A couple of days are enough for most entry-level jobs.

When the candidate accepts your offer, you should have the candidate sign this sheet and keep it with your files.

### Be Prepared & Persistent

Your best candidates may not accept your first offer. You should decide, in advance, just how far you are willing to go with an increase in salary, perks, etc. If you do this prior to a rejection, you will be more apt to keep your emotions out of the equation.

## EMPLOYMENT AGREEMENTS

Employment agreements are becoming more popular, particularly in the most highly competitive industries. An employment agreement protects both the employer and the employee. An agreement especially benefits the employer in areas where trade secrets, clients and prospect lists must be protected.

An employment agreement should detail:

- Job Title

- Duties (job description)

- Expectations (responsibilities, obligations and conditions of employment)

- Damages & Remedies

# SELLING THE JOB TO THE RELUCTANT CANDIDATE

If a candidate doesn't accept an offer, this does not necessarily mean that they won't come to work for you. Your candidate may need time to process the offer or speak with others, such as a spouse or parent.

Some candidates must still be "sold" on your company. If this happens, be careful not to push too hard. Inquire politely if there is any information you can provide that will help them make a decision. Ask if there is something in particular that is making them hesitate.

At this point, you may need to make a decision about whether or not to sweeten your offer. You should already know what terms (and how far) you are willing to adjust. This may depend upon whether or not you have other qualified candidates for the job.

If you are light on qualified candidates, you may be more apt to adjust your offer. If you have a dozen similar candidates, you will be less inclined to budge.

Salary is often the most important impediment to someone accepting a position with a private company. This is not always the case, so don't rush to increase pay until you understand just *what* is keeping your best candidate from coming to work for you. Sometimes family issues are involved. Commuting considerations can play a factor. Advancement opportunities are usually more limited within a small company environment.

Do your best to find the true reason for a candidate's reticence, before improving your offer. It may be as simple as letting her leave early on Thursdays so she can coach a child in soccer or basketball. Maybe the candidate wants *less* salary and *more* incentive pay. You don't know until you have asked. So, ask.

Once you understand the true reasons why you have been rejected (Yes, it will feel that way.), you will know how to react. Don't respond frantically. Be polite and professional. Woody Allen once said, "I'd never join a club that would accept me as a member." No one wants to work for someone who is too desperate to have them. Your best employees want to be appreciated, not worshipped.

# Chapter Twenty-Two
## HR
### People

# SETTING THE GROUND RULES

There is an old saying that says: When you start something new, you want to "get off on the right foot." This cliché holds true when you hire a new employee.

When an employee comes to work for your company, you should set the ground rules at once. This way, new employees will know what is expected of them. This will enhance productivity and avoid mistakes.

Make the transition to your company as easy as possible. You work far too hard to hire good employees, only to lose them (physically or emotionally) in the first week on the job.

### Reduce Stress

Starting a new job is stressful. Stress reduces one's ability to perform at peak ability. Therefore, you want to make every new employee's transition to your company as stress-free as possible.

# NEW-EMPLOYEE ORIENTATION

Large companies are famous for handing out stacks of folders that detail every aspect of a new job. They conduct employee orientation meetings and prepare hundreds of online videos.

Small businesses tend to thrust a new employee into their new job and expect them to perform at once. Training might consist of the words, "There is your new desk. Go get 'em tiger."

Too many employers think that "on-the-job" training is all a new employee needs to reach his full potential — by noon. Don't make this mistake.

Orientation should not take place by osmosis. It should not be conducted in puppy dog fashion by following good ol' Joe around the office for a few days. New employee orientation should be a well thought out process designed to acquaint your employee with the job, to get her working efficiently, as soon as possible.

### Welcome Packet & Procedures Manual

Every new employee should be given a *Welcome Packet* and *Procedures Manual.* This should include all of the information they will need to navigate the job. I'll discuss this later in this chapter.

# A FRIENDLY ENVIRONMENT

You must develop and support a company culture where existing employees welcome new ones and make them feel comfortable from the start.

### Encourage Inclusion

It is natural for employees to remain focused on the tasks of their *own* jobs, rather than be sensitive to the feelings of someone who is new to the company. It is easy for employees to maintain existing cliques, without letting the new guy or gal in. Make sure that your current employees know that it is part of *their* job to help new employees assimilate into your company.

### First Impressions Matter

You don't want a new employee's first impression of your company to be a bad one. First impressions last a lifetime and you only get one chance. The right impression can foster company loyalty from day one. The wrong impression can plant a seed that will lead to discontent and increased employee turnover.

Your company (you and all your employees) should do everything you can to make new employees feel part of the team. You should:

- Have someone (preferably you or the employee's new boss) meet each new employee at the company entrance on their first day.

- Personally introduce each new employee to your company receptionist, and to your employee's new team members.

- Give each new employee an orientation packet. This should include a phone and email list, a company hierarchy chart, a Policies and Procedures Manual, etc.

- Set up an informal meeting (perhaps in your lunch room) where you can introduce your new employee to the team.

- Actively encourage current employees to welcome new ones.

   o   This can be done through your company newsletter. If you don't have a newsletter, this can be done through a company-wide email or a simple hand out sheet. This should include a short bio (and perhaps a picture) of your new employee, along with her job title.

- Schedule lunch for your new employee with at least one member of her team, and/or with you.

# YOU GET WHAT YOU EXPECT

In life, we often get what we expect. If we set high goals, we will often achieve them. If we don't, we won't. The same holds true with new employees.

If you don't tell a new employee what you expect, you generally won't get what you want and what need.

# INITIATE NEW EMPLOYEES INTO YOUR CORPORATE CULTURE

If you hired correctly, you reviewed your company's products and services during the interview process. You shared your company's mission statement and company goals during interviews. You told your candidate how great you are.

Now that your candidate has become an employee, you need to do this again. A candidate's mindset is far different than that of an employee. You must understand this and act appropriately.

Just as you get one chance to make a first impression, you get one great chance to shape a new employee to your corporate culture.

When an employee walks through that front door on their first day, think of them as a lump of clay, ready to be shaped to what you want and need them to be. After a few short days or weeks, they will begin to harden into place. You need to make sure that they settle properly into their job, that they assimilate into your corporate culture, and that they develop the habits that will make them great. In this meeting, you should:

> • Give a complete review of your company's evolution. If you are the owner, you should tell the story of how the company came to be. If you are not, you should learn the story and relay it to every new employee.

> • Describe your company's industry and where you fit within it.

• Give a detailed review of your company's products and services. Every employee should know what you do.

• Review your company's mission statement. Read it out loud. Have your new employee read it out loud. Tell them that they must have it memorized before their first review.

• Review your company goals. Break these down to department goals, particularly as they relate to your new employee. Then explain the part that your new employee plays in helping reach these goals.

• Describe how all of this fits into your **corporate culture**. Remember, this is the time that your new employee is most impressionable. Make sure that she understands what your company is all about, and how she fits into the whole.

• Make your new employee feel important. She *is* important, critical in fact. Every new employee is worth more to your company than your car, or your finest piece of jewelry. Treat her that way, not like she doesn't matter and you have more important things to do.

*Write this all down! Be organized.*

## HOW TO SET THE GROUND RULES

Every new employee should:

• Receive a clear *job description*. This is something they should hang up beside their work chair, maybe even memorize. Remember, a job description should prioritize *tasks* so that your new employee works productively. You must take the time to review this with every employee to make sure that it is well understood.

- Write out a goal list. You should sit with each new employee and help them write out their goals, as they pertain to the new job. This will help keep your employees on task and keep them productive.

You, the employer, should:

- Establish your performance standards and the way in which your employee will be evaluated.

- Establish a review schedule, where your employee's performance will be evaluated.

# THE WELCOME PACKET

On every employee's first day, someone should sit down and explain what is expected. Your employee should be given a road map to help him navigate the job and reach his destination — success with your company.

### Procedures Manual

Every new employee should receive a Procedures Manual. This manual will detail *where things are* and *how things work* in your company. Your manual should be a reference that every employee can review any time they need to find or do something.

A procedures manual should answer the questions your new employee might ask of a co-worker. Anything an employee may need to find should be listed in the guidebook. This saves interruption and maintains productive work time. Your manual should explain where to go for things and who to call. Who does one go to for supplies? Who arranges travel? Who hands out paychecks? This includes where things are situated, such as rest rooms, lunch rooms, fire exits, first aid kit, copiers, security office, parking spaces, etc.

### Organization is Critical

The best way to accomplish all of your first-day tasks is to keep things organized. You should set up a schedule where your new employee receives everything she needs, and meets with the appropriate people. For some companies, this could be a meeting with one person. For others, it could be a full day of shuffling from office to office.

A new employee may have a first-day agenda that looks like this.

| | |
|---|---|
| 7:30 a.m. | Meet with Jim CEO for breakfast |
| 8:30 a.m. | Review with Sandy Beach, head of HR |
| 9:30 a.m. | Coffee break with staff in small lunch room |
| 10:00 a.m. | Meet with Sally Sales to meet your new team |
| 10:45 a.m. | Tour of facility with Sandy Beach |
| 11:15 a.m. | Meet with Tom Comfort to review benefits |
| 12 noon | Lunch with Jim CEO, Sally Sales and Sandy Beach |
| 1:00 p.m. | Policies & Procedures review with Sandy Beach |
| 2:00 p.m. | Coffee with your company mentor, Al Friendly |
| 2:45 p.m. | Meeting with office manager, Sally Smart |
| 3:15 p.m. | Meeting with Jack Safe, director of security |
| 3:45 p.m. | Office organization with Sandy Beach and Sally Smart |

# EMPLOYEE REVIEW

Once your new employee has had a chance to settle into your company, and once she has been through orientation, you should have a sit-down where you ask about the effectiveness of your process. Get feedback from every new employee about how well you managed the process.

Prepare an employee review sheet that allows new hires to respond, explaining how well you handled the orientation process. Did you explain everything your employee needed to know? Did you make your employee feel comfortable with his new business home? Was your employee productive from the start, or did it take too much time to get oriented to the job? Does your employee understand your corporate culture and his place within it? What could be improved about the process?

Here are a few questions that you may wish to ask:

- What was it that made you want to work for our company?

- Do you understand our company mission and your role within it?

- Have we met your expectations?

- What could we do better?

- Were other employees helpful when you first came to work with us?

- Were the materials you were given adequate? What could we improve?

- Do you perceive your job differently now than before you came to work with us? What are the differences? How can we improve our hiring process?

## GIVE YOURSELF A SCORE

Set up a process to evaluate the effectiveness of your hiring procedures. Make a note of what you are doing well and what could be improved.

## Chapter Twenty-Three
## _____ HR _____
## People

# POLICIES AND PROCEDURES MANUAL

Even if your company is small, you need to have a Policies and Procedures Manual. A P&P manual is like a business plan for your employees. It gives them a single resource that tells them how things work. It is also designed to give employees all of the information that is required by law.

Your P&P manual does not have to be a thick and imposing document. However, the more comprehensive you can make it, the better off you'll be.

**HINT** — While your manual may contain a breadth of information, you should put as much of it as possible into a format that is simple to read and easily accessible to your employees.

## BUILDING A MANUAL

There are many places to get help building a policies and procedures manual. Type the key words into your search engine and you will find thousands of sources to help you. These are the areas that should be covered in your document:

- You should address all of the applicable state and federal laws regarding:

- o   Hiring and Reporting

- o   Employment Practices

- o   Sexual Harassment Issues & Training

- o   Exempt & Non-exempt Employees (discussed in Chapter 29)

- o   Wages

- o   Overtime

- o   Benefits

- o   Antidiscrimination Practices & Remedies

- You should discuss state and federally mandated programs and benefits, such as:
  - o   Social Security
  - o   Workers' Compensation
  - o   Unemployment
  - o   Jury Duty
  - o   Military Leave
  - o   School Visitation Rights
  - o   The Age Discrimination in Employment Act of 1967
  - o   Equal Employment Opportunity (EEO) Laws
  - o   Fair Credit Reporting ACT (FCRA)
  - o   The Federal Fair Labor Standards Act of 1938 (FLSA)
  - o   The Women's Health & Cancer Rights Act (WHCRA)
  - o   Uniformed Services Employment & Reemployment Rights Act
  - o   National Defense Authorization Act of 2008
  - o   Caregiver Leave

- o   HEART Act of 2008
- o   Wages & Hours
- o   The Occupational Safety & Health Act (OSHA)
- o   The Employee Retirement Income Security Act (ERISA)
- o   Uniformed Services Employment & Reemployment Rights Act
- o   Employee Polygraph Protection Act
- o   Garnishment of Wages
- o   The Family & Medical Leave Act
- o   Plant Closings & Layoffs

- • Give an outline of company policies regarding:
  - o   Salary & Wages
  - o   Payment Dates
  - o   Telephone Use
  - o   Internet Use
  - o   Email Use
  - o   Standard Mail Practices
  - o   Confidentiality Practices
  - o   Standards of Conduct
  - o   Performance Reviews
  - o   Disciplinary Policies

- • Include a list of the appropriate Department of Labor laws.

- • Provide information on company sponsored benefits:
  - o   Life & Health Insurance
  - o   Disability Insurance
  - o   Retirement Plan(s)
  - o   Vacation Time
  - o   Sick Leave
  - o   Holidays

The preparation of a policy manual is usually a collaborative effort, with contributions from all divisions of the company. A copy should be made available to all employees. This can be a hard or electronic copy. Electronic copies can be forwarded anywhere, so you may wish to safeguard these with a password.

# Chapter Twenty-Four
## _____HR_____
### People

# EMPLOYEE COMMUNICATION & TEAMWORK

We examined communication in the Big Picture section of this book. Because of its importance, we are now going to review this in greater detail.

In the early 1990s, W. Alan Randolph, a professor of management at the University of Baltimore's Merrick School of Business, conducted a detailed study of ten major corporations. Randolph concluded that open communication was one of the most important predictors of corporate success. Randolph concluded that the most successful companies had multiple lines of employee communication. He also found that these companies communicated constantly, through:

- Regular emails

- Daily briefings

- Corporate meetings

- Computer access to information

Randolph also concluded that the most successful companies

had a free flow of information in *both* directions, up and down the corporate hierarchy. This communication gave employees a sense of empowerment. It also kept the companies fresh with ideas.

Successful corporations tend to share items like their company vision, financial data, market share and profitability. Compensation in upper management is often incentive-based, with bonuses, stock options, etc. This makes the sharing of financial information rather critical.

Private companies do not have the same financial reporting mechanisms as large, public corporations. Also, it is not always prudent for a small business owner to share key financial data with employees. In some situations this can alert competitors or even breed discontent. However, private companies should emulate the practice of open communications.

**What To Communicate**

Even in small companies you should be sharing your:

- Strategic vision

- Sales initiatives

- Service initiatives

- Some sales data, even if it is listed as percentage increase or decrease

- Production rates

- Competitor activities

You can keep communication open between management and employees in many ways. The traditional suggestion box can still be utilized. Electronic versions can be implemented on your website, or in blogs, podcasts, videocasts and emails. You can also use social networking sites like Twitter, Facebook or LinkedIn. You can use posters, company meetings, even papers pinned in the lunch room.

Anything to keep the lines of communication open will help employees remain engaged in your company. You may even wish to have your CEO meet regularly with employees.

Communication shows that management cares. It builds loyalty with employees. It is a valuable source for new ideas. It can help make your company great. Empowered employees are more creative; they work harder; they are better with your customers.

Another function of the communication system is to reward employees for outstanding performance. Remember our example from McDonalds? Simple recognition can create powerful incentive for employees at a negligible cost.

## TEAMWORK

Communication is also important in building effective teamwork. The success of a private business is often determined by how well its employees can work together. Think of an eight-man scull rowing in a regatta. If the eight rowers are not stroking together, if just one is paddling against the others, there is no way to win. It is the same with a small or mid-sized business. Every employee must be working with, not against, the others.

### Reduce the Hierarchy

One of the keys to successful teambuilding is the reduction of the corporate hierarchy. A manager who is afraid of criticism, and reacts negatively to it, will miss out on constructive criticism that would make him a better leader. A boss who hogs all the credit will reduce incentives for initiative, and won't get much help.

A business leader that can learn to praise employees for useful criticism, and reward employees for speaking up about problems or solutions, is the type of leader who gets the best from his people.

# TEAM MISSION

We talked a lot about your mission statement. Teams work best when they are working toward a clear, common mission.

Large companies have groups of teams. A small company might have just one.

Regardless of size, every team must have a shared mission and a common, strategic focus. With every team, you should:

- Set the ground rules. What are you trying to achieve?

- Assign duties within the team.

    o   Write these out.

    o   Clarify the roles, but allow for flexibility and the crossing of duties.

    o   Allow your team members to suggest better ways of accomplishing tasks, even if it is not their specific duty.

- Have realistic targets and expectations.

- Establish measuring sticks for progress.

- Hold people responsible for their duties.

- Establish team rewards for excellent ideas and production.

- Establish a mechanism for suggestions and criticism.

Take great care to see that your employees function together well as a team. The more you can do this, the greater your profits will be.

## Chapter Twenty-Five
## HR
### People

# UNDERCOVER BOSS

The television show, *Undercover Boss*, is a fine example of communication in action. Corporate executives go under cover inside their own companies. They interface directly with employees as they embark upon the most menial tasks within their company.

The results of raw, first-hand communication are extraordinary. Executives come away with a far greater appreciation for what their employees endure. Employees come away with the feeling that management cares about them.

The results of effective communication are clear and powerful. Executives learn new ways to improve their company. Employee morale is boosted. This results in a better company.

You may not have the opportunity to go undercover within your own organization. But your executives do have the power to work side-by-side with employees and help build a better, more efficient company.

# Chapter Twenty-Six
## HR
### People

# PERMANENT OR TEMP

One of the most debated topics in business today is whether or not to have "employees" at all. With so many government requirements, including the new financial reforms and mandated health care, companies are employing strategies to shift the paperwork, liability and costs away from themselves, and onto others.

Functions and benefits that were once provided by employers are increasingly being *outsourced* to others.

In some cases, this can be an effective strategy. In other cases, the results can be disastrous. You will need to assess your own company's needs and resources to determine the best mix of employees and non-employees for you.

## OUTSOURCING

Outsourcing involves the practice of shifting an entire function of your company to an organization that specializes in that area.

If you call for technical support on an electronic product or software, you may experience outsourcing first hand — as many of these calls are now handled from overseas.

Outsourcing can be enormously cost-effective. Outsourcing companies can utilize economies of scale that you could never have.

They can employ experts that you can't afford. They can perform all of the administrative functions related to the outsourced activity, allowing you to focus upon your core business.

Smaller companies are often forced to outsource, particularly when the requirements (or technology) of a particular task become too complex to manage.

For example: With all of the government requirements, using a payroll company has become more of a necessity than a choice.

Other outsourcing decisions might be made by choice, simply because they make functional and economic sense. Besides payroll, here is a list of other areas where outsourcing is commonly used:

- Benefits

- Shipping

- Billing

- Internet & Computers

- Administration

- Security

- Communications

- Marketing

As an HR manager, you should be aware of all of the ways that you can outsource company functions more efficiently. Do the research. Talk to consultants. See where you can use outsourcing to improve efficiency, profitability and customer service.

# LEASING

Leased employees look and feel like real employees. They usually work in your company on a full-time basis, just like any other.

By leasing employees, you can outsource key corporate functions, like hiring and training and benefits.

### The Leasing Industry

Professional Employment Organizations (PEOs) are usually very large. They have economies of scale. PEOs offer benefit and training programs that smaller companies can't afford. They may be able to deliver high quality "pseudo-employees" for less than what it costs for you to hire them.

Unfortunately, leasing companies often fail to deliver productive employees at a total lower cost. In some cases, they cause more problems than they solve. Be **very** cautious when handing your business over to a large, bureaucratic organization that is focused on their profits, not yours.

# INDEPENDENT CONTRACTORS

Companies are hiring more independent contractors than ever before. Much of this is being driven by financial need. Why hire a full-time accountant when all you need is five hours a week? Why pay the high cost for benefits if you can avoid the expense?

Independent contractors are *not* employees. They are self-employed and work on an as-needed basis. They manage their own benefits and taxes.

### Independent Experts

In today's business climate of high unemployment, many highly skilled individuals have opted (often by necessity) to become independent contractors. A former (large company) CFO might contract with half a dozen smaller companies to provide this same function.

There is a great deal of talent out there. You may be able to engage contractors that once earned high six-figure incomes with other companies, and pay them a fraction of their former salaries — for the same work.

You should constantly assess the quality of outside independent contractors versus full-time employees. Contractors may provide talent you can't afford on a full-time basis, but is within your part-time budget. This is especially true when unemployment is high.

### Know the Law

When engaging contractors, you must take care that you don't abuse employment laws. De facto employees cannot be paid as contractors without running the risk of severe financial consequences.

Government regulators don't look kindly upon employers who hire employees as contractors, simply to avoid paying benefits and payroll taxes. In recent years, state attorney generals have become increasingly aggressive in enforcing such HR laws.

## JOB SHARING

Job sharing is another effective way that employers are able to manage costs, without sacrificing the quality of work.

You may have a full-time need that can be performed by more than one person. Some employees prefer to work on a part-time basis. Mothers who want to spend time at home with their children are the classic example. Retired executives also provide another great source of job-sharing talent.

Utilizing part-time employees can also help save on company overhead. You may need less office space. Job sharers often don't need benefits. They just want a steady income without the requirement of a full-time commitment. This can be a win-win for you.

Take care to ensure that your job-sharers are compatible. Make sure that all parties to the sharing are comfortable and confident in their roles.

## TEMPORARY WORKERS

We've all heard the Accountemps commercials saying something like this, "No problem, Jim. Take as long as you need...*Bob* is here."

Temporary workers can be hired for virtually any position, even as a CEO. Businesses use temp workers to fill a void left by sickness or family leave. They are hired to manage part-time tasks, like accounting. In times of high unemployment, highly skilled individuals can be found everywhere.

In years past, temp workers were engaged through temporary agencies. Recently, websites like Craigslist and LinkedIn have become an inexpensive and effective alternative for finding temporary help.

As with independent contractors, there are many legal issues surrounding the use of temporary workers. You should consult outside counsel if you employ contractors or temp employees for positions that could be deemed full-time. I will discuss some of the legal issues in the compliance this book.

# Chapter Twenty-Seven
## HR
**People**

# TRAINING & DEVELOPMENT

Trained employees work more effectively than untrained employees. Yet, too many private companies ignore the importance of vital, organized training.

Great workers are well trained. So train to be great. Here's how.

### All Training Is Unique

Training will not be the same between industries, or even companies within a common industry. Products and services vary. Therefore, each organization has a unique corporate culture.

As an HR specialist, your challenge is to develop the best training program for *your* company. Make it your own.

### Training Never Stops

The world stops for no business. Products continue to evolve. The economy remains a moving target. Consumers' tastes change with the seasons. Technology advances at an ever-increasing pace.

HR managers must embrace the challenge of a changing world, and adapt the content of employee training continually. As business morphs around you, so must your training. Speak with your company managers regularly. Make sure that you understand the current and future skill sets needed by your company.

Your greatest challenge is to decide which training methods to employ, and to conduct your training in the most cost-effective and productive manner possible.

Think of a chess board, with employees as your pieces. The world around you keeps changing. This is like an opponent making chess moves. You must always think several moves ahead, anticipating what your opponent will do next. Sometimes an opponent will surprise you, with moves you didn't anticipate. It is the same in business.

You must hire employees that have the skills necessary to fulfill your current job needs, but also have the ability to *adapt* to the changing needs of your company.

## TRAINING PROGRAMS HELP RECRUIT GOOD CANDIDATES

If you are hiring new employees, remember this: Your training program is a valuable recruiting tool.

People like to work for employers that help them improve their skill set. The best employees don't want to be trapped into dead-end jobs, or fall behind peers in their skills. They want the ability to rise in station, as well as improve their financial and emotional standing in the workplace.

A well-constructed (and communicated) training program is a valuable tool in your recruiting tool box.

## TRAINING PROGRAMS RETAIN LOYAL AND PRODUCTIVE WORKERS

If you don't train your work force to grow with the rest of the world, you will have to replace them. This will be costly. You expend valuable resources to recruit candidates with today's skill set. Without training, these employees will fall behind the outside (employee) marketplace and become obsolete. Then, you will have to replace *them* with new ones. This sets up a costly revolving door of employees, which you cannot afford. It also creates a poor corporate culture and destroys morale.

Training, particularly in the area of technology, should be mandatory and monitored for its effectiveness. You should also monitor the training received by terminated employees. This may help point out weaknesses in your current training programs.

## TRAINING BOOSTS TEAMWORK

Training is like a tide that raises all ships. Comprehensive training programs will help shape your corporate culture into one that helps all employees work better together.

Training helps your employees "speak the same language." This helps employees work better together as a team, which is critical to maximizing efficiency and running your business in the most profitable manner.

## HOW TO BUILD A TRAINING PROGRAM

As we have discussed, employees in private companies must often function in multiple roles. Your owner might be your biggest salesman. Your CFO may also be your operations manager.

Smaller companies don't have the resources for a CTO, a chief training officer. As a result, too much training is done informally, or simply on-the-job by osmosis.

A formalized training program will enhance employee knowledge and lead to far greater productivity. It will lead to greater employee job satisfaction and a greater consistency of output across all areas of your company.

# DEVELOPING A PLAN

Before you begin training, you need to ask the following:

- Do you need a training program? Will new training improve employee effectiveness, and bring more money to your bottom line?

- Who needs to be trained? Technologies change. Products change. The competition changes. Every company should take a hard look at all of their employees, to gauge who could benefit the most from new training.

- What resources are available? Do you have internal resources to help with training, or must you go outside your company?

- Who will do the training? What form will it take?

- How will your training be evaluated?

- What problems will result if you don't train your employees?

- How will newly-trained employees share that knowledge with others?

While there are many training strategies, private business HR executives rarely have the financial resources, or the time, to build effective, comprehensive training programs on their own.

## Good News About Training

In many business areas, training can be outsourced. The world is filled with companies that want to help train your employees. If you search "employee training programs" in Google, you will get more than four million hits. While this is data overload, it should let you know that you are not alone in your need.

There are thousands of generic training programs, covering everything from sales, to management, to team building. You may also find specialized training programs within your industry. Many of these resources can be accessed for free, or at very little cost.

As you review potential training programs, you should try to quantify the benefits that new training will bring. Will your program make everyone feel better, or bring substantive results that will lead to greater profitability? Will your training match that of your competitors? Does it lead to excellence?

At the end of your evaluation, you must decide what resources, in time and money, you are willing to devote to your new program. Then do it.

## IDENTIFY YOUR NEEDS

The first thing that you must do when constructing (or modifying) your training program is to assess your needs. You can hire outside consultants to help you do this. You can do it internally. If you choose to do this yourself, I have included a list of strategies below to help you.

Outside vendors and product specialists (within your industry) will often provide expert training at no cost. Before spending large sums of money on training, see what is out there for free. It is often as good as what you must pay for.

## EMPLOYEE SURVEYS

If you have been doing your assignments in this book, you should already have a good idea about where your company needs more training. You should review your:

- Competency Models
- Skills Inventory
- Employee Templates
- Job Descriptions
- Training Manuals

Using these studies and documents, you can develop an employee survey which helps you evaluate the specific skills and knowledge required in your company. Make a list of questions that focus on the key skills your employees need to be at their best. Then give this survey to employees and their managers.

Suggestion Box – Don't be afraid to ask employees for their feedback on what questions should be asked in this survey.

## FOCUS GROUPS

Set up meetings with key employees (not just management) to assess the training needs of your company. Consider meeting for a day or two off-site, at a place where you are removed from the normal day-to-day distractions of business. If this needs to be on a weekend, and you have to pay employees for their time, so be it. This is critical.

Choose one person to direct your focus group. This may be someone from inside the company, like your CEO. Or, you may wish to hire an outside consultant to moderate your focus group.

Whoever facilitates, make sure that he or she keeps the meeting focused on the positives, not all the negatives of the company. This isn't a bitching session; it should be a positive step toward company growth and renewal.

## OBSERVATION

Take a walk around your company. Watch employees as they go about their jobs. Ask your management personnel about their most productive employees. Watch how *they* conduct their days. How are they different from employees who are less productive in the company? Talk with them. Get some feedback. Make a list of the best practices in your company.

## MISSION STATEMENT

Review your company mission statement. What training policies can you put into place that can help you better achieve your mission?

Answer these questions:

- What are the major goals of your company?

- What skills do your employees need to achieve these goals, such as:

  o Sales training

  o Customer service instruction

  o Product knowledge

  o Communication skills

  o Technology skills

There are probably dozens of things you can add to this list, and variations of each. As you build *your* list, you should also establish *priorities*. Remember, training works along the same 80/20 principle as everything else. Don't waste time. Here are more questions you need to ask:

- What competencies will help develop the skills needed to run your company more efficiently?

- What are your current strengths and weaknesses?

- What are the areas that need the greatest improvement?

- What is your competition doing that you aren't?

Once you understand the training deficits within your company, you must decide how much effort to put into your training program. If your training needs are small, you may only tweak a few things. If you find that your company skills and knowledge gaps are the size of a small country, you should address the problem (and opportunity) with time, money and concerted effort.

Here are a few of the factors that will help influence your decision:

- The labor market. Is it cheaper to hire new, more highly skilled employees than to train existing ones?

   o Many companies face high turnover, particularly among their less highly trained workers. In a tight job market, you may be able to import new talent more easily than you can teach new skills to your current workforce.

- How big is the skills (and knowledge) gap in your company?

   o Sometimes, new information can be imparted easily. If not, you will have to address the problem in a more formal manner.

   o Is this something you can bridge with a few company meetings or seminars?

- What is the workload status for employees with the greatest training need?

   o If employees are running flat out, it may be difficult to take them off the job in order to train them. Then again, if your employees are working inefficiently, you will be able to train them to do more in less time. This is most apparent with technology. Today's technology can help one person do the work that it took three people to accomplish twenty years ago. If your employees are hampered by old technology and poor technological competence, you must bring them closer to the cutting edge.

- Who will implement your training? At what cost?

  o Few companies are awash in cash and time. Most private businesses must squeeze a dollar from every quarter. Therefore, training decisions must be implemented within clear sight of the bottom line.

  o Can you train existing employees to become inside "experts" that can train others?

## TRAINING OPTIONS

Your training options are endless. The ones that *you* choose will be dependent upon:

- The extent of your training needs

- Employee time constraints

- Your financial resources

- The financial benefits of training

- The individual learning styles of your employees

Professional educators understand that everybody learns differently. For example, some people are auditory learners. Auditory learners absorb new information better when they *hear* it. Others are better when they *read* it. Still others learn better with *touch* and *feel*.

As you develop your training, you should be aware of these different learning styles. Someone who falls asleep during seminars is not absorbing the information. This same employee might thrive with interactive computer learning.

Use end-of-training testing and evaluation to ensure that employees understand what they have learned, and as a way to continually improve the process.

# IN-HOUSE TRAINING

In-house training has advantages over other forms of learning, particularly for smaller companies. You don't need to pay for hotel space, or pay big seminar fees. If your employees are housed in one place, they won't have to waste time traveling to outside locations. In-house training can allow even your most critical employees to attend learning sessions. You should also get good group interaction among employees, as they learn together.

In-house training requires a good deal of logistical planning. Someone at your firm must co-ordinate the training, as well as manage the details around it. If your company has multiple locations, it may not be practical to have all of your employees converge on one location.

# SEMINARS

Seminars are an effective method of training, and can be used by nearly every company. Seminars may be conducted at your company location, or at off-site locations. They can be moderated internally, or by outside professionals. They come in every form of media.

### Public Seminars

Public seminars can teach skills and impart knowledge effectively. They can be reasonably priced, or outrageously expensive. It usually won't break your budget to send a few executives to a seminar. It may crumble your bank account to send all employees to a weekend retreat.

Public seminars are most helpful with generic knowledge and skills. They tend to be less industry specialized and more personally driven.

When evaluating a seminar, you must make sure that it is teaching information that *directly translates* to skills needed for your company. Sending your salespeople for sales training may sound like a great idea, but how will it translate to selling your product or service?

Make sure it's relevant.

# PRE-PACKAGED TRAINING PROGRAMS

You may be able to find pre-packaged training programs that are specialized for *your* industry. Look through your trade journals. You may find them advertised.

You will find training for everything. Every piece of software has a training program somewhere. Every piece of equipment has a manual. The same holds true with each function in your company.

You can find free instruction all over the Internet. Blogs offer tutorials. Companies do the same for their products. A little searching over the Web can help find much of what you need. Ask your employees to help with this. They have skills that will surprise you.

### Effective Combination

Many companies find that combining pre-packaged materials with customized, in-house programs offers the most cost-effective solution to training.

# COLLEGE TRAINING

Most colleges offer programs to help employees improve their skills. Colleges offer executive programs during the day or at night, intensive weeks-long programs and weekend retreats. Others offer on-demand programs over the Internet. We've all seen the University of Phoenix advertisements. Even Ivy League colleges offer distance learning from the comfort of one's living room.

# INDUSTRY EXAMS & CERTIFICATION

Most industries have certification programs that can be taken individually, or on a group basis. Certifications are usually maintained with continuing education requirements. Certification training can be an effective way to train employees at reasonable costs.

# INTERACTIVE LEARNING

With today's teleconferencing and high-speed Internet, employees can attend interactive seminars (webinars) from a conference room, a personal computer at their work desk, or a television at home. Tele-seminars can be very cost-effective, allowing employees to "meet" and converse with some of the greatest minds on the planet.

Bill Gates, the founder of Microsoft, has spoken of how he regularly uses interactive seminars to stay current with social and technological trends.

# TRAINING PROGRAM SUMMARY

- An effective training program should address a fundamental need for improvement in the knowledge and skills of your employees. It should produce more in profits than it costs.

- It should be designed around your company's mission statement. Your training program should help employees better accomplish the goals of your company.

- It should be built around the fundamental needs of your company.

- Your program should be implemented only after you have conducted a thorough review of your company employees.

- You should develop your training program to incorporate the different learning styles of employees.

- The training should be appropriate to the needs of each employee. For example, don't waste time teaching your accountant how to sell widgets.

- Thoroughly evaluate the training systems in the

marketplace. Look for programs that are available for free or at little cost.

• Ask employees to provide examples of training that they feel would be helpful.

• Look for programs that are industry-specific. Evaluate the quality of each program. Get referrals. Talk to others who have used them.

• Get feedback from your employees. Ask them what knowledge and skills they need to better do their jobs. Once they undertake any new training, ask them (in person and with surveys) to evaluate the effectiveness of the training.

• Use the proper training venues. You can't teach soccer on a hockey rink. The same holds true in business training. Make sure that you train employees in an environment that is conducive to the best learning.

• Where appropriate, make sure you have an agenda. Share it with participants in advance so that they understand the program.

# CREATE A LEARNING CULTURE

The most effective companies have created a culture of learning. Employees within these organizations are expected to seek continual improvement in their personal and business lives. Effective companies encourage employees to learn. They also provide a learning path. They often provide the resources. They make learning easy. They reward it.

You may not be able to afford to reimburse employees for furthering their education. But you can make it easier for employees to improve their skills. You can encourage them to do so. Here are a few things you can do:

- Create a list of all of the learning resources available to employees.

- Demonstrate to employees how learning has improved the performance of others.

- Build a company library. Collect books, courses, CDs or DVDs teaching the skills of the job. Your employees may have items to lend or donate to the library.

  o Consider having a training room, where employees can read or watch programs in a good learning environment.

- Consider tuition reimbursement for relevant course training and seminars.

- Establish a culture of communication between all levels within your company.

- Continually measure the results of your training program. Survey employees (and even customers) about the effectiveness of your training. Evaluate the efficiency of employees and departments that utilize your training. Make sure it works.

**Summary**

With all of the tasks you must complete in your daily work-life, building a comprehensive training program may seem like an impossible fantasy. It doesn't need to be. You can begin with small steps. By reading this text, you are already well underway toward improving your company's training program. Ask your employees to help you. Some will surprise you — with their willingness to contribute, and with their ability to create something great. If you set better training as a goal, it will happen. So do it now.

# Chapter Twenty-Eight
## _____HR_____
## Attract & Retain

# WORK ENVIRONMENT

Employees work more productively in places they enjoy. They work longer and harder if they like their jobs and feel appreciated.

This concept seems so basic that you wouldn't think I would need to state it. You are probably saying to yourself, "Of course, people work better in jobs they enjoy."

Why then, do so many small businesses ignore the concept?

What active steps have *you* taken to make your business a great place to work? What policies and procedures have you implemented to make your employees' jobs more enjoyable?

HR executives working for small and mid-sized businesses are often overwhelmed with "getting things done." They rarely have time to address issues that aren't specifically on their job description. It is easy to ignore little things that can make huge differences in employee attitude and productivity.

### Don't Overlook

Our basic animal senses are programmed to keep us safe. By nature, we become accustomed to various stimuli, to the point where we no longer notice things that many outsiders will. For example, people who live near a highway or train tracks, often won't hear the noise. Their brains learn to filter out the normal, so that they can focus on more important stimuli. In our own homes, we won't hear a ticking clock. We won't see the dust on the window panes or in the corners of our floors. We no longer smell the unique odors of our own residence, as we do when we visit others'.

### Don't Be Complacent

We get used to our surroundings, wherever we are, and we begin to overlook, and not even notice, things that can be very significant. The same holds true in business. Over time, we begin to overlook little thing that can dramatically enhance productivity. *We become complacent. We stop doing the little things that aren't essential, but still matter greatly to certain employees.*

## RETHINK YOUR WORKPLACE

When employees know that management cares about them, they will be more inclined to care about management.

Take a walk through your business with a fresh pair of eyes. Are the bathrooms clean? Are the floors clean? Are supplies in order? Are employees bickering among themselves, protecting turf rather than supporting each other? Are employees getting the recognition they deserve for outstanding performance? Are *you* doing the little things to keep your employees motivated? Are employees willing to take on extra responsibility, or work loner without complaint? Is management interacting with the rank and file? Do employees feel empowered and valued, or do they feel ignored? How full is your suggestion box? Does your CEO routinely greet employees by name and with a smile?

### Make Things Fresh Again

There are dozens of little things you can do to keep your business fresh. It starts by taking a walk around your offices. Notice the little things that your senses have tuned out. Sit down with employees and ask them how things are going, and what you can do to make things better. This will go a long way toward improving morale and productivity, with virtually no cost.

The following chapters will discuss other techniques to make your workplace more productive. But don't forget to use your own eyes and ears.

# Chapter Twenty-Nine
## HR
### Attract & Retain

# WHAT TO PAY & HOW TO FIGURE IT OUT

Private employers have a fair understanding of what sort of salary it takes to hire good people. Most of this knowledge has come through experience, sometimes simple trial and error. An offer is made. It gets rejected. A new offer is made, which gets rejected again. Finally, a compromise is reached and a standard gets set.

### Be Efficient with Salaries

A general understanding of appropriate salaries is not the most efficient way in which to compensate employees. You should know more.

Large companies employ specialists who continually monitor the marketplace for salary data. They subscribe to services which develop complicated salary matrixes. They use the law of large numbers to develop salary algorithms that pinpoint the relative value of each position within a company. This value gets augmented by relative productivity within that position. With salary caps in professional sports, some teams have developed relative value into a true science.

Systematic salary planning is *not* the playground of the small or mid-sized business HR manager. Smaller businesses often have employees that fulfill multiple roles. Paying someone "what they are worth" is far more subjective than a point on a salary scale.

As the HR manager for your company, there **are** some things that you can do to make sure that what you pay employees is commensurate with their value.

## TYPES OF COMPENSATION

Before we work on building a compensation system, let's discuss the various ways in which employees can get paid.

- **Salary**. Salary is a fixed amount paid on a regular basis. Base salary is the amount paid before deductions are taken from pay.

- **Base Wage**. This is an hourly wage paid only for hours worked. Base wages are typically paid for a normal work week, traditionally forty hours.

- **Overtime**. Overtime is typically paid when the normal work week has been exceeded. Time and a half (150% of base wage) is the standard overtime wage.

- **Bonus**. This is an incentive on top of base compensation, which is usually paid for outstanding performance.

  o   Bonuses are typically paid in cash or with shares of company stock.

  o   Privately held companies may use such variants as "shadow stock," and "stock appreciation rights." This type of bonus is beyond the scope of this book.

- **Stock Options**. Public companies often pay incentive compensation in the form of stock options. These are options to purchase company shares at a specific price. If the company does well, and the stock price increases, options can become quite valuable. Privately held companies can employ variants of public stock options.

• **Benefits**. Benefits can be offered to all employees, or to just a selective group. Benefits come in many forms, such as health and life insurance, retirement plans, deferred compensation, etc.

• **Commissions**. Commissions are often paid to sales people. Typically, commissions are paid as a percentage of the sales price for a particular product or service. Commissions can be "straight," with no base pay. They may offset a "draw against commissions" that is paid on a regular basis. Commissions may be paid in addition to a salary. Employers may also pay a regular "draw," which is treated as an advance against future commissions.

• **Exempt workers**. Exempt workers are a classification of employees who receive salaries (typically on a weekly, bi-weekly or monthly basis). Exempt workers do *not* normally receive overtime pay, when they work more than a typical work week.

• **Nonexempt workers**. These are full-time employees who receive an hourly wage. Nonexempt employees are covered under the provisions of the Fair Labor Standards Act (FLSA), as well as similar state laws. These laws set out regulations regarding minimum wages and *overtime pay*.

• **Total Compensation**. Total compensation is a combination of all of the forms of compensation.

# BUILDING AN EFFECTIVE COMPEN-SATION STRUCTURE AND SYSTEM

Establishing a functional compensation system must begin with a *compensation philosophy*. Do you want to pay the highest compensation for the best talent? Do you want employees within various teams to be paid the same, regardless of position? Do you want lower base earnings with lots of incentive pay? Each strategy can be effective, but you cannot employ all at once. Here are some of the questions that you will want to answer:

- Do you want to pay employees fairly, but not excessively, running the risk of losing some employees to higher compensation offers? Or, do you want to be at the top of the compensation scale, ensuring a low turnover because of compensation issues?

- Do you want to structure compensation based upon positions within your company? Or, do you want to pay compensation on an individualized basis? For example, do all administrative assistants receive the same salary? Do all sales people have the same base salary and commission percentage? Or, are some more valuable than others?

- Do you want to make *individual* or *collective* incentives a major part of compensation? For example, many investment management firms pay a modest base salary, with a hefty bonus based upon individual performance and/or that of the entire firm.

- Do you want to offer a lot of benefits and lower base pay, or fewer benefits and higher pay?

- How much do you want incentive compensation to be part of the total pay package? Are you paying Christmas bonuses to all employees, or are you establishing incentive compensation as the major part of total compensation?

- Do you want to pay "above and beyond" bonuses for exceptional effort or production?

- Do you want to pay salaries or hourly wages?

- Do you want part-time employees and independent contractors to be part of the mix?

Your compensation philosophy can vary between departments of your company. Sales departments tend to be highly incentive based. Administrative functions tend to be far less incentive-laden. Once you have determined your compensation philosophy, you will want to build it into a system. An effective compensation system should have the following attributes:

- Compensation should be perceived as fair by your employees. Nobody likes to be treated unfairly, particularly with compensation. Employees who feel they are unfairly compensated will be unproductive. They will speak poorly of your company. They won't stay with you for long (unless they really aren't worth what you are paying them).

  o You need to communicate why you pay what you do. You should explain all of your costs that don't show up in regular paychecks. Benefits and taxes can easily exceed thirty percent of an employee's total compensation. Employees should know this. If you don't explain it, employees will be less content with their pay. Benefit statements are a great way to communicate the unseen compensation that employees receive.

- Nepotism should be avoided. Don't pay unusually high salaries to non-productive family members of the ownership group. Employees resent working with members of an owner's family who simply sit around and collect a big paycheck.

• Make sure that the pay scales within your company reflect the *relative value* of the job, and the skills required to do that job. Don't let one employee set an unreasonable bar that forces you to pay all others more than they are worth.

• Keep your pay competitive, so that you are not losing your best and brightest to your competitors.

o Be willing to adjust your pay practices as the business climate and job market changes around you.

• Manage your total compensation as a percentage of your total company revenues. Review industry data to see where you should be and manage your pay accordingly. Payrolls, including benefits and taxes, generally run about thirty to forty percent of total revenues.

• Communicate your compensation policy to employees. Make sure your compensation strategy has the support of management. Don't make compensation a complete mystery.

• Don't play favorites. Employees should be paid what they are worth. Employees should not receive greater compensation because they are a friend or better window dressing than someone else.

• Stay within the law.

## ESTABLISHING COMPENSATION

Compensation is normally a function of how important a job is to your company.

Since nothing happens without sales, salespeople are usually among the most highly paid employees. A company without effective leadership goes nowhere, so effective leaders are also among the most highly paid employees. Employees that are easily replaced will be at the lowest end of the salary scale.

## COMPENSATION PROCEDURE

Earlier in this book we discussed the following.

- Organizational Hierarchy Chart – Position and Duties
- Competency Models
- Skills Inventories
- Employee Templates
- Detailed Job Descriptions

Hopefully, you have completed these tasks for your company. Now, we will put that information to further use. Make a list of every job within your company. Group them into categories, such as sales, management, and customer support. As you outline the jobs and categories for your business, don't be afraid to solicit help with this from your senior management and key employees.

Once you have a full list of jobs within your company, you should rank them according to the following criteria:

- How important is this job to your company's mission?

- How hard is this job to fill? Are there many qualified candidates? Is there a scarcity of talent in the marketplace for this job?

- How valuable is this job to your company? Can you survive without it?

- What skills are required for this job? Does one

need a Ph.D. or a law degree, or a high school education?

- · Does the job help pull the company train? Does the job produce something of measurable value or enhance revenues?

- Are there other factors that make this job more valuable than others?

## SETTING THE PAY

Once you have a greater understanding about the relative value each position has within your company, you can set appropriate pay. This will help you become more efficient and more profitable. Pay scales will need to be adjusted, based upon other factors, such as:

- **The marketplace**. How easy is it to replace someone in this job? Teachers and day care workers are often underpaid, relative to their value in society and the training necessary to qualify for the position. This is because there is a ready pool of candidates available to replace a lost worker. If an employee is easy to replace, their compensation value is limited.

- **Comfort & Fit.** In private businesses, pay is often determined by an owner or manager based upon the *comfort level* of an employee. Employees that don't require supervision, who know what they are doing and do it well, are worth keeping happy.

- **Dedication.** Does this employee possess the traits you desire for your company? Does this employee represent your company well, work long hours without complaint, or seek personal improvement without requirement?

# ASSESSING YOUR PEOPLE & FINE-TUNING COMPENSATION

Many factors go into an employee's value to a company. Some of these are tangible, such as skill level or productivity & output. Other contributing factors are far more difficult to measure and quantify. What is the value of loyalty? How much does an employee raise the productivity of the people around her?

Other factors come into play on a macro, rather than individual, level. Rewarding individual employees for excellence can be a motivator to other employees, thereby improving overall productivity. Rewarding employees for loyalty (longevity) can encourage newer employees to remain with your company, thereby reducing turnover costs.

Everybody brings something different to a company. Here are a few things you should consider:

- Current and previous experience. Employees with a great deal of experience and knowledge are able to function well and *adapt* with the changes around them. This type of employee is often difficult to replace. It may be far more costly to replace this sort of employee than to retain them with a little more compensation.

- Education regarding your products and services can be invaluable. Overall education may or may not be critical. Employees who have learned the ins and outs of working within your company can also have an added value over outside candidates, who would need to be trained and initiated to your business methods.

- Longevity within a company matters. Rewarding employees for their seniority sends a powerful message to newer members; remaining with your company has advantages. Employees who know that compensation increases are a reward for maintaining their productivity will be more prone to keeping it high.

• Individual performance comes in many forms. The value of players like Larry Bird to the Boston Celtics, or Tom Brady to the New England Patriots extends beyond their individual ability to perform. The examples set by Bird and Brady, as well as their leadership qualities, made all the players around them better. The same holds true with some of your employees. Don't overlook the intangibles that an employee brings to your company.

• Marketing savvy and contacts. Some employees just have a knack for making things grow, like a business "green thumb." Maybe it is cocktail conversation, community service, or golf course connections. While it may be hard to quantify, don't overlook this hidden value that some employees may bring to your company.

# SETTING WAGES

Setting wages can be challenging. Private businesses are far less academic than their large counterparts, but usually have a very good idea about the prevailing wages in their industry and region.

Still, private businesses must eke out as much productivity per dollar as they can. If you can get the same productivity for smaller wages, you should do it.

## Get Organized

If you are like most small businesses, your current compensation structure was established over time. You paid what you "needed to" when any new employee was hired. An as-needed strategy usually results in a haphazard payroll structure. Compensation varies from employee to employee and department to department, without any rational thought or explanation. It happened on its own. It is costing you money. You should review the pay for all your employees, and bring it into proper balance.

### Prevailing Rate

What is the prevailing wage rate? The prevailing rate is what you must pay to get the quality of work that you need. You should understand these rates, by position, within your particular marketplace. If you have a rational explanation for why you pay a particular wage for a particular job, you can often reduce employee grumbling and increase the overall satisfaction within your work force.

There are several concepts you should understand when establishing the prevailing wages within your company. If you must deal with collective bargaining, this can be particularly challenging. If employees are not union-based, this can be much easier. You can set prevailing base wages by using the following methods:

# BROADBANDING

Broadbanding is widely used to develop pay systems within a company. Broadbanding is used scientifically and systematically within large organizations. It happens organically within most smaller ones. Private companies usually broadband without using the term or actively practicing the methodology.

In broadbanding, a number of related jobs are grouped into one category, or "band." Rather than having a National Service Manager, Regional Service Manager, District Service Manager, Branch Service Manager, Service Tech, Telephone Service Support, Media Service Support, etc., you create one large category entitled "Service." In this example, base salaries might range from $15,000 to $80,000. Individual managers will have the ability to adjust pay based upon job performance rather than a specific job title.

Broadbanding gives flexibility to managers, allowing them to adjust compensation based upon productivity. It reduces excessive pay required by a simple title, rather than job performance.

Like any method designed to adjust pay, it can create morale problems, particularly among long-time employees who are past their most productive days. Broadbanding allows for favoritism and discrimination — which can create conflict and inconsistencies. Managers can reward employees for their productivity, or they can pay their friends more than others, simply because they like them. Beware.

## SKILLS

Paying wages based upon *skills,* rather than position, is a growing trend within national management circles. Employees in the same position, but with different skills, will earn differently. This allows you, the employer, to differentiate pay based upon *productivity*, rather than position. Implementing skills-based compensation allows you to:

- Pay less to younger, less skilled workers.

- Create incentives for employees to increase skills.

- Empower employees who want to grow.

Setting up a skills based system will take some effort on your part. You will have to establish rules. You will have to monitor skill levels regularly. However, this will enable you to start younger (or newer) employees at a smaller wage, without creating resentment.

**Note:** You will have to monitor this system, adjusting it along with the requirements of the job and the marketplace.

## PROFICIENCY

Another way to establish wage scales is through *proficiencies* rather than skills. Think of this as measuring an employee's attributes rather than their specific skills. Here, you would develop a list of core competencies for each job. (See your Competency Models) An employee's pay will be based upon that employee's ability to acquire and master the competencies required to earn the maximum pay.

Just like the skills paradigm, this pay system encourages employee growth. It attracts employees who want to get paid "what they are worth," and discourages employees who simply to clock in for the paycheck.

This type of system can be a challenge to develop and monitor. You must get your employees to accept the system. Established employees who are past the stage of youthful ambition may feel that they are being unfairly treated. Employees who have grown too comfortable, or too stagnant, in their jobs will complain. If you can handle the initial grumbling, you may be able to significantly energize your employees with this strategy.

Switching to this type of incentive-based compensation may cause early turnover, particularly among your less productive employees. But, it will increase motivation and growth within your work force.

# VARIABLE PAY FOR PERFORMANCE

Variable pay systems tie a percentage of an employee's pay to performance. Performance can be measured on a company-wide level, by department or by the individual. This can be a form of *profit sharing*, where individuals and departments are rewarded for their contribution to the overall well-being of a company.

With a variable pay system, employees receive a guaranteed base pay. This gives employees the comfort of an ongoing income. Incentive is created by rewarding employees with an additional ten or twenty or thirty percent of pay, which is based upon predetermined goals. These goals may be individual, department or company-specific.

### Payroll Flexibility

Variable pay creates payroll flexibility for private companies, allowing them to pay more when business is good, and less when business turns downward. It reduces the morale-crushing problem of having to cut salaries when business is bad. It also keeps employees focused upon the most profitable uses of their time. Employees will often police each other, making sure that everyone keeps on task.

This type of compensation structure can hurt morale when a company is not able to reach its goals. This may occur because of faulty projections, or because of economic conditions outside the control of employees, or the company.

Care must be taken with this arrangement, making sure that certain employees are not favored over others.

When making promises of incentive compensation, be sure that you can back up what you promise. You must have a system in place that can accurately monitor the variables needed to trigger your incentives.

## SUMMARY

As you can see, there are many ways that compensation can be structured. Changing from haphazard pay to a systematic compensation structure can help reduce your payroll costs without sacrificing productivity. An incentive-based corporate culture can be highly effective and profitable. Both take thought and ongoing attention.

Creating a systematic compensation structure is much like a farmer growing a crop. Care must be taken to plow, plant, fertilize and water the field. Time and money must be spent, long before any crop yields its bounty. The yield can be great, and the profits rewarding, provided all of the critical steps are followed.

Creating this type of compensation arrangement can dramatically increase the yield for *your* company, but you must be as diligent as any good farmer and tend to your crops. Don't start it unless you are willing to see it through.

# Chapter Thirty
## HR
### Attract & Retain

# YOUR CORPORATE HIERARCHY — WHO DOES WHAT

Employees who understand their place within a company...employees who know what is expected of them...are far happier and more productive than employees with no clear vision of their role.

Too many private companies manage without detailed job descriptions, or any clear-cut corporate hierarchy. Smaller companies tend to have a CEO (usually the owner) who makes the ultimate decisions. There might be various managers who perform key tasks and help implement the company's mission. Then there is everybody else.

If you establish detailed job descriptions and place these jobs within a corporate hierarchy chart, you will give employees a greater understanding of what you need them to accomplish. This will help you establish clear lines of function and communication. Employees will know who to contact when they have questions or problems. They won't waste time doing work that should be done by others. They will spend more time on task.

# Chapter Thirty-One
## _____HR_____
## Attract & Retain

# EMPLOYEE COMMUNICATION

We have already discussed the importance of employee communication. In the following paragraphs, I will show you how to use communication to help your business function more efficiently and profitably.

**SHARED VISION** — Mission Statements & Sub-mission Statements

You are probably tired of hearing us talk about mission statements and, as George H. W. Bush once put it, "the vision thing." The fact is; sharing your company vision is critical to creating and maintaining robust company efficiency. When employees know their mission, they have a goal. Everybody works better with goals. In order to communicate a cohesive company vision you should:

- Create and distribute a clear mission statement.

- Make sure that all of your employees understand your mission and are working in sync with that mission.

- Create a culture where your employees help others remain focused on the company's mission.

# DEFINING ROLES

Establish a group of **sub-mission statements** for the different departments within your organization. Create mission statements for sales, marketing, service, management, customer service, etc.

Make sure that every employee understands the mission of the company, as well as their individual mission.

# STRATEGIC FOCUS

Make sure that each manager within your company has a clear understanding of your company's mission, as well as the mission of his or her team. Once you are sure that management and employees understand the mission, you should take steps to see that everyone maintains a strategic focus upon the mission.

- Establish clear and realistic goals.

  o Lay out your strategy to achieve these goals.

  o Establish and clarify the tasks, roles and responsibilities of every team and team member.

  o Establish rewards for success and penalties for failure.

- Establish your methodology for measuring success.

  o Set up regular meetings to discuss each group's or employee's status.

  o Establish procedures to monitor progress.

  o Be organized and consistent.

  o Praise success.

o    Establish protocols to help avoid and mitigate failure.

o    Make teams and individuals accountable for their actions.

o    Make appropriate changes to employees and teams that are not meeting your goals.

o    Set the rules for resolving conflicts. Conflict can be a good thing, as long as it leads to correcting mistakes and increasing performance. Employees should be encouraged to voice their differences and concerns, provided you have a procedure in place for resolving any lingering issues between employees.

# Chapter Thirty-Two
## HR
## Attract & Retain

# EMPLOYEE ADVANCEMENT

Large companies have significant advantages over smaller ones when it comes to advancement opportunities. Big companies have many spaces to fill. They have turnover. They have the resources to train employees for roles with greater responsibilities and greater incomes.

Private companies run the risk of losing their greatest talent because there is no place to promote them, or enough resources to pay them. The best and brightest may go to work for the competition. They may even become the competition, by going into business for themselves. This can lead to low morale and create staleness within a company.

**What can you do to keep employees who need to stretch beyond your ceiling?**

Banks are famous for paying modest wages to their officers — but everybody gets a title. Titles can be an effective substitute for greater pay, to a point. They help build self-esteem and maintain job satisfaction.

If an employee is outgrowing the responsibilities and positions you can offer, sometimes a new title can be enough to keep them happy, at least for a while.

You may also be able to come up with special projects, for which you can pay additional compensation. Special projects can boost esteem and create loyalty. They can make underemployed workers feel essential, which they may very well be.

Don't be afraid to help employees improve their knowledge and skills. When employees feel thwarted, they begin to look elsewhere.

Selective compensation and benefits can also become an alternative to employee advancement. These are discussed in Part Eight of this book.

# Chapter Thirty-Three
## HR
### Attract & Retain

# EMPLOYEE RELATIONS

When employees are happy, they work better. A bigger paycheck does not always solve this goal.

Too many small employers make the mistake of focusing solely upon increased compensation and job advancement as their method for maintaining and improving job performance.

As we have discussed, psychological factors can also have a direct impact upon productivity. Many of these cost you nothing at all.

Having a workplace with good employee relations is critical toward achieving maximum output from your entire workforce.

As we discussed earlier, companies that foster good employee communication are far more productive than ones that don't. Communication is critical in maintaining good employee relations.

Communication is not the only low-cost way to boost productivity. Many strategies can enhance employee relations. Here are some of the others.

## EMPOWERMENT

Employees that have reasonable autonomy and control of their individual actions are more likely to perform better. When bosses are not trying to micro-manage every activity, employees will tend to take "ownership" of their actions. They will have more pride in their work, since it is theirs.

Employee empowerment occurs when individual judgment is allowed to replace restrictive rules and procedures. Here are some effective empowerment strategies that you can employ with very little outlay.

- ALLOW INITIAL FAILURE. You must be willing to allow employees to fail at the outset. When they fail, you should help them correct their mistakes and do it right the next time.

- TRAINING. If you are going to allow employees to take more initiative, you must provide appropriate training that will allow them to succeed.

- INFORMATION. We have already discussed the need for communication. You must ensure that employees have access to all of the information they need to make informed and appropriate decisions.

- REDUCE THE HIERARCHY CLUTTER. Too many cooks spoil the meal. The same holds true with employee empowerment. It is fine for an employee to answer to a boss. But when an employee constantly fears reprisal, which can be caused by pleasing too many masters, paralysis can set in.

- In some cases, you might pay more attention to *results* than *how* the work gets done. Certain employees may work more efficiently with some down time. They may need extra coffee breaks or water cooler conversation. Others may need to work off-site, at the local Starbucks, or at the library. Don't penalize a highly productive employee just because they make it look easy.

• SHOW YOU CARE. It is easy for business managers to forget about the warm and fuzzy little things that can affect a company's overall mood. Employees work harder when they feel that their work is appreciated. We have already discussed some of the simple strategies that you can employ. Other effective, "mental health" policies, are more difficult to justify, because they involve expenses that can stretch a challenging budget. It has been shown, however, that certain policies can return more to employers than they cost. Such policies include:

     ○ Time off. Everybody needs time to recharge their batteries. Vacation time is essential. Companies generally give time off for holidays and vacations. Others allow a certain number of off-days to be taken at any time. **Note:** Be sure to examine your policies with regard to accrued time off. Accrued vacation time can become a significant, hidden liability for a company.

     ○ Leaves of Absence. Sometimes employees have issues that make it impossible to work effectively. Large companies generally allow employees to take unpaid leaves of absences. This is far more difficult for private companies, as every employee can be critical. Newer laws force companies to allow leaves under certain conditions, so every employer should have a plan in place to manage such events. This is especially true for employers with more than 50 employees.

          ▪ When you have clear job descriptions and written procedures for each position, existing employees may be able to fill a void created by a leave of absence. Or, you may be able to hire temporary workers to do the same.

o  Sick days. Large companies typically allow 5-15 paid sick days per year. Private companies don't have the resources to pay employees when they are sick, at least for very long. Many smaller companies allow sick days on an "as needed" basis, without creating a formal, sick-day policy. Beware: If you don't have a formal sick day policy, the courts may create one for you, mandating a policy that is "customary" to that of larger companies. So, create one. Whatever your policy, make sure to formalize your sick day policy and communicate it to employees so that they understand it.

o  Telecommuting. With today's technology, it is often more efficient for employees to work from home, rather than face long commutes while they juggle the requirements of business and family life. Don't be afraid to utilize telecommuting in your business practices.

o  Casual Fridays help some employees remain fresh at the end of a week. Allowing employees to leave early on Friday (when weekly or monthly performance is outstanding) can also become a powerful incentive for maintaining excellence.

## LET MANAGERS MANAGE

Private businesses face management challenges which are not present in large companies. One of these can be particularly vexing to business owners. This has to do with authority.

It can be very difficult for a private company CEO to let go, such that they allow their managers to actually manage.

Private company CEOs often feel that it is their obligation to remain accessible to their employees. On the whole, this is a very good thing. However, if a CEO allows employees to come to *them* to resolve conflicts with their *managers*, and then overrides management decisions, this can seriously undermine the effectiveness of the management team.

**A manager whose decisions are constantly reversed by ownership will lose the ability to lead.** No manager likes to see employees going behind their back to their bosses.

**Note:** If your CEO has fallen into this trap (which is quite normal), you should encourage your CEO to resolve issues with managers first. There may be very good reasons for a manager's decisions. In cases where a decision is still reversed, the reversal should come from the manager, not the CEO. This will allow managers to maintain their integrity and avoid inefficient micro-management, where it is least efficient.

# Chapter Thirty-Four
## HR
## Attract & Retain

# GENERAL & SELECTIVE BENEFITS

Later, we will discuss specific details of benefits that companies can offer to employees. The purpose of this chapter is to discuss *how* benefits can be used to help you attract and retain productive employees.

If you don't offer competitive benefits, it is unlikely that you will attract and retain the type of full-time employees that you need. Even companies without formal benefits must usually provide something else to their employees.

**Mandated Benefits**

Most company benefits are voluntary to employers, but there are three that are not.

- Social Security & Medicare.

    ○ Employers must withhold Social Security taxes from employee incomes. The rate is 6.2% for employees. An additional 6.2% is paid by employers. (At the time of this writing, there is a temporary reduction in employee withholding to 4.2%). Withholding must be made on the first $110,100 (in 2012) of earned income.

o   Withholding for Medicare is 1.45%, with no cap. The Medicare rate is scheduled to increase to 2.35% (for individuals earning $200,000 and couples earning over $250,000) with the Health Care Reform Bill.

- Unemployment Insurance. Unemployment insurance was established in the Social Security Act of 1935. Unemployment insurance is managed by the under a loose set of laws. Employers typically pay unemployment insurance premiums to a state fund, based upon an overall experience rating that is set by the fund. **Note:** On an individual company basis, the more people you lay off, the higher your premiums might be.

- Workers' Compensation. Workers compensation was designed to provide benefits for workers who become injured or ill on the job, regardless of who is at fault. Workers comp (as it is called) will often pay medical bills, death benefits, and disability (partial income replacement) benefits to permanently disabled workers. Workers comp is an insurance program. Premiums are paid upon a per-employee basis. Premiums may be paid to a state fund, to private insurers, or to a mixture of both. Workers' comp structures vary from state to state. As a general rule, premiums are experience rated, based upon the number of claims filed against *your* company.

o   As an employer, you will want to have good workplace health and safety practices.

Note: You can research various Federal tax topics at the following Internet address:

http://www.irs.gov/taxtopics/

Besides the three mandated company benefits, there are many other benefit programs that companies can offer to their employees. Some may be provided to all employees, while others can be offered to a selective group.

### Deductibility

As a general rule, benefits that are offered to *all* employees (and paid by the employer) are tax deductible to the employer and not taxable to the employee.

Benefits that are offered *selectively*, to just a small group of employees, are usually not deductible to the employer and may be taxable to the employee.

Small companies typically provide the least amount of benefits that they can, while still being able to attract and retain the type of employees that they need.

Company-wide benefits, such as health insurance, are expensive, but often required to compete for a productive workforce. You may lose your best employees if you don't provide health insurance. You may find it difficult to recruit talented employees without it.

Selective benefits can be provided to specific workers, as an incentive for them to work for, and remain with, your company.

Managing benefits efficiently is critical to the ongoing success of every company. A full understanding of what is available, and how best to integrate company-wide and selective benefits is one of the most important functions of all HR managers.

# Chapter Thirty-Five
## HR
### Attract & Retain

# AWARDS & RECOGNITION

On April 17th, 2011, McDonalds announced that they would hire fifty thousand new, low-end workers. Some of these employees will see their name upon the wall as employee-of-the-month. Some may eventually become CEOs of major companies. Others may one-day own a franchise.

McDonalds is famous for providing both tangible and intangible *incentives* to employees who barely earn the minimum wage. At Mc-Donalds, employees are taught that everyone is critical to the success of a franchise, and to the company as a whole. The majority of the employees hired on April 17th will move on to other organizations, but while they are with McDonalds, each will be productive, and essential to the success of their company.

As an HR manager, you must ask yourself, "What is my company doing to provide awards and incentives to help improve employee productivity?"

While you may never grow to be as large as McDonalds, or even a single franchise, you *can* implement programs that will keep employees motivated, and make your company a better place to work.

# EMPLOYEE RECOGNITION

Employee recognition programs are part of every large company. They should be part of every small and mid-sized company as well. When designed correctly, and implemented properly, recognition programs improve productivity, enhance morale and increase employee loyalty.

Employee recognition programs should begin with one basic question in mind: **What behaviors are you trying to encourage?** Recognition programs should be designed to encourage and reward *specific* job actions. Are you looking to increase sales? Improve company service? Produce higher quality products? Eliminate company down time? Improve employee safety?

Whatever your company needs to improve and maintain can become a target for employee recognition. Employee recognition can come in the form of:

> • Spot bonuses. Bonuses can be awarded at any Spot bonuses should be reserved for outstanding performance that is above and beyond the norm. They are usually given in cash, gift cards, travel vouchers or trips.

> • Performance Awards. Performance awards are typically given in the form of cash, gift certificates, merchandise, travel vouchers or trips. What employee won't work hard after you have sent them to Bermuda for five days?

> • Recognition Awards. If you have ever watched college football, you have seen the stickers on player helmets. Ohio State gives out buckeyes. Florida State sports little tomahawks. Years ago, some brilliant football coach realized that, if he asked players to run through a wall, they would look at him cross-eyed. But if he said, "If you run through that wall, I will put a sticker on your helmet," he found that players

would line up for the chance. Employees in your company are the same. Recognition awards matter. So, use them.

- Service Awards. Service awards are generally given for length of service. However, they can be given out for other events and occasions. For example, if your company has just initiated a new product line, a service award might be given out to the individuals or team most responsible for its successful launch.

- Teamwork Awards. Teamwork awards are given to employees who make personal sacrifices for the good of their team.

- Idea Awards. Idea awards recognize employee suggestions that have led to improvements in any facet of the business.

When you establish awards, make sure that they are given for good reason only. Make your rewards matter. Rewards that are given for fairly good performance will result in just fairly good, not great production. Rewards that create clutter or become a nuisance are worthless.

If you use rewards correctly, they can become a powerful incentive that drives greater productivity in your company.

# Chapter Thirty-Six
## _____HR_____
# Effective Performance Management

# GOAL SETTING

**If you don't know where you are going, you won't get there**. This may sound like a Yogi Berra cliché, but it is one of the most fundamental business truths.

Think of it this way: When you decide to travel to a specific destination, you have a goal. If the destination is far away, you choose a method of transportation. Let's say your transportation is a car. The minute you sit in the seat, you have a plan; you know where you want to go. If you don't know what route to take, you might use a map or GPS. When you combine your destination objective, your car, your directions, and your efforts, you reach your destination.

With any company, **goals** determine your **destination**. Your business resources, and your people, become the method used to reach that goal.

**Goals must be specific**.

A goal of attending a wedding, "somewhere in Massachusetts," won't bring you to a ceremony on at the First Parish Church at 19

Town Square in Plymouth.

Companies that have clear cut, **written** goals are more efficient and more profitable. Employees who have a target destination, such as a "12% increase in sales," or a "99% employee service satisfaction rate," or a "99.85% quality control standard," will be more likely to reach their potential.

Employees with general goals of "better service," "greater sales," and "better quality control," will have a far more difficult time achieving excellence.

### Management by Objectives

Goal setting is often called Management by Objectives. In practice, a manager will sit down with an employee and set up targets for performance. These goals should be as specific as possible. The manager and employee should determine a method to measure the achievement of these goals. They should establish a time frame in which to measure progress and a time for review. In many cases, there should be a reward for success and a penalty for failure.

Management by Objective (MBO) works because the employee is *part of the planning process*. When an employee "owns" the goal, they are much more apt to achieve it, particularly if there is an incentive. In our car example, MBO provides the GPS. MBO directs employees to achieve their individual goals.

MBO can also be implemented on a *company-wide* basis, with each employee, team, department, division, region, etc. working toward common goals.

MBO requires organization. You must know what specific goals to expect. Employees must have the motivation and the means to achieve the objectives. You must also be prepared to follow through on your part of the process — performance management and rewards.

# Chapter Thirty-Seven
## HR
## Effective Performance Management

# PERFORMANCE ASSESSMENT

Measuring performance is critical to any company that wants to improve its efficiency and profitability.

### Facts are Facts

A sales goal is usually black and white. Ten percent growth is quite specific and easy to document. You have a benchmark.

### Intangible Factors

Assessing other areas of achievement is not so simple. Many factors come into play. For example: Your office manager, Judy, may be one of your most indispensable employees. It may be difficult to explain exactly why, but you just *know* it. Perhaps everyone says so.

### What to Measure

When measuring employee performance, it will be helpful to focus on the following areas:

- Quantity

- Quality

- Timeliness

- Intangibles

- Customer and peer feedback

# EVALUATION REPORTS

When managers prepare regular evaluation reports (or employee reviews), they become more aware of the efficiency of employees. When employees know that they are being reviewed, they adjust their behavior to achieve a good review. This is basic human nature. We like praise. We dislike criticism.

## Make them Count

Be sure that reviews don't become too routine and/or too biased. Vary their structure if you can. If a manager simply rubber stamps a review, he is wasting everybody's time. Make reviews count.

## Critical Incidence Reporting (CI Reports)

Critical incidence reporting is a common method of review and evaluation. CI reports try to measure an employee's intangibles, such as leadership ability, creativity, motivation, interpersonal skills and team orientation.

Critical incidence reporting should be far less regular and routine than employee evaluation reporting. It occurs "as things happen." As such, this type of reporting can capture the intangibles an employee brings to a company, traits that often don't show up in other places.

CI reporting does not need to be long and detailed. Even so, it may be extremely helpful in capturing the essence of an employee's value to a company.

A CI report might look like this: "We weren't sure how to approach this problem until Bill came up with a creative solution that was way out of the box. This is the second time this year that Bill has saved our department. Kudos to him!" This is a valuable report to have in Bill's employment file, as it demonstrates Bill's intangible value to the company.

### Checklist

Another employee rating system is the checklist. By establishing a pre-determined list of functions, traits and behaviors that are expected from an employee, a manager can complete employee evaluations in just a few moments. This type of evaluation is helpful in monitoring the ongoing pulse of your employees' job performance.

### Behaviorally Anchored Rating Scale (BARS)

A Behaviorally Anchored Rating Scale is an effective method of analyzing employee behaviors, as they relate to job performance. Look back to your job descriptions. Each one should identify the most important performance factors (dimensions) of each job. Make a list of the important job attributes and assign them to a rating scale (known as an anchor).

A rating scale of 1 to 5, with 5 being the highest, is generally sufficient. A simple BARS rating scale might look like this:

### JAMES DEAN – CUSTOMER SERVICE: PERFORMANCE RATING

| Attribute | Rating |
|---|---|
| Greets customers in friendly manner | _____ |
| Maintains positive service attitude | _____ |
| Knowledgeable about our products | _____ |
| Finds answers fast | _____ |
| Services customers efficiently | _____ |
| Gets to work on time | _____ |
| Does extra things to help others | _____ |
| Available on short notice | _____ |
| Presents a professional image | _____ |

Speaks well of company                                    _____

Dependable                                                _____

**Total Score**:                                          _____


A BARS scale gives your managers a quick way to keep track of an employee's behaviors, as they relate to their job. It can be especially useful when kept over a long period of time. It can help you spot behavioral trends and performance changes over time.

### Graphic Scale

A Graphic Scale is similar to the BARS, but with added dimensions. A graphic scale helps you appraise three distinct levels of employee performance. It helps you measure descriptive *attributes* (such as quantity of work, attendance, reliability), job *functions* (similar to the BARS and taken from the job description), and *behavioral* dimensions (such as decision making skills, creativity, attitude, communication abilities, product knowledge, personal development, etc.).

When using a graphic scale, you will want to establish specific standards for each category of job. You may use the same 1-5 scale, or general ratings such as "outstanding," "average," and "below average."

### Summary

Whenever you decide to implement a job rating system, make sure that your system gives you fairly accurate information that is pertinent to job performance. An employee who doesn't communicate well may be great as an accountant, but not productive in customer service.

Make sure that your rating system is fair, and not biased by the person who does the rating.

Make sure that the managers who are doing the rating are taught how to do it properly. Training is essential in the effective use of any rating system.

Employee rating can be an enormously helpful management tool, when used correctly. You must be thorough and organized in your approach to evaluating employees. If you do this properly, you will always have accurate moving snapshots of every key employee and department within your company.

Suggestion: Ask employees to appraise their own performance. Employees usually have a good idea of their own strengths and weaknesses. If employees are asked to evaluate their performance, they will often improve efficiency on their own.

Self-evaluations can be used in conjunction to with management appraisals. Together, they can help managers consistently monitor and improve employee performance.

## COMMUNICATE APPRAISALS

Just as employee appraisals must be conducted properly, they must also be *communicated* effectively. Employees that are being evaluated should *understand* the process, and should be told about the *results* in a *private* session *without* bias. Employees should be allowed to dispute findings, and to make improvements before the next rating session.

For each appraisal interview, your manager should:

- Prepare for the interview. Do not "wing it." The manager should prepare documentation for his findings.

- Allow employees time to prepare for the meeting.

- Allow sufficient time for the meeting.

- Have the meeting in a private place, where disagreements can be aired without distraction.

- Focus on an employee's performance and how to improve it.

- Make it a positive interview focused on improvement, not on failure.

- Be able to defend your ratings with specific examples.

- Allow the employee to respond to criticism and suggest ways to improve.

- Distinctly praise good performance and reinforce it.

- Develop a game plan to improve. This includes ways in which the manager can improve her performance.

When conducting a performance interview, the manager should not:

- Do all the talking.

- Concentrate solely on poor performance.

- Compare the employee with others. This is like criticizing a sibling by saying, "You should be more like your brother…" It only creates animosity.

Before you launch any rating system, you should:

- Establish clear cut goals for the system.

- Be sure that the system can improve employee performance.

- Get employees to embrace the system as a means to improve their job performance, leading to a healthier company and (maybe) promotions or better pay.

- Establish how reviews may be tied to pay.

- Develop an appropriate timeline for appraisals and reviews.

- Establish the ground rules for reviews, including how employees can dispute findings.

- Establish a training program (if needed) so that managers will conduct appraisals effectively.

## EMPLOYEE RATING OF MANAGERS

When you allow managers to rate the employees beneath them, you may not get a completely accurate picture of performance. When evaluating employees, you should also allow your employees to **evaluate their managers**. You should develop a similar system where employees are allowed to evaluate the people above them. This can be rather delicate. Employees may not want to criticize their bosses, for fear of losing their jobs.

Employee rating of bosses should be done when managers are being evaluated by *their* bosses. In many private companies, the managers' boss is the company CEO.

CEOs and managers should speak privately with employees when evaluating their managers. Employees should be given the equivalent of attorney/client privilege, where their individual criticism will **not** be shared with their boss. Keep it private. You'll get better feedback. If you request anonymous, written evaluations from a manager's team, you will get a good sense of how a manager is perceived by others, and a better idea of their strengths and weaknesses.

## MANAGE RESISTANCE

Nobody likes to be criticized, but most people want to improve their lives. Employee evaluations should be addressed as an effective method of improving overall company performance, as well as the lives of individual employees.

### Don't Threaten

Employees may feel threatened by an appraisal system. You need to assure them that it is necessary for maintaining overall corporate health. Communicate that appraisals are in the best interest of the company and each employee.

Communicate to employees that appraisals will be used to help improve employee performance, not punish them.

Communicate that good and improved performance, as measured by your appraisals, can lead to promotions and increased pay.

### Make Time

Managers may not want to take the time to conduct employee appraisals. Make it a requirement, at least annually. Stress that appraisals can lead to greater job performance and improved productivity. This may result in greater profits, which ultimately leads to greater pay for your managers.

### Minimize Paperwork

Do your best to minimize additional paperwork. This can be done by organizing your appraisals into a well-designed system.

### Follow Up

Once appraisals are completed, you must set up a plan to address the results and improve performance.

## APPRAISAL SUMMARY

Every company should have a way to measure and improve employee performance. By setting goals, and evaluating employee performance in achieving those goals, companies can dramatically improve their efficiency and profitability.

## Chapter Thirty-Eight
## _____HR_____
## Effective Performance Management

# EMPLOYEE MOTIVATION

People are motivated in many different ways. Some are primarily motivated by money. Others see status as more important than pay. That V.P. next to a name, or a plaque on the wall, can be far more important than a raise. Other employees value relationships, job flexibility, or the feeling of "making a difference" with a company or corporate society.

### What Motivates

As you establish the mechanisms to motivate employees, you must be aware that many employees are motivated differently than you are. If money is important to you, you will be predisposed to think that money is the greatest motivator for everybody. This is not the case.

In order to motivate effectively, you must be sensitive to the differences between individuals, and learn to adjust rewards and incentives accordingly.

Years ago, the "gold watch" was the ultimate reward for an employees' loyal career. In today's world of rapid job-switching and performance driven, productivity-based management, the gold watch has been replaced by different rewards, ones which have a greater impact upon a company's bottom line.

# DEVELOP YOUR OWN MOTIVATORS

Every company is different — by industry, by location, by dominant corporate culture. As such, what works as motivation for your company may not work effectively for the employer next door.

# COMPENSATION

Most people are motivated by money. Few employees feel that they are adequately compensated. An employee who feels fairly compensated, may still want more. This isn't bad; it's human nature. It drives us to succeed.

The easiest way to increase compensation is for your company to improve sales, work more productively, and make more money. This should be regularly communicated to your work force, on an individual and on a company-wide basis.

If your employees don't buy into the productivity concept, if your employees want higher wages or fewer work hours for the same productivity, then you must change your corporate culture.

### Discussing Compensation

As you discuss compensation, you should stress that greater pay comes from greater productivity. Increased productivity leads to greater profitability, which leads to higher incomes.

If an employee wants higher compensation, they must deliver more value. Value can be enhanced by assuming greater responsibilities, by delivering greater productivity and by helping others achieve higher production.

### Bonus Payments

Bonus payments can be an effective motivator, when warranted.

- Bonuses can be paid as part of incentive programs, retention programs, or recruiting programs.

- Bonuses can be paid annually, or on a spot basis.

- When you pay bonuses, give them for greater production, and actions that lead to greater profitability.

- Make sure that bonuses are part of an organized structure that treats employees fairly.

## COMMISSIONS & INCENTIVES

Nothing connects compensation more fairly to value than commissions and incentives.

Before you pay commissions, you want to make sure that you have an accurate measure of value. Make sure that your incentive structure is actually profitable. I have seen instances where incentive compensation actually causes a company to lose money rather than make it.

Incentives may include such items as customized benefits, individual learning opportunities, flexible scheduling, even a piece of the company.

## TEAMWORK

Many employees work more effectively when they are part of a team, rather than alone. There are many reasons for this.

- Working with a team can be fun. Job enjoyment can lead to greater productivity.

- Employees will do things for others than they would not do for themselves. Some employees will perform more tasks, or work longer hours, to support a team than they will for themselves.

- Peer pressure is powerful. The thought of letting others down can be a great motivator.

Many of us have seen a sports coach single out a player for lack of effort. A smart coach might not force this player to run extra laps or do more push-ups. The smart coach will make all the *other* players do this, while the offender is forced to watch. This puts major team-building dynamics into play, usually causing the offender to increase his or her effort to match the others.

The same happens with business teams. As a manager, you should understand that well-run teams can produce more than the team members working individually on their own.

## AWARDS

Don't be afraid to reward employees for their achievements. Sales awards, service awards, or any kind of award that creates incentive can lead to greater production. Make sure that the awards you give are meaningful. Don't give participation trophies; they are a joke in business and not worth the time or expense.

## EMPLOYEE CULTURE

If parts of your company are dysfunctional, or if you have employees who bicker or display Machiavellian tendencies by "stabbing each other in the back," you need to fix the problem. Nothing poisons productivity faster than a poor working atmosphere.

You want employees to look forward to coming to the office. Do everything in your power to make your company environment a friendly and supportive place to work. This might mean firing employees who bully others. It might mean hiring people that fit a certain profile. It might even mean making changes in the way you do business.

## TRAINING

If your employees lack the skills to do their jobs effectively, they won't be happy and they won't be productive. We've already discussed training programs in detail. Review your training program and make sure that it is getting the job done.

# COMMUNICATE

Companies with clear lines of communication have more contented, more productive, employees. Don't stifle your employees' creativity or enthusiasm. Make sure that your managers keep the lines of communication open. This includes allowing employees to voice their suggestions on how to improve your company.

## SAFETY

Employees want to feel safe at work. This means physical and emotional safety. If you have a work environment that causes employees physical and emotional stress, find ways to fix it.

## BENEFITS

No company can provide all of the benefits that employees need. Even the largest companies don't have the resources.

If you do provide benefits, you should communicate the *extent* and the *cost* of those benefits to employees. Many employees are not aware of how much you spend to keep them healthy and safe. Make sure they know. **Benefit statements** are a great way in which to do this.

Many employers give employees the opportunity to purchase their own, self-paid benefits through company payroll deductions. These will cost you little, if anything. But they can help reduce employee stress and increase productivity.

## SURVEY YOUR EMPLOYEES

If you ask employees what will make your company a better place to work, they will tell you. If you ask them what would provide greater motivation, they will give you some good ideas. Never be afraid to ask employees what they want. Even if you can't deliver what they ask for, at least they will know that you care.

## Chapter Thirty-Nine
## HR
## Effective Performance Management

# CONFLICT MANAGEMENT

Conflict is part of the human condition. At any given time, there are wars between nations, wars within nations, and disagreements in the halls of all governments. There are disagreements between spouses, between parents and children and between children. Conflict is as inevitable as breathing.

Conflicts within a business are just as normal. Managers argue among themselves. Managers disagree with employees. Employees do the same among themselves.

Sometimes the disagreements are meaningful. Sometimes they are petty. Most conflicts can have a successful resolution. The challenge for HR professionals is to solve conflicts in a manner that all sides feel that they are treated fairly.

### Conflict is Essential

In HR, you must accept the fact that conflict is normal, often healthy. You should even put systems in place to create (or at least encourage) conflict. You must also develop strategies to manage disagreements, so that they produce productive results.

If your business lacks conflict, then you are stifling creativity and healthy dissention. If you can't encourage and then manage conflict properly, you will have less innovation, lower output, greater employee turnover and poorer company morale.

The following pages discuss how to manage conflict. Good conflict management can help a business run more effectively.

### Forms of Conflict

Conflict comes in different forms. We will focus on three.

- **Emotional conflict** can come from such things as sexual harassment, racial taunting, or a simple lack of respect from one employee to another. This type of conflict might not be apparent to others, but it can cause enormous pain to the afflicted. This form of conflict must be eliminated.

- **Business conflict** arises out of normal business activities. Employees might disagree on how best to achieve a task. A manager might want to do things differently than the person she manages. One employee's poor performance may be holding back the performance of a whole team. This type of conflict should be encouraged, but managed carefully.

- **Legal conflicts** can cost you money, or even your business. Avoid them.

## HIRE CORRECTLY

Unhealthy conflict often begins with the hiring process. If you hire brawlers, you get brawlers. If you hire men who are insensitive to women, or women who don't like working with men, you will rarely get them to work well together.

If you find that you must manage an inordinate amount of non-productive employee conflict, one of the first things you should review is your hiring policy.

## SENSITIVITY TRAINING

Private businesses usually compete in a far less "civilized" world than major corporations. While big companies are able to make time for sensitivity training…having meetings on gender and race issues, or sponsor weekend retreats where they sing Kumbaya around a campfire…private business managers are far more focused on paying the bills, making the next sale or solving a delivery problem than they are on managing the feelings of employees.

Small retail and service establishments tend to be simpatico. But businesses with 25, 50, or 200 employees can become battlegrounds where the wounds of conflict go unnoticed, ignored and untreated. As an HR specialist, you need to be keenly vigilant, making sure that your employees don't suffer from excessive mental or physical duress.

No employee should be forced to endure sexual harassment or racial taunting. Every employee deserves to be treated with respect.

If sexual harassment or racial taunting is occurring at your company, you should do everything in your power to stop it. It is not profitable. It is not right.

Some conflict is a simple misunderstanding. What one employee sees as a compliment may be viewed by another as demeaning. "That dress looks great on you," might make one employee smile. The same compliment might give another employee the creeps.

You don't want to have employees walking around afraid to make comments or give compliments. Sensitivity training should be designed to educate **both** sides — the offender and the offended. Sometimes, a compliment is just a compliment. Sometimes a joke is just a joke.

Employees should be trained on how to avoid being oversensitive, just as they should be trained to respect the feelings of others.

You do *not* want to foster a culture that punishes disagreements — because healthy disagreements can make your company better. Just see that disagreements are civilized, and don't erupt into outright hostility or hidden cold wars.

# COMMUNICATION

The key to managing personal conflict is fostering a culture of open communication. Employees should be able to discuss issues that make them feel uncomfortable, without the fear of reprisal.

All employees should be told that personal harassment will not be tolerated in your company. Make it part of your Policies and Procedures Manual. Make it law.

Business disagreements should be encouraged, because disagreements help keep a company fresh. A manager who insists upon conducting business the "way it has always been done," might need a wake-up call. That old paper rolodex might have seen better days.

# CONFLICT MANAGEMENT

Here is a system to help you manage conflict. When conflict arises, you should:

- **Acknowledge that conflict exists**. All parties should acknowledge that there is a conflict. You may wish to employ an arbiter, who will listen to all sides of the issue and help mediate the problem. You must insist that all parties be honest in their appraisal of the situation and commit to honesty as they present their cases.

- **Express all feelings**. Conflict often becomes emotional. Emotions can make it difficult to solve problems. Conflict creates feelings of anger and hurt. Employees should understand that these feelings are normal. They should understand that emotions must be set aside before any resolution can occur. Therefore, you must see that these emotions are expressed and acknowledged without judgment.

- **Define the problem**. Once you have moved past the emotions that were triggered by conflict, all parties must define the problem. All parties must come to an agreement, defining the conflict in concrete terms. What problems is the conflict creating? What is the impact upon job performance, working relationships, etc.? Is the conflict the result of different personality styles, or is it a functional issue? Your arbiter should question each employee separately about the situation, before determining a course of resolution.

• **Determine your goals**. Managing conflict resolution is not deciding who is right and who is wrong. The best solution is usually a compromise that everyone can accept. Therefore, rather than looking for a solution, the first thing you should look for is needs. What is it that your employees need, emotionally and physically? Is it a matter of respect? Autonomy? Credit? If you look for needs first, then win/win options can often become quite apparent. Ask your employees why they want the solutions they have proposed, and what the results would be with these changes. Once you understand what an employee hopes to achieve with the change, you will have a much greater understanding of his or her needs.

• **Find common ground.** You should work with conflicted employees until they:

> ▪ Agree upon the problem.

> ▪ Determine procedures that all parties can live with.

> ▪ Agree upon changes (even minor ones) that can give the parties a feeling that they are moving toward resolution.

• **How to agree on solutions.** At times, it can be a challenge to get employees to agree upon solutions.

The following is a strategy that is employed by many successful businesses:

> ▪ Sit together and discuss all of the possible solutions to the problem. Put them on a board or in a notebook.
>
> ▪ Agree upon a course of action.
>
> ▪ Make sure all parties agree to the action.
>
> ▪ Make sure that the agreement is genuine.
>
> ▪ Make each employee look you in the eye and tell you that the solution is agreeable.
>
> ▪ Implement the solution.

• **Decide upon how you will monitor your decisions**. You should schedule a follow-up meeting in the near future to determine how the agreement is working. Typically, two weeks is enough time to see if your compromise is working.

• **Determine a plan of action if your solution does not work.** Conflict resolution does not always work right away. The solutions you devise may work well for one party and not others. They may cause disruption within various departments, even among parties that were not part of the initial dispute. Take heart; this is normal. Be sure that you have planned, in advance for another set of meetings if things don't work out the first time around.

## LEGAL CONFLICT RESOLUTION

Employment laws are complicated. There are so many rules and regulations, so many things you can and cannot say and do, that it is impossible for any business to avoid making mistakes. Usually the mistakes are small and go unnoticed. But mistakes like "wrongful discharge" and "discrimination" can bring you to court faster than you can say "Are you married?" or "I'm sorry, but I'm just going to have to let you go."

Here are a few things for you can do to avoid costly legal mistakes:

- Make sure that none of your recruiting materials imply a guaranteed position with your company.

- Remove the word "permanent" from any recruiting documentation.

- Establish a clear set of standards for evaluating job performance. Make sure that these standards are reasonable.

- Document job performance reviews. Make sure that managers keep careful notes regarding all disciplinary actions and warnings.

- Make sure that employees are warned repeatedly before any termination. Put these warnings in writing. Document the behaviors or work standards that must be improved and outline a strategy to improve them.

- Give employees the ability to dispute your findings and produce proof to support their claim.

- Complete a true, documented investigation before any disciplinary action. Make sure that this investigation is fair and non-biased, and that any discipline is reasonable.

- Have a clear-cut, written termination procedure and follow it. Be consistent with how you terminate employees.

- Understand that any employee who quits may come back and sue you for any reason.

## Plan in Advance

As long as we are human, we will have conflict. Accept it as normal. Managing and avoiding conflict is easier if you have planned for it in advance. If you establish clear and logical procedures, and execute them consistently, you will minimize conflict and keep productivity as high as possible.

## Chapter Forty
_____**HR**_____
## Effective Performance Management

# PERFORMANCE APPRAISAL MEETINGS

Managing business productivity is like navigating a sailboat. While your business goals may be clear and tangible, the means of achieving them may require many steering changes. While we would all prefer to sail in a straight line, without effort and conflict, the fact is, we can't. Regular performance appraisals act as an ongoing steering and correction mechanism that will help keep your company moving efficiently forward.

### Performance Appraisal

If you want to get the most out of your employees, you must continually monitor their performance and seek ongoing improvement. Performance appraisal allows managers to evaluate employee productivity and seek ways to improve it.

Performance appraisal is not always fun. Few employees like to be monitored and graded like a school child. Managers rarely enjoy the process. It takes time. Imparting criticism is not easy. Appraisals may lead to employee termination. This, in itself, is a challenge. As we have already discussed, firing employees isn't easy anymore. It must be done with care and forethought.

# THE GOOD NEWS ON APPRAISALS

When informing employees about your appraisal process, you should stress, and reinforce, the reasons for it. Appraisal, and the appraisal interview, can help you:

- Assess employee skills and knowledge.

- Determine ways to improve company-wide performance.

- Review and reinforce company goals and values.

- Give underperforming employees a strategy to improve performance.

- Create a basis for evaluating individual performance and the justification for greater compensation.

- Establish methods to increase compensation for achievers.

- Create a forum for managers and employees to improve synergy.

- Motivate employees to improve job performance.

# CHOOSE AN APPRAISAL SYSTEM

Regardless of the type of appraisal system you employ, the process should:

- Establish performance criteria.

- Create a way to measure performance.

- Document employee performance.

- Provide a forum for managers to detail performance successes and failures.

- Provide a forum for employees to dispute findings and evaluate managers.

- Establish a system to improve individual and company performance.

Your ultimate appraisal system will depend upon your company's overall needs and resources.

**Evaluation is worth the effort.**

Although you may find it difficult to devote time and resources to a systematized employee evaluation process, you should understand that a well-run program will return more than it costs.

When building a program, you should consider and evaluate the following:

- The degree to which employees are allowed to help establish performance criteria.

- The time commitment required by all employees.

- The methods used to track and evaluate performance.

  o Are they fair and unbiased?

  o Can they withstand a challenge in court and support any actions you take as a result of your evaluations?

- What tools will you use to integrate your findings into improving individual and overall company performance?

- Have you made effective provisions for all employees to perceive value in the process?

The appraisal meeting should not be dreaded by managers, or

by any productive employees they manage. Good workers will see this as way to improve performance and enhance their standing within the company. Managers should perceive the process as a way to improve productivity and the performance of their units. Dedicated, but poorly performing employees should view this as the company's sincere effort to help them. Employees who continue to perform poorly, or who don't work to improve, should see this as their invitation to seek work elsewhere.

# Chapter Forty-One
## HR
### Effective Performance Management

# CORPORATE WELLNESS

Private companies don't have the resources to undertake the types of corporate wellness programs that exist in many large corporations. It is the rare private company that has the physical space to put in a company gym and sauna, or a "de-stressing" suite with pool, ping pong tables and a company theater.

This doesn't mean that corporate wellness should be ignored.

- You can make your office a safe place to work.

- You can make your office as stress-free as possible.

- You can eliminate sexual harassment and bigotry in your company.

- You can encourage healthy workforce behaviors.

Take a look around. Meet with your employees and ask them what would make your company a better place to work. Sure, employees will tell you that higher pay would help; but they will also help you determine ways to improve employee well-being in ways you cannot imagine.

**Chapter Forty-Two**
## HR
**Effective Performance Management**

# IT'S ALL ABOUT SALES & MARKETING

If you are working for a small or mid-sized company, you have a far different perspective on business than those who work for large organizations.

If business were a football game, you wouldn't be in the stands in some luxury box, cheering between sips of Chablis. You would be in the "trenches," banging your shoulders against an opponent across the line, pushing and clawing to gain a precious yard forward. You aren't the white-robed Roman senator; you're the gladiator.

Small business is mano-a-mano. And it all begins with sales & marketing.

**Everyone sells.**

Virtually every small business owner was the company's first salesperson. While many have progressed beyond that title, many of them still make the rain...even if it is on the golf course.

If a company doesn't produce new sales, it slinks quietly into the night and dies quickly. If a private company fails, it is usually because they failed at selling their goods and services effectively.

# SUCCESSFUL COMPANIES ARE GREAT AT SALES & MARKETING

Think of the most successful companies in today's competitive, world marketplace. The names are on the tip of your tongue: Apple, Amazon, AT&T, Google, IBM, McDonald's, Verizon, Wal-Mart… These companies are *always* in the news. They are in your face with marketing and advertising.

The biggest companies are also constantly reinventing themselves and telling us about it, as if their very survival were at stake. They never let their company names fall out of the public consciousness. They are as ubiquitous as air.

Private businesses don't have the financial resources of the corporate behemoths. The finances of a private business tends to be held together with duct tape, Crazy Glue and chicken wire. However, private businesses share the same needs as big ones.

Smaller companies must continually change with the marketplace. They must reinvent themselves to stay in the lead. And they must continually let their customers know that they matter. They must make the sales.

Everyone in your company should be part of that selling process.

## Chapter Forty-Three
## HR
### Effective Performance Management

# BUILD A WINNING SALES TEAM
# ATTITUDE, TRAINING & EXECUTION

**Every successful business has a winning sales team.**

Your sales team may consist of one person, or it may be a group of hundreds. Whatever the size, you want your salespeople to be effective at helping your company grow. You want them to be profitable and self-sustaining. You want them to be the engine that powers your company forward. You want them to be the superstars of your industry. So, how do you do this?

## ATTITUDE

There is a common saying in sales training: "Attitude brings Altitude."

If you have been in business for more than a day or two, you know that nothing kills sales more than a bad attitude. Nothing succeeds better than a great attitude. It is almost that simple.

**Hire the right salespeople.**

When you are hiring salespeople, the most important trait your candidate must possess is attitude. Good looks or an Ivy League resume will not guarantee sales success. A cheerful, but pugnacious and determined attitude almost always will.

# THE SALESPERSON INTERVIEW

When you are interviewing candidates for a sales job, don't throw them softballs and let them hit it out of the park. Give them your best fastball. Challenge them with a high one right at the chin. Reject them and see how they respond. Throw them some curveballs and see how they behave. Give them some questions like:

"I'm not sure that I see anything here that shows me how you will succeed at this job…"

"Why should I believe you…?"

"What made you choose the clothes you are wearing for this interview? … Are you sure they are appropriate?"

"Why do you say that?"

"Why is that important?"

"Do you like yourself? … Why?"

"Why should I like you?"

"Tell me about your worst characteristic…Does that disqualify you from working for our company?"

**Intelligence and good looks are not the key attributes for selling.**

Employees who can easily memorize a sales presentation may freeze when the pressure is on. Employees who look great in a suit may be better off with a modeling agency.

Employees who can absorb rejection and keep a positive attitude will be resilient in sales. *They* will be your superstars.

The intangibles that are important in sales are difficult to measure. It usually doesn't matter if your sales people went to Harvard or dropped out of the local university. Sure, graduating from a top college indicates intelligence and the ability to achieve. But it does not always give a reliable measure of the "fire in the belly" that it takes to thrive in sales. Your college dropout might now understand the importance of hard work. He may have a chip on his shoulder the size of Colorado.

## I REPEAT: ATTITUDE IS KEY

Never forget that the most reliable indicator of sales success is attitude.

- You must hire sales people who will set concrete goals, and let nothing stop them from achieving them.
- Hire resilient people with an unshakably positive attitude and your sales will soar.

## TRAINING

I understand how precious business resources can be. I've been there. Every dollar counts. Time is at a premium. Perhaps you are shuffling bills just to meet payroll. This is not uncommon.

The implementation of a comprehensive sales training program costs money and time. That is why so few small businesses become big ones. Few small businesses have the resources to develop the kind of sales training that will turn them into the next IBM or Johnson & Johnson.

Here is why you should install a formal training program in your company:

There are few problems in your business that more sales won't fix.

While the above statement is highly simplified, its essence holds true for most small and mid-sized businesses.

## THE ECONOMICS OF SALES TRAINING

Fixed costs for small companies are usually quite high, relative to sales. You have a lease or a mortgage. You have your management salaries, equipment leases, etc.

In most cases, a ten or twenty percent increase in sales does not impact fixed costs. Therefore, an increase in sales will often produce much higher profit margins than existing sales. The math is simple.

Why then, do so few small companies have formal sales training programs? Is this mystery as unfathomable as the meaning of the Mayan pyramids or Stonehenge? No. Most private businesses just don't know how and why they should do it.

If you conduct a Google search for "sales training," you will receive more than thirty-five million hits. This is a bigger response than if you searched for something as basic as "walking." This is because sales are the cornerstone of any business.

Ask yourself this question: "Can my company benefit from increased sales?" Of course, you will answer, "Yes." Ask yourself these questions:

- What training programs do we have in place to help increase sales?

- Are our training programs effective?

- Can we do better in sales?

## SALES TRAINING PLAN

Most companies approach selling their product or service as an information session or a persuasion event. Companies train their sales people about their products or services, then send them out into the world to *tell* prospects how great they are, and why they should *buy* their product or service. Selling in this manner can be an enormous waste of talent, time, energy and money. Nobody likes to be "sold." It is a four letter word.

Prospects don't like to be told how good a product or service is. Hearing about them means nothing. Prospects need to *feel*; they need to escape their intellect and experience *emotions*. Emotions make the sale. When prospects imagine the experience, and feel the emotions of owning your product and service in their minds, they will rationalize the purchasing decision with their intellect.

While prospects and customers don't like to be sold, they love to own things. The effective salesperson *asks* many questions, and then asks more. The effective salesperson allows the prospect to experience emotions, such as fear, love, or greed.

Selling products and services the old fashioned way, by telling, is like trying to run your business software on the first PC. The first PC had a 10 megabyte hard drive and 32k of RAM. This wouldn't power any of today's mobile phones.

So, why do so many company executives send their sales representatives out to sell something intellectually, rather than allowing their prospects to own emotionally? Poor training.

### Be Sincere

While effective communication is important, sincerity is critical. Prospects want to know that you care and that you have their best interests at heart. Remember this: If you help your prospects get what they want, you will get what you want - greater sales and higher profits.

### Training to Communicate

Effective selling in today's world requires an understanding of how people communicate. Proper sales training should incorporate an understanding of how human behavior interacts with the specifics of you company's products and services. In addition to face-to-face marketing, you should utilize other sales methods — such as direct marketing, media and social marketing.

Let's give a simplified face-to-face example of proper versus improper selling:

An untrained salesperson might approach a prospect and start by saying something like, "Let me tell you about how great our widgets are…" An effective sales person might approach the same prospect by asking the question, "Tell me, John…What areas would you like to improve about the performance of your widgets…" An untrained salesperson tells. A trained salesperson asks questions first, and then listens intently.

Training will teach your salespeople that there are many strategies or techniques involved in successful communication. Appearance…Body language…Planned pauses…Answering questions with a question…Negative reverse selling…The list is almost endless.

Effective sales techniques are simply better ways to help us communicate with prospects. Effective communication leads to a prospect asking for the features and benefits of our products, rather than forcing a salesperson to try to stuff the features and benefits down a prospect's throat.

Effective communication skills will help your sales grow exponentially. So, start today.

## COMMIT & EXECUTE

Commit to take the required steps to dramatically increase your sales. Then set about to build a training program that teaches your salespeople how to communicate effectively, in a manner that will help people make the decision to own your product or service.

## RESOURCES

There are many sales training resources that can help you develop a winning sales team. Some training programs are expensive, costing more than a new addition on your home. Others programs involve the cost of a few books, DVDs or a couple of online seminars.

Your needs and resources will determine the right training programs for your company. At the least, you should see that your salespeople fully understand that selling is not something that you do *to* a prospect or customer, but something you do *with* and *for* them.

## Start Cheap

Sales training books are modestly priced. They can enhance any salesperson's performance in very little time. Many books are offered in conjunction with audio and video programs, which can dramatically enhance the learning process. Here are a few resources you should consider:

- *You Can't Teach A Kid To Ride A Bike At A Seminar*, by David Sandler and John Hayes. Sandler (www.sandler.com) also provides direct individual and corporate sales training.

- Stephen R. Covey has written several books on peak performance and sales. Franklin Covey (www.franklincovey.com) provides direct sales training as well.

- Tom Hopkins has written very effective books that teach sales techniques. He has developed seminars using these techniques, which help salespeople develop their skills. He speaks worldwide on the subject of selling. (www.tomhopkins.com).

- Zig Ziglar has conducted seminars and written sales training books for decades. He has developed a number of effective programs to help salespeople develop their skills. Ziglar (www.ziglar.com) provides both personal and corporate training programs.

Do not be afraid to sell your way to greatness. Sales training is not learning how to manipulate, but how to *communicate* effectively with your prospects. If you do it well and do it often, your company will prosper like never before.

## Chapter Forty-Four
## HR
## Benefits Management

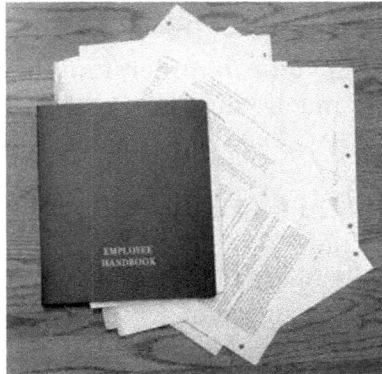

# DEFINING YOUR BUDGET

## THE BENEFITS REALITY

Benefits are great. In a perfect world, we would provide as many as our employees need and want.

The world isn't perfect. We must make very difficult choices regarding benefits, because they are expensive.

In HR, your task is to offer enough benefits to remain competitive within the job marketplace. If you offer benefits that are significantly less than your competitors, you will have difficulty hiring (and keeping) the highest quality workers.

If you work for a private company, you don't administer benefits from the tenth floor of a corporate office a thousand miles away from the work force. You work side-by-side with your employees. And, unlike Congress, you must live with the same benefits that you mandate for others. So, how do you get the most from your benefits dollar?

## BUDGETING

Defining a benefits budget is like trying to predict the weather. It is nearly impossible. The benefit landscape changes daily, both legally and financially.

**The one thing you *can* understand is your budget.** You have a good idea how much you can spend on benefits. This is rarely enough; you are forced to make choices. It isn't easy.

## AN AMOUNT OR A PERCENTAGE?

If you are like many private company HR managers, your approach to benefits management goes like this: You buy the basic benefits (health insurance and a retirement plan), then purchase more benefits if you have any extra money. This haphazard strategy can be inefficient and costly.

HR managers usually rely on their insurance broker to tell them what is available, and then commit to whatever they think they can afford. When they review their choices, they might say to their broker, "I can't afford that. What do you have that's cheaper?" The broker might say something like, "We can change to a plan with a deductible..." And so on.

This strategy can make you feel powerless against the benefit providers. You might view insurance companies as adversaries rather than partners. It doesn't have to be this way.

### Efficient Benefits Management

Efficient benefits management starts when you define a specific benefits **budget**, as a specific dollar amount, or as a percentage of company revenues.

Just like a mortgage, rent or payroll, every year you should define a new dollar amount for benefits, then build it into your company budget. Many companies attempt to hold benefits costs to a specific percentage of revenues, and make adjustments as things change.

### What to Budget

In developing your benefits budget, it might be helpful to know what other companies are spending. The following is an employee compensation analysis made by the U.S. Bureau of Labor for 2010:

http://www.bls.gov/news.release/ecec.nr0.htm

# EMPLOYER COSTS FOR EMPLOYEE COMPENSATION - DECEMBER 2010

"Private industry employers spent an average of $27.75 per hour worked for total employee compensation in December 2010, the U.S. Bureau of Labor Statistics reported today. Wages and salaries averaged $19.64 per hour worked and accounted for 70.8 percent of these costs, while benefits averaged $8.11 and accounted for the remaining 29.2 percent.

"Total compensation costs for state and local government workers averaged $40.28 per hour worked in December 2010. Total employer compensation costs for civilian workers, which include private industry and state and local government workers, averaged $29.72 per hour worked in December 2010."

Use this national summary as a guide to understanding where the cost for benefits might fit within your company budget. Adjust your amounts by industry or region of the country. Then you will have a better idea of what your benefits budget should be in order to remain competitive within your industry.

Your insurance broker can usually provide more specific information regarding your region and industry.

The Department of Labor website is also a helpful, free resource.

**Note:** If you don't have the resources for the suite of benefits that you need to remain competitive, do what you can. Hopefully, some of the chapters in this book will help you increase your sales and profitability, and get you on your way to greater prosperity.

## SUMMARY

Once you know your budget, you should go to your benefits brokers and tell them what you can afford. Tell them what you need to offer to remain competitive in the marketplace and see how the numbers play out. Good luck. I know that this is one of your greatest challenges.

## Chapter Forty-Five
## HR
## Benefits Management

# MAXIMIZING YOUR BENEFITS DOLLARS

Private companies cannot afford to waste resources on excess benefits. In HR, you must scrutinize every benefit to determine its worth to employees and the company. You must continually monitor the benefits marketplace to see that the ones you do offer are priced competitively, and that they remain competitive.

All too often, HR managers maintain the status-quo. If a manager gets a rate increase, she grumbles, but then pays it. Managers worry about rising costs, but sometimes do little to control them, until it is too late. When costs get too large for a company to pay, a manager might make sweeping changes, such as dropping valued programs without warning. This can shock employees and disrupt productivity.

The smart HR manager analyzes the benefits market continually. She looks several years into the future, taking steps today to manage current and future costs.

Ask yourself these questions: "What steps have I taken to see that I am getting the most for my benefit dollars?" "What steps am I taking to manage future costs?" "Will employees want to pay some of the costs if my company can no longer afford its current share of premiums?"

Here is what I recommend:

- If you do not fully understand the benefits landscape, then you should find someone who does.

- If you are not analyzing costs and competitive programs on a regular basis, then you should do so.

- If you are not exploring strategies to manage future benefit costs, then you should ask your benefits advisors what steps you might take to minimize future cost increases.

- If you handle benefits alone (or your current benefit specialists cannot do the job) find someone who can help you. Your local benefits broker might be the first place to look.

# Chapter Forty-Six
## HR
## Benefits Management

# COST MANAGEMENT STRATEGIES

## LET EMPLOYEES CHOOSE

Every employee has unique benefit needs. An employee with a working spouse, whose employer provides health insurance, may not need you to provide it. Why pay for it and waste the money? This same employee might prefer dental coverage, life or long-term care insurance.

### Cafeteria Programs

One of the most effective cost management strategies is to provide benefits in a cafeteria style. Cafeteria programs offer a menu of benefits that allow employees choose which ones are right for them. This strategy allows employers to eliminate coverage that isn't needed, and allows employees to obtain the coverage that is best for them.

## PAY ONLY FOR *CURRENT* EMPLOYEES

Make sure that all former employees have been removed from your billing database. Inform your payroll company and/or insurance carriers when an employee leaves your company. Constantly check their records against your own. Many a business has been billed (sometimes tens of thousands of dollars) for employees that were not on their payroll!

## SHARING COSTS

More and more companies are asking employees to share in the costs of benefits. This is a delicate issue, particularly as costs increase. Effective employee communication is critical in maintaining high employee morale, as they are asked to shoulder more and more of the benefits load.

### Experience Rating

Healthy companies may be able to implement health insurance strategies that allow them to benefit from lower claims in the future. In Massachusetts, this applies only to companies with more than fifty employees. Check with your state for your local regulations.

### Lifestyle Benefits

Companies are introducing lifestyle benefits, which are inexpensive to offer and allow employees to receive some benefits at a lower cost.

## INCREASE DEDUCTIBLES

Many employers are being forced to switch to health insurance plans with increased deductibles. By choosing this option, employers are able to significantly reduce benefit costs. While employees must pay all or a portion of the deductible, there are ways to reimburse employees for some or all of their expenses.

## LEASE EMPLOYEES

Small companies do not have the same economies of scale as large companies, particularly with regard to benefits. In some situations, leasing employees may be a solution to this problem.

Leasing companies usually employ thousands, giving them the flexibility and the resources to mix and match benefits to the needs of their clients (you). By leasing employees, a small employer may be able to provide a big-company suite of benefits, at an affordable price. The small company pays the cost of benefits to the large company by including these payments in the terms of the lease.

Beware. Leasing employees can cause significant problems. By leasing employees, you are transferring partial control of your company to a far larger organization. The leasing company will have its own agenda, which may be far different than yours. Don't get trapped into an arrangement that can be difficult to unravel.

## CONTRACTORS

By using independent contractors, employers may not be required to provide benefits at all. Contractors provide their own benefits, and are "independent" of the companies that hire them.

Be careful when establishing contractor relationships. A full-time contractor relationship that is established "solely for the purpose of avoiding benefit costs," will not be regarded kindly by governmental authorities.

## PART-TIME EMPLOYEES

Employers are not required to offer the same benefits to part-time employees that they offer to their full-time work force. If you have ever visited a Wal-Mart, you have seen this policy in action on a nationwide scale. Wal-Mart hires many seniors (who have Medicare Insurance) on a part-time basis. This strategy allows seniors to earn a supplemental income. It also allows Wal-Mart to avoid paying for benefits. These savings get passed on to the consumer in the form of lower prices. "Welcome to Wal-Mart" might be translated into "Welcome to the new American Way..."

### Summary

Today's private businesses must deliver high-quality goods and services at the best price possible. A good understanding of benefits, and how they can be acquired more cost-effectively, is essential in this endeavor. Do your homework. Hire knowledgeable professionals to help you. Monitor everything.

# Chapter Forty-Seven
## _____HR_____
## Benefits Management

# TAX STRATEGIES

The United States has a long-standing competition with Japan for the dubious distinction of having the highest corporate tax rates in the world. Recently, America has taken the lead in that race.

Any private business knows that every dollar matters. A dollar paid in taxes is a dollar that could have been used to help grow the company, replace outdated equipment, pay the past-due rent or mortgage, or even catch up on back salaries for senior management.

Therefore, it is critical for every HR manager to understand what benefit expenditures are _deductible_ for corporate tax purposes, and which are not.

The same holds true for what benefits are taxable to employees and which are not. Some benefits may be deductible from an employee's federal income, but may still be subject to FICA deductions or state income taxes.

### Arduous Tax Code

In typical fashion, the U.S Government (and its muscle-man, the IRS) have created a tax code that is so arduous that it makes rocket science look like a kindergarten class. In the following chapters, I will attempt to simplify the tax nature of benefits as best I can.

## Chapter Forty-Eight
## _____HR_____
## The Benefits Landscape

# QUALIFIED VERSUS NONQUALIFIED

Money that is allocated to benefits which are "qualified" for favorable tax treatment is *deductible* to employers and *non-taxable* to employees.

Nonqualified benefits do not receive favorable tax treatment.

As a general rule, benefits provided to all employees, without discrimination, are tax deductible to the employer and non-taxable to employees. In many cases, like with retirement plans, the government sets limits to what is deductible and what is not.

In most cases, the following benefits are deductible to an employer and non-taxable to employees:

## Employee Benefits

- Medical insurance

- Group term life insurance (up to $50,000)

- Group disability insurance

- Group long-term care insurance

- Prescription insurance

- Vision insurance

- Dental insurance

- Dependent care plans

- Flexible spending accounts

- Retirement plans

    o Pension

    o Profit sharing

    o 401(k)

    o SEP IRA

    o 403(b)

- Child care benefits

- Adoption assistance

- Legal assistance plans

- Transportation plans

- Wellness programs

- Employee discount plans (with many exceptions)

- Meal & lodging benefits/plans (especially when for the employer's benefit)

# SELECTIVE & "FRINGE" BENEFITS

In order to supplement basic employee benefits, many companies offer additional, selective & indirect benefits. These are often called "fringe benefits." Fringe benefits usually don't receive the same favorable tax treatment as qualified benefits. They are not deductible to the employer and are fully taxable to employees.

### Fringe Benefit History

As an historical note, the term "fringe benefits" arose during World War II. At that time, many wage increases were prohibited by law. As a result, companies began to devise alternative ways to attract and retain valued employees. The term was created by the War Labor Board as a way to delineate (and monitor) how companies were circumventing the wage restrictions in place at that time. The government continues to monitor, and discourage, certain benefits today.

Fringe benefits that favor one employee group over another will not generally receive favorable tax treatment. Benefits that rarely receive favorable tax treatment include such items as:

- Deferred compensation

- Golden handshakes & golden parachutes

- Group term life over the $50,000 limit

- Some stock options

- Selective long-term care insurance

# OWNER/EXECUTIVE BEWARE

Employees that are 5% owners or "highly compensated" face additional hurdles in meeting the tax deductible standards for many benefits.

## IRS PUBLICATION

The IRS has published a substantial document, Publication 15b, which describes the taxability and non-taxability of fringe benefits in great detail. You can order this document from the IRS, or read it online at:

http://www.irs.gov/publications/p15b/ar02.html.

# Chapter Forty-Nine
## _____HR_____
## The Benefits Landscape

# HEALTH INSURANCE

Buying health insurance is like buying a car. There are many models to choose from, and each comes with a list of options. Determining which type of coverage is right for your company can be complicated.

Many of the complexities of health insurance coverage derive from policies developed to serve the customer — your company and your employees. Some features have evolved to manage costs and deliver efficient care. Other complexities derive from the contortions that insurance companies must go through to follow federal and state regulations.

You will make better decisions regarding health insurance if you understand what drives it. This may also reduce the frustration (or anger) that you might feel toward the insurance companies that are taking your money and paying for care.

Health insurance companies help manage health care services for their policyholders — you. Each insurance provider tries to develop the most competitive, risk-sharing products, in the hope that you will choose them over their competition. If they do this effectively, they will have enough policyholders to make money.

Health insurance is a very competitive industry. Insurance companies do not make exorbitant profits. Some make a reasonable return for their stockholders, while others struggle to make anything at all. Insurance companies are not your enemy, as many in today's media would like you to think. They do the best that they can to deliver the best coverage, at the best possible price. That is how they stay in business.

Insurance companies face many challenges that are outside their control. The cost of medicine is expensive, and growing all the time. Medical technology doesn't come cheap. Its advancement will never slow down. Patients constantly sue their doctors. This dramatically inflates the cost of care. Our federal and state governments continually issue regulations that mandate costly changes to care. It isn't fun for anyone.

In the following pages, we are going to review some of the factors that contribute to the cost of your benefit choices. I will also explain how you may be able to navigate through these factors to manage your company's health care costs.

## LIMITATIONS & REGULATIONS

### Federal Law

Many of the laws regarding insurance are mandated on a federal level. The controversial Health Care Reform bill passed in 2010 is just one example of how national policies shape the health insurance landscape. This bill requires many employers to offer "affordable" health insurance coverage to employees, or be forced to pay substantial fines.

### State Regulation

While Congress may create the laws regarding health care, its actual regulation is conducted by the states. Each state regulates insurance differently. Therefore, insurance companies wishing to do business in all fifty states must submit separate applications to *each* state, and comply with the regulations for everyone. Before an organization can offer insurance plans to your company, its programs must be approved by your state insurance commission. This is complicated, costly, and time consuming. Any modifications, including rate changes, must often be re-submitted to each individual state.

Because of the intense federal and state regulation, discussing specific details of any health insurance program is futile. Therefore, we will limit our discussion to the basic types of care that may be available to your company.

In the following pages, we will discuss the major forms of coverage you can offer your employees. We will review the advantages and disadvantages of each, so that you can determine which type, or mix, is right for your company. I will also give you strategies to help you reduce the cost of your coverage.

# How Insurance Companies Work

Before reviewing the particulars of insurance plans, you should know a little bit about how insurance companies work, and how they determine insurance premiums. Why? So you won't become so frustrated when they ask for so much information, or make it so difficult to obtain coverage.

## Adverse Selection

Insurance companies must manage the risk of adverse selection. If they don't, the premiums for existing policy holders will become far more expensive than they are today.

We would all prefer to pay for health insurance only when we need it. Why spend thousands of dollars when all we need is an annual checkup? This trait of human nature has led many individuals to seek coverage *only* when they know that they are facing significant medical bills.

To combat such adverse selection, and maintain reasonable premiums for policyholders, insurance companies have been forced to place limits on who they insure and when.

If an individual, or a company, is simply switching coverage from another insurer, this may not be a problem. If a company, or individual, applies for coverage, and they do not currently have it, the new insurer must ask, "Why now?"

Depending upon your company size, and the existing health characteristics of your employees, you may have to manage against adverse selection when purchasing health insurance for your company.

## LARGE NUMBERS

A key component of determining insurance premiums is something known as the *law of large numbers*. In simple terms, this means that the more people that are insured, the easier it is to predict expenses.

Insurance company actuaries determine their company's average current, per-insured expenses, and predict future expenses. If a company insures a million individuals, a cancer claim for $1,000,000 will add $1 to the average cost of each person that is insured. This cost will not affect premiums or profitability, and has already been built into premiums. If the same company insures a hundred people, this cancer claim will represent $10,000 per insured, and will dramatically affect future premiums.

If insurance companies do not closely monitor the companies (and individuals) who wish to purchase their insurance, they will quickly get themselves into a position where they lose money, or even go out of business.

Let's explain:

- Insurance companies guarantee to pay claims, using premiums they receive from their policyholders.

- Insurance companies need to have the money available to pay all claims.

- Policyholders want to pay as little in premiums as possible.

- The insurance company wants to charge as little as possible, so they remain competitive in the marketplace.

- Insurance actuaries determine current and future costs. They build in a competitive profit margin and determine premiums.

If an insurance company does not monitor new eligibility closely, they will assume many large claims due to pre-existing conditions. This can become a significant expense. If a company develops a reputation for regularly allowing pre-existing conditions, they will have a long line of uninsured sick people at their door.

Insurance underwriting may present a problem for the uninsured. But, allowing instant access to insurance for the sick, particularly for those who haven't paid for coverage until they need it, is bad business and a quick path to insolvency.

If you are a small business, you may understand the frustration and limitations that this close attention can create.

If you have been forced to go without coverage because of financial reasons, you may have to work harder to get new coverage, especially if you are sick. The 2010 health care legislation removes some of the barriers for uninsured individuals and companies.

## THE BIGGER THE BETTER

The larger your company, the more options you have with regard to health insurance. This is a working example of the law of large numbers in practice. As a general rule, insurance companies segment insurance choices based upon the number of employees. Your premiums, and your available options, will be significantly influenced by where your company fits into the following employee brackets:

- 0 – 10 Employees

- 10 – 25 Employees

- 25 – 50 Employees

- 50 – 100 Employees

- 100 – 250 Employees

- 250+

## TYPES OF COVERAGE

There are five main types of health insurance coverage available in the United States today, with many variations of each. Different companies offer different features in order to compete. Some carve out niches. Each state mandates its own options, including the premiums that can be charged.

The basics of coverage remain the same. The types of plans are as follows:

- Indemnity (Reimbursement Plans)

- PPOs (Preferred Provider Organizations)

- POS (Point of Service Plans)

- HMOs (Health Maintenance Organizations)

- HSAs (Health Savings Account Plans)

## INDEMNITY PLANS

An indemnity plan allows policy holders to go to their doctor of choice, at any time they want. Each insured files an insurance claim after service. So does the doctor or hospital.

The insured will be reimbursed for all "covered" medical expenses. Most normal procedures are (usually) covered under indemnity plans. A full list of covered services will be provided to every person who is insured under a plan.

Indemnity plans break services into various categories. Depending upon the category, the insurance company will pay a certain percentage of the claim.

- **Deductibles:** Most indemnity plans have an annual deductible that the insured must pay *before* the insurance company will reimburse for covered expenses. This deductible will be determined in advance. Typically, the higher the deductible, the lower the premium. Deductibles might be $500, $1,000, or even $10,000.

- **Co-Insurance:** Once a deductible has been met, indemnity plans will pay a certain portion of covered expenses (see Usual and Customary below).

- **Out of Pocket Maximum:** Indemnity plans usually have an annual, calendar-year, out-of-pocket maximum. Once covered expenses have reached this figure, the insurer will pay the usual and customary fee *in full*. If providers charge more than the usual and customary fees, an insured may still be required to pay a portion of any bills.

- **Usual and Customary**: The insurer generally pays a percentage (usually 80 percent) of what is considered usual and customary care. The insured pays the balance, or *coinsurance*, which is typically 20 percent. Health care providers and insurance companies generally agree upon payment rates in advance. However, if a provider charges more than what the insurance company deems to be fair, the insured may be required to pay the additional balance.

  o   For example: If the insurer determines that the usual fee for a doctor's exam is $200, it will pay $160 for the visit. The insured will pay $40. If the doctor charges $210, the patient will need to pay $50.

# PPOs

A preferred provider organization (PPO) is somewhat similar to an indemnity plan. PPOs negotiate rates (discounts) with doctors, hospitals and other providers. These providers become part of the PPO "network." Like an indemnity plan, the insured can typically visit their doctor at any time, provided they are within the PPO network.

### Copayment

When an insured visits a physician within the network, the insured typically makes a copayment. The PPO pays the rest. The traditional copay is $20 to $25.

If an insured sees a physician outside the network, the insured (usually) will still receive coverage. However, rather than pay a normal copay, as under the PPO arrangement, the insurance arrangement works much like the standard indemnity plan. The insured might pay 20% - 30% co-insurance, while the PPO pays the balance.

For example: If an insured's doctor is outside the network, the insured can still see that doctor. If a visit costs $200, the patient (insured) might pay 20%, or $40. The PPO pays the balance. With some plans, the patient may be responsible up-front for the entire payment to the doctor. The insurance company will then *reimburse* the insured. With other plans, the insured will just be required to pay his portion up front.

If an insured chooses a $30,000 surgery outside the PPO network, the insured will be responsible for his portion of the bill. If the patient responsibility is 20%, the patient would pay $6,000 of the bill, or the out-of-pocket maximum, whichever is less.

### Deductibles:

In addition to coinsurance, PPOs may also have deductibles. As with indemnity plans, the deductible is the amount of covered expenses that the insured must pay before the PPO will begin reimbursement for any medical expenses.

Deductibles typically range from $100 to $2,000 per year per individual. There is usually a "family" deductible as well. This will typically range from $500 to $5,000 per family.

In most cases, the higher the deductible, the lower the premium.

The insured (employee) is often given the ability to choose a deductible and premium level that fits her budget and lifestyle needs.

### Self-Referrals

One of the popular features of PPOs is that referrals are not needed from a primary care physician. With PPOs, the insured is able to see *any* doctor, including specialists, at *any* time without a referral. This includes doctors inside and outside the PPO network.

### Premiums

PPO premiums are usually lower than indemnity plans. This is due to the negotiated provider discounts.

# HMOs

With a health maintenance organization (HMO), the insured does not pay for each individual service that they receive. Instead, the insured pays a set premium for all coverage.

HMOs offer a full range of health benefits, including preventive care. The HMO negotiates discounted rates with doctors, labs, hospitals and other providers within the network. In return, the HMO will send a steady stream of patients to providers within the network.

Negotiating discounts and volume service are the primary methods that HMOs use to keep healthcare costs in check. HMOs are generally the most affordable type of health insurance plan.

### Primary Care Physician

With an HMO, the insured chooses a *primary care physician* that is affiliated with the HMO plan. This is normally a general practitioner. This physician will then coordinate all of the insured's care from that point forward.

In order for the insured to see a specialist, the primary care physician *must* provide a referral. The referral will be made to a provider within the HMO network. HMO generally require that the insured seek care within its own network of specialists.

### Copayment

Most HMOs require a modest copayment for services. This might be $10 or $20 for an office visit, perhaps slightly more for a specialist. Some HMOs apply copayments to hospitalizations as well.

### Direct Care

HMOs seek to deliver the full range of care, from within the network, to those insured under their plan. Insureds (patients) are expected to go to the HMO's own medical facilities to see nurses, doctors and specialists, in all disciplines.

## POS PLANS

A point-of-service plan (POS) combines the elements a health maintenance organization (HMO) and an Indemnity Plan.

POS plans typically allow the insured to have a primary care physician, who coordinates all care. The insured can also *self-direct* her care at the "point of service."

When medical care is needed, the insured will generally have several treatment options. The particular choices will depend upon the specific health plan. The choices might be as follows:

1    The insured can seek treatment through a primary care physician. Service coverage and payments will be similar to an HMO, usually with a modest copayment.

2    The insured can access care through a PPO provider. In this case, services and payments will be similar to in-network PPO guidelines. A copayment is usually required. The insured may also be responsible for coinsurance as well.

3    The insured can seek services from providers outside of the HMO network. These services will typically be reim-

bursed according to out-of-network rules. This usually means higher copayment and coinsurance amounts.

### Co-Insurance & Deductibles

Depending upon the type of care needed, an employee insured through a POS plan may have to pay deductibles and/or coinsurance. Deductibles might range from $100 to $2,000 per year per individual. There is usually a family deductible of $500 to $5,000.

As in other plans, the higher the deductible, the lower the premiums.

## EMPLOYEE ASSISTANCE PROGRAMS

Some health plans also offer Employee Assistance Programs (EAPs) as part of their suite of benefits. Other EAPs are stand-alone plans that can be added to employee health coverage.

EAPs can be used by employees and their household members to help manage non-health issues in their work and personal lives. Most EAPs provide counseling services, including assessment and support. They may also provide referrals to additional resources.

EAPs provide support for many personal issues, including:

- Emotional Stress, often in the areas of:
    - Work Environment
        - Safety
        - Relationships
    - Health Concerns
    - Financial Problems
    - Legal Problems
    - Marital or Relationship Problems

- o   Child Behavior Problems

- • Stressful Life Events, such as:

  - o   Marriage or Divorce

  - o   Births

  - o   Accidents

  - o   Deaths

  - o   Aging Parents

- • Substance Abuse

# HSAs

Health Savings Accounts (HSAs) allow individuals to save money to pay for medical expenses (current and future) on a *tax-free basis*.

Employers can offer HSAs to employees as a benefit. Like a qualified retirement plan, monies accumulate inside the plan on a tax deferred basis. If used for eligible expenses, the funds come out of the HSA tax-free as well.

In order to be eligible for an HSA, an employee must be covered by a qualified *high-deductible* health insurance plan. The insured cannot have any other health insurance.

HSAs are attractive to individuals who want to protect themselves from catastrophic health-care costs, but don't expect many current, day-to-day medical expenses. HSAs can also act as a lower-cost alternative to more traditional health plans for private businesses. Because of this, they are growing in popularity.

Smaller businesses rarely have the resources to pay for first-dollar, low-deductible medical coverage. A high-deductible plan, combined with HSAs, can be an attractive alternative to employee health care coverage.

Here's how HSAs work:

In 2012, an HSA plan must be paired with health insurance coverage that requires an annual deductible of at least $1,200 for individuals or $2,400 for families. Total out-of-pocket costs for these plans, including deductibles and copayments, cannot exceed $6,050 for an individual or $12,100 for a family. These amounts change from year to year. Contribution limits to HSAs in 2012 are $3,100 per individual and $6,250 per family.

Some qualifying plans offer full coverage or require only a small copayment for preventative care, such as an annual physical, or a well-child checkup.

The following is a summary of features and benefits for high-deductible plans combined with HSAs:

- Premiums for high-deductible health plans are typically lower than those for HMOs, PPOs or POS plans.

- The disadvantage is the potential for higher out-of-pocket costs.

- To offset the risk to employees, employers can contribute to an HSA account. These contributions are deductible to the employer in most cases, depending upon the type of business entity.

- Employer contributions are tax-free to employees.

- The funds grow tax-free in employee accounts.

- Tax-free withdrawals can be made to pay any qualified medical expense, now or in the future.

- HSAs can also be used to pay for expenses that typical health insurance plans do not cover, such as eyeglasses and hearing aids.

The U.S. Treasury Department offers more information about HSAs at this address:

http://www.treasury.gov/resource-center/tax-policy/Pages/Health-Savings-Accounts.aspx.

## THE FUTURE OF HEALTH CARE

The cost of health insurance is growing faster than most companies' revenues. While Congress has passed legislation aimed at reducing the growth of these costs, many experts feel that this will have little positive impact. It could make things worse.

Private employers are being forced to examine their health care expenditures and make continual adjustments. Employees are being asked to share more of the direct cost for these benefits. Deductibles and copays are increasing.

As an HR specialist for your company, you must continue to monitor the benefit landscape. You must reduce costs wherever possible, while still trying to maximize the benefits to your employees.

Don't be afraid to seek help. Call your insurance broker first. Brokers usually know the marketplace better than anyone. Ask for advice and new options. Always.

## Chapter Fifty
## HR
### The Benefits Landscape

# VOLUNTARY BENEFITS

The Declaration of Independence says, *"We hold these truths to be self-evident, that all men are created equal, that they are endowed by their Creator with certain unalienable rights, that among these are life, liberty and the pursuit of happiness..."*

The United States was founded upon the concept of equality. Our forefathers believed that every person should have the right to freedom, life and be allowed to pursue their own happiness.

While it may be a stretch to assume that our Founding Fathers fought the Revolutionary War to allow companies to offer voluntary benefits to employees, the concept of such benefits has roots that are deeply planted in the American Way.

Voluntary benefits treat all employees equally. They give employees the freedom to choose benefits that will enhance and protect their lives.

Voluntary benefits can be offered to employees with little or no cost to the employer. They can be used by employers to attract and retain productive employees. They can be used by employees to supplement benefits that are not provided by the employer.

## How They Work

Voluntary benefits are typically offered to employees on a payroll deduction basis. The employer chooses what benefits are to be offered under the program. Employees choose which of these benefits they desire, and in what quantity. The employer withholds the benefit premiums or payments from employee pay and forwards the money to the insurer or provider.

Employer-sponsored benefits have several important advantages over similar, individually owned benefits. Among these are:

- **Convenience**. Payroll deduction gives employees an easy way to own benefits that they desire, but often don't get the chance to purchase.

- **Underwriting concessions**. Benefits offered on a group basis often have more lenient underwriting standards. This can allow some, less insurable individuals, to own coverage they may not be able to purchase on their own.

- **Volume discounts**. Because company-sponsored benefits are offered in larger numbers, providers can often pass volume savings to participants.

- **Access to expertise**. Enrolling in employer-sponsored benefits may give rank and file employees access to professionals they would never meet on their own. Advice from a highly-trained professional can often be a life-changing event.

Voluntary benefits can be funded completely by employees. Employers may also choose to fund a portion of the expenditures.

Some employers choose to fund a base amount and then allow employees to purchase additional benefits. Others fund a portion of the expenditure. This may or may not have limits.

With today's computer and payroll technology, voluntary benefits can be offered easily and efficiently. Any expenditure of time by employers can be recovered by increased productivity within the work force.

Most voluntary benefits programs are nonqualified. This means that:

- Employee withholdings are still taxed to employees as compensation.

- Employer contributions are taxed to employees as compensation.

- Benefits, when received, are generally non-taxable to employees.

Typical voluntary benefits that are offered by employers include:

- Life Insurance

- Disability Insurance

- Long-term Care Insurance

- Medical Prescription Insurance

- Dental Insurance

- Vision Insurance

- Cancer Supplement Plans

- Legal Assistance

- Hospital Confinement

- Accident Insurance

- Child Care/Dependent Care Benefits (In Section 125 Plans)

- HSAs

- Individual Retirement Plans

- College Savings Programs

Every employer should consider the use of employee-paid benefits. It is an effective way to give employees what they want and need, without much expense to the company.

## Chapter Fifty-One
## _____HR_____
## Retirement Plans

# RETIREMENT PLAN HISTORY

Retirement plans have evolved over the years and will continue to do so. This change has been driven by financial and macroeconomic trends. Evolution has also responded to various social trends that have occurred within the job marketplace.

As business and employee needs change, Congress continues to introduce legislation to meet the goals of both.

Years ago, most Americans worked for large companies. Little changed within those companies, and employees often spent a career working for the same organization. A large company would promise an employee a pension and gold watch at retirement, in exchange for that employee's long-term loyalty to the organization.

With such stability, there was little demand for a diverse array of retirement plans. For many years, there were just two types of pension plans. Companies could implement a *Defined Benefit Pension Plan,* a *Money Purchase Pension Plan*, or both. Pension plans were loosely regulated until Congress passed the ERISA legislation in 1974. ERISA established concrete guidelines (and penalties) with regard to retirement plan management, eligibility, contribution limits, investments, fiduciary responsibility, etc.

In addition to pensions, companies could also implement *Profit Sharing Plans,* where employers shared a portion of profits with all employees. These became regulated under ERISA as well.

Since ERISA, Congress has made many changes to our laws. Congress has created new regulations, bringing additional features to traditional retirement plans. Congress has also made changes that allowed for new types of plans.

The following chapters highlight the features and benefits of the various types of retirement plans that can be offered to employees. My goal here is to:

- Help you choose plans that are right for your company.

- Help you manage your plan(s) more efficiently.

- Help you become better informed about your responsibilities.

# RETIREMENT PLAN OVERVIEW

Retirement plans come in many forms. Some are funded completely with company monies, while others are funded solely by employees. Some are negotiated and customized with bargaining units, while many are off-the-shelf plans with no customization at all.

Most private companies have similar objectives when implementing retirement plans. Most employers want to:

- Offer plans that are owner/executive friendly.

  o Most smaller companies are privately held. When the company contributes to a retirement plan, the contribution comes from money that would otherwise be retained by ownership.

- Offer plans that attract and retain highly skilled employees.

    o Businesses cannot afford to lose key employees because they don't keep pace in the retirement plan marketplace.

    o These plans should be managed well, and they should offer employees the best possible mix of investment options.

- Minimize plan expenses. This is important for several reasons.

    o Plan sponsors have a fiduciary responsibility (see below) to manage plan expenses.

    o Employers generally seek to minimize their own out of pocket costs.

    o Excess plan expenses can reduce investment returns for employees.

- Communicate effectively. Companies want their employees to understand how to make the best use of their retirement choices.

- Minimize fiduciary liability.

    o Since plan trustees/sponsors can be held personally liable for breaches in fiduciary duty, private companies are particularly attentive to fiduciary risk.

- Minimize plan administration requirements.

- Provide accurate and timely information to the plan trustees and beneficiaries.

## QUALIFIED PLANS

Retirement plans must qualify for favorable income tax treatment. Plan qualification allows contributions that are made by an employer to be tax deductible. Qualification also allows plan investments to grow on a tax-deferred basis. Qualification rules vary depending upon the type of plan. We will review these in greater detail later in this chapter.

### The IRS Rules

The Internal Revenue Service is responsible for ensuring compliance with the Internal Revenue Code. The Internal Revenue Code establishes specific rules for operating tax-qualified plans, including plan funding and vesting requirements.

## ERISA

Qualified retirement plans are governed by an act of Congress that is known as ERISA. Under ERISA, the U.S. Department of Labor's *Employee Benefits Security Administration* is charged with enforcing the rules governing the conduct of:

- Plan managers

- Investment of plan assets

- Reporting and disclosure of plan information

- Enforcement of the fiduciary provisions of the law, and

- Workers' benefit rights

If you are going to sponsor a qualified retirement plan you should understand the law. I have included the Department of Labor's ERISA explanation in this book. Many plan sponsors hear about the law from advisors, but never understand the essence of its rules. Because of its importance and complexity, I have decided to include the exact text of what the DOL has to say about ERISA. It is as follows:

## *"WHAT IS ERISA?*

*"The Employee Retirement Income Security Act of 1974, or ERISA, protects the assets of millions of Americans so that funds placed in retirement plans during their working lives will be there when they retire.*

*"ERISA is a federal law that sets minimum standards for pension plans in private industry. For example, if an employer maintains a pension plan, ERISA specifies when an employee must be allowed to become a participant, how long they have to work before they have a non-forfeitable interest in their pension, how long a participant can be away from their job before it might affect their benefit, and whether their spouse has a right to part of their pension in the event of their death. Most of the provisions of ERISA are effective for plan years beginning on or after January 1, 1975.*

*"ERISA does not require any employer to establish a pension plan. It only requires that those who establish plans must meet certain minimum standards. The law generally does not specify how much money a participant must be paid as a benefit.*

*"ERISA does the following:*

*"Requires plans to provide participants with information about the plan including important information about plan features and funding. The plan must furnish some information regularly and automatically. Some is available free of charge, some is not.*

*"Sets minimum standards for participation, vesting, benefit accrual and funding. The law defines how long a person may be required to work before becoming eligible to participate in a plan, to accumulate benefits, and to have a non-forfeitable right to those benefits. The law also establishes detailed funding rules that require plan sponsors to provide adequate funding for your plan.*

*"Requires accountability of plan fiduciaries. ERISA generally*

*defines a fiduciary as anyone who exercises discretionary authority or control over a plan's management or assets, including anyone who provides investment advice to the plan. Fiduciaries who do not follow the principles of conduct may be held responsible for restoring losses to the plan.*

*"Gives participants the right to sue for benefits and breaches of fiduciary duty.*

*"Guarantees payment of certain benefits if a defined plan is terminated, through a federally chartered corporation, known as the Pension Benefit Guaranty Corporation."*

You can read the full text of this article at the following Internet location:

http://www.dol.gov/ebsa/faqs/faq_compliance_pension.html

When you think about ERISA, you must understand that this law has teeth the size of a bear. Unfortunately, abiding by every ERISA statute requires the Wisdom of Solomon and the Patience of Job. None of us are perfect, but you must do everything in your power to abide by ERISA's regulations.

## FIDUCIARY RULES

If you are a retirement plan trustee, or business owner, you will (almost always) be considered to be a plan *fiduciary*. Plan fiduciaries have specific obligations under the law. If you breach those responsibilities, the Department of Labor may hold you *personally liable* for asset losses in your plan, even if those assets are self-directed.

Here is what the Department of Labor has this to say about fiduciary responsibility:

*"The Employee Retirement Income Security Act (ERISA) protects your plan's assets by requiring that those persons or entities who exercise discretionary control or authority over plan management or plan assets, anyone with discretionary authority or responsibility for the administration of a plan, or anyone who provides investment advice to*

*a plan for compensation or has any authority or responsibility to do so are subject to fiduciary responsibilities. Plan fiduciaries include, for example, plan trustees, plan administrators, and members of a plan's investment committee.*

*"The primary responsibility of fiduciaries is to run the plan solely in the interest of participants and beneficiaries and for the exclusive purpose of providing benefits and paying plan expenses. Fiduciaries must act prudently and must diversify the plan's investments in order to minimize the risk of large losses. In addition, they must follow the terms of plan documents to the extent that the plan terms are consistent with ERISA. They also must avoid conflicts of interest. In other words, they may not engage in transactions on behalf of the plan that benefit parties related to the plan, such as other fiduciaries, services providers or the plan sponsor.*

*"Fiduciaries who do not follow these principles of conduct may be personally liable to restore any losses to the plan, or to restore any profits made through improper use of plan assets. Courts may take whatever action is appropriate against fiduciaries who breach their duties under ERISA including their removal."*

You can read the full text of this article at the following Internet location:

http://www.dol.gov/dol/topic/retirement/fiduciaryresp.htm

**Note:** Private retirement plans are regulated under Title I of ERISA, which is enforced by the U.S. Department of Labor. Plans run by public entities — such as federal, state and local governments — may not be governed under Title I of the law.

### Summary

You've now got a general view of retirement plans and their regulation. It is time to discuss the particulars of plans that you may offer to employees.

As you read about the various plan structures, you will find that certain ones, and their variations, provide significant advantages for small and mid-sized employers. Depending upon your objectives, you will choose one plan, or a combination of plans, that will best satisfy your needs.

As we go along, I will also try to help you understand your legal responsibilities regarding plan management, as well as the tax implications of any plan you choose.

# Chapter Fifty-Two
## _____HR_____
## Retirement Plans

### DEFINED BENEFIT PENSIONS

Defined benefit pensions pay employees a benefit that is *defined* at retirement. With this type of plan, an employer tells employees: "If you work for our company for X number of years, and you earn Y, we promise to pay you Z…"

An employee's benefit under any plan is determined by a formula. Formulas are flexible at the formation of a plan. Typically, the employer agrees to pay retirees a certain percentage of their salary (or total compensation), adjusted by the number of years of service with the company. Most employers pay a much higher retirement benefit to employees with the longest company tenure. It often takes many years of work before an employee earns a meaningful pension at retirement.

Once a formula has been chosen, great care must be taken if you decide to change it.

In a typical defined benefit pension plan, an employee with thirty years of service might expect to retire (at age 65) with 60%-80% of their final salary. This is in addition to Social Security and other benefits — provided the company is still in business and the pension has been fully funded.

A typical benefit formula might credit employees 2% of pay for each year worked with the company. Under this formula, an employee who has worked with the company for 35 years would receive

70% of pay at retirement. Pay (under this formula) is the *average total income* for the last *three years* of service with the company. If the average income was $100,000, this retiree would receive $70,000 per year in retirement. There may also be a cost of living adjustment included, where benefits increase over time with inflation.

Benefit formulas might pay 1%, 1.5%, or 2.5% per year. They might cap retirement pay at 50% or 60% of compensation. Some might cap benefits at 20 years' of service, 25 years, or 35 years. The variations are flexible and can be mixed and matched, depending upon the goals of the company.

### Payout

Payments at retirement are typically made on a monthly basis. Under current law, the most that an employee may receive in retirement is $195,000 per year.

Some plans allow for a lump sum payment in lieu of monthly benefits. The actual lump sum payment would be determined by the plan's actuaries. The amount paid would be the *present value* of the *future benefits*. This is the lump sum of cash that it would take, today, to provide the promised future benefits. This formula is a function of the employee's age, benefit and the prevailing interest rates in the financial marketplace.

If you pay attention to lottery winners, you will notice that some of them choose to receive the annual payments. Others choose an "equivalent lump sum" payment. The lump sum payment is significantly lower than the sum of the annual payments. This is because the lump sum can be invested to earn a rate of return, which (in theory) would ultimately equal the sum of the payments.

When an employee leaves a company *before* retirement, they may be entitled to a lump sum payment from a defined benefit plan. The plan may also keep the money, continue to invest it, and pay the employee in the normal manner at retirement. The amount that an employee is "owed" by the plan will be the present value of the vested benefits. We will review both of these concepts below.

# VESTING IN A DEFINED BENEFIT PLAN

There are legal requirements that require employees to be "vested" in benefits provided under defined benefit retirement plans. Vested benefits are *owned* by the employee, and *owed* by the plan.

Vesting in defined benefit plans is fairly complicated. Your retirement plan administrator should be able to explain the particulars of any plan. Essentially, employees become vested in their benefits, as earned. If a plan is terminated, employees will become immediately and fully vested in their benefits.

### Present Value

If an employee leaves a company before retirement, the plan owes the employee the *present value* of the vested *future benefit.* This benefit may be less than the money put into the plan to fund it. This is because your plan funds to pay the full vested benefit, given a rate of return, many years in the future.

If employees leave a company after relatively short periods of time, much of the money that has been set aside for their retirement may come **back to the plan**.

**Here is a simplified example:** An employee has worked for your company from age 20 to 25. He is fully vested in his benefit, and has been earning $20,000 per year. Your employee has been credited with 2% of pay each year. Therefore, he is vested in 10% (2% for five years) of $20,000. The plan owes this employee $2,000 per year *forty years* from now.

What does the plan actually owe this employee today? The amount owed today is the present value of the future benefit (which is $2,000 per year in forty years).

How much money will it take to provide this benefit? ERISA law gives ranges of returns that actuaries are allowed to use for rate of return calculations. Your actuary will choose a rate from within this range (which is derived from historical interest rates) and use a prevailing life expectancy table to determine the present value of the future benefit. For simplicity, let's assume that your actuary determines that 5% is a reasonable return on investments. $40,000 invested at 5% would yield $2,000 per year. Your actuary will also calculate in a reduction in principal. This would reduce the $40,000 to a lower figure, because the $2,000 benefit would be calculated only over the employee's life expectancy, about 20 years. Let's say that your actuary reduces this future amount to $35,000.

$5,000 invested today, at 5% per year, would grow to $35,200 thirty years from now. Therefore, the *present value* of the benefits earned by your 5-year employee is about $5,000. This is what your plan would owe this employee with five years of service.

In order to fund the full retirement benefit of this employee, you may have set aside $2,000 per year. The money may have grown to $12,000. Therefore, you would segregate the **$5,000** that is *vested* by your employee. This may or may not be paid today. The balance of **$7,000** would *revert* to your plan.

### Defined Benefit in Private Business

Defined benefit plans can be extremely attractive to private businesses, particularly if they have older owners who want to set aside much larger sums of money than are allowed by traditional retirement plans.

# Chapter Fifty-Three
## HR
## Retirement Plans

## MONEY PURCHASE PENSIONS

With a money purchase pension, a company guarantees to make pension contributions for all eligible employees, such as 10% or 15% of pay each year. These funds are often held in a pooled account which is managed by the company. Independent, third party administration firms are hired to keep track of how much is in the account for each employee.

Some employers allow employees to take control over their own investments, in a manner similar to 401(k) accounts. 401(k)s are explained in a later chapter.

As business has become more competitive and less predictable, large companies have been scaling back on defined benefit and money purchase pension plans. Employers are less able to make long-term commitments to pension accounts.

Many defined benefit pension plans, particularly those for union employees such as laborers and state workers, are in deep financial trouble. Because of this, employees have become far less willing to stake their financial futures on a forty-year promise made by a company that might not exist when the time comes to retire.

As the use of traditional pension plans has dwindled, the use of other forms of retirement plans has grown. We examine additional plan options in the following chapters.

# Chapter Fifty-Four
## HR
## Retirement Plans

## CASH BALANCE PLANS

Large companies have migrated from traditional, defined benefit pensions toward the use of Cash Balance Pension Plans. Cash balance plans use similar funding formulas as defined pension plans. However, rather than make a thirty or forty year promise, companies make annual contributions into employee-owned accounts that are based upon defined-benefit-type formulas. Employees take on the investment risk. Employees are usually subject to vesting in their investment accounts. The company (plan sponsor) is *not* obligated to continue future funding if business conditions change.

This hybrid pension significantly reduces long-term liabilities to companies. It also gives employees tangible assets that can't be forfeited, provided they hold up their end of the loyalty bargain by remaining with the company.

# Chapter Fifty-Five
## HR
## Retirement Plans

## PROFIT SHARING PLANS

Profit Sharing Plans have become the retirement cornerstone for most American workers. Profit sharing plans do not have the same long-term liabilities to employees as pension plans. Contributions do not have to be made every year. They are made at the employer's discretion. In addition, employees do not accrue future benefits, simply by working another year for the company. In a competitive and uncertain business climate, this is a more attractive option for most employers.

Employers establish profit sharing plans as an incentive to attract and retain productive employees. Contributions are normally made from company profits, although contributions can still be made in a money-losing year. A ten or fifteen percent (of salary) annual profit sharing contribution can be a powerful incentive for employees to see that a company remains profitable.

Deductible contributions to profit sharing plans are limited by tax laws. The maximum annual company contribution to a plan is twenty-five percent of payroll. The individual amounts are detailed in chapter eighty-eight.

**Note:** There are variations to profit sharing formulas that can be rather advantageous to the owners and executives of smaller businesses. We will review these over the next few chapters.

# Chapter Fifty-Six
## _____HR_____
## Retirement Plans

## 401(K)

In the late 1970s, Congress reacted to the changing business marketplace by adding an *employee-deferral feature* to the traditional profit sharing plan. Deferral profit sharing plans became known as 401(k) plans, because they utilize sub-section (k) of Section 401 of the Internal Revenue Code. The first plan using the employee-deferral concept was created in 1981.

Insurance companies dominated the early 401(k) market, particularly for private businesses. An insurance company would choose a set of mutual funds from several fund families (typically ten to forty funds) and place them inside a *group annuity* contract. They would then add an asset charge on top of the normal mutual fund fees (typically 1% - 2%) to cover expenses.

Insurance companies still offer some of the most competitive plans for smaller businesses. Asset charges are much lower today than at the inception of the first 401(k)s.

The earliest *mutual fund* 401(k) programs consisted of funds offered solely by the sponsoring company. If a company went to Fidelity Investments, that company could choose from Fidelity funds only for their plan.

In the early 1990s, the nation's first *Open Architecture* 401(k) was created. Open architecture allows employers to choose from thousands of investment options for their plan. This lets employers offer the best mix of investment choices for their plan. Open architecture can also include the use of individual brokerage accounts by plan participants.

The earliest open architecture 401(k)s were built in conjunction with independent third party administrators (TPAs). A company (plan sponsor) would hire a TPA who would work with an independent investment specialist to create a completely customized plan.

Mutual fund and insurance companies were quick to embrace the open architecture concept.

Today, virtually all plans offered by TPAs, mutual fund companies and insurance companies now utilize some variation of the open architecture concept.

## HOW A 401(K) WORKS

A 401(k) is a "qualified" plan that receives favorable tax treatment under the law. In order to remain qualified, the plan must follow a complex set of regulations. The primary focus of these laws is to ensure that the plan does not discriminate against any group of employees.

### The Essence of 401(k)

In HR, you already know that a 401(k) is one of the most popular benefits that you can offer your employees.

There is a common misperception that 401(k)s are expensive, particularly to the smallest employers. This is not the case. A 401(k) can be offered at little or no cost to your company. Another misconception is that employees won't participate. They will, particularly if they are educated properly.

Don't avoid implementing a 401(k) because you think you cannot afford it, or that your employees don't want it, even if they tell you they don't. Affordable plans are available to your company. Nearly all employees welcome the chance to participate once they are properly educated.

As an HR manager, or private company executive, you should know how a 401(k) works. You should understand your responsibilities, and what you must do to fulfill your duties in managing the plan. Here is a list of the key features of any 401(k).

- A 401(k) is a profit sharing plan with an employee salary-deferral feature.

- The plan sponsor (company) nominates trustees (usually the business owner/executives) to establish the plan for employees.

- The plan trustees become Fiduciaries — with specific requirements and liabilities for breach of duty.

  o Fiduciaries are entrusted with seeing that the plan does not discriminate in favor of certain employees, and that the management of the plan is made for the welfare of its participants.

  o Fiduciary obligations involve aspects of employee education, plan administration and cost control.

  o Most plan providers can help you execute your fiduciary obligations in a stress-free manner.

- An *Investment Policy Statement* must be prepared by the plan trustees. Think of it as a business plan for your 401(k).

- *Individual accounts* are established for all participating employees.

  o The company withholds a percentage of employee income (as determined by each employee) and contributes it to the plan.

- A third party administrator (TPA) is hired to manage the accounting and *recordkeeping* for the plan. The TPA may be completely independent. The TPA may be owned by your 401(k) provider. Or, the TPA may be specifically contracted by the 401(k) provider to do the work.

- A company is hired to *manage* the investments (usually mutual funds).

- An advisor is engaged by the plan trustees to help manage *Fiduciary* obligations.

    o The advisor helps the trustees choose investments for the plan.

    o The advisor usually helps with the Investment Policy Statement.

    o The adviser usually educates employees regarding the plan and its investments.

- Employees usually determine where their individual funds will be invested.

- The investment company and the TPA provide accurate *information* regarding plan investments.

- Employees are allowed to *change* their allocations regularly (daily in some plans).

- *Eligibility* is determined by the plan.

    o Under most circumstances, all employees that are over the age of 21, with a full year of service (1,000 hours) must be included in the plan.

- The *average* deferral percentage of highly compensated employees (HCEs) may not exceed 2% more than the average deferral percentage of non-highly compensated employees.

- The plan sponsor (your company) can *match* employee contributions.

  o Matching contributions will be determined by a customized formula.

  o Company matches can have a *vesting* schedule.

- Specific rules *regulate* how much of the company *contributions* can be allocated toward the ownership/executive group.

  o Limits to highly compensated employees (HCEs) are based upon company ownership and income levels.

- Additional *profit sharing* contributions can be made to the plan.

- *Loans* can be made available to plan participants. These will be subject to certain limitations.

- *Hardship withdrawals* can be allowed from the plan. These will be subject to limitations.

- Employee contributions into a 401(k) are typically *tax deductible* when going in.

- Investments grow on a *tax deferred* basis.

- Employee deferrals are still subject to *Social Security taxes.*

- When distributions are made from the plan (or any subsequent IRA), all proceeds will be subject to *income taxation.*

In a ***Roth 401(k),*** contributions are made on an *after tax basis*. The investments grow on a tax deferred basis and come out *tax free*. We will discuss the details of a Roth 401(k) in chapter sixty-nine.

# Chapter Fifty-Seven
## HR
## Retirement Plans

## 401(K) RULES:

### Contribution Limits:

The government sets limits on how much can be contributed annually to any retirement plan, including a 401(k).

With a 401(k), these limits consist of maximum annual contributions by employees, as well as combined employer and employee contributions. These limitations include plan forfeitures.

Plan forfeitures are non-vested employer contributions that were made on behalf of participants that have left the company and the plan. We will review vesting on the next page.

The annual limits to contributions made into a 401(k) are the lesser of:

- 100 percent of the employee's compensation, or

- $50,000 (for 2012).

The amount that employees can *contribute* under any 401(k) plan is limited to $17,000 for 2012.

401(k) plans can allow *catch-up* contributions of $5,500 (for 2012) for any employee who is age 50 and over. This provision was created to allow older workers to save more than younger employees, as they have less time to see their investments grow.

## Vesting:

All salary deferrals made by an employee are owned by that employee. Company contributions can be subject to a vesting schedule. Once a company contribution is vested, it is owned by the employee. Vesting is determined individually for each employee, and is based upon years of service with the employer.

There is a maximum amount of time that can elapse before company contributions become vested and owned by each individual employee. Vesting can occur gradually or all at once (cliff vesting). The following is the most restrictive, company-friendly vesting schedule allowed by law. This schedule can be found at the U.S. Department of Labor website: http://www.dol.gov/ebsa/publications/401kplans.html

### Graduated Vesting

| Years of Service | Non-forfeitable Percentage |
|---|---|
| 2 | 20% |
| 3 | 40% |
| 4 | 60% |
| 5 | 80% |
| 6 | 100% |

### Cliff Vesting
Less than 3 years of service - 0% Vested
At least 3 years of service - 100% Vested

# ANTI-DISCRIMINATION RULES

Retirement plans must treat all employees equally, and may not discriminate in favor of owners and top executives. Anti-discrimination rules govern how much employers can set aside for various employees, and how much employees can set aside for themselves.

Anti-discrimination rules limit the amount that can go into a plan for highly compensated employees (HCEs). This holds true for profit sharing contributions, as well as 401(k) deferrals.

HCE rules are complicated, and the percentages differ based upon a number of factors. The bottom line is this: Employers have limits that they can put into retirement plans for highly compensated executives. The same holds true with 401(k) deferrals. If highly compensated individuals defer too much, the plan must return contributions to bring deferral percentages into balance.

You can learn more about 401(k) testing requirements at the following IRS website:

http://www.irs.gov/retirement/article/0,,id=112858,00.html

**What is an HCE?**

An HCE is anyone who is a *5% owner* or is *highly compensated*, earning over $115,000 in 2012. In some cases, HCEs are anyone in the top 20% of company earners.

Note: There are several strategies that companies can use to allocate greater funds to owners and executives, without violating anti-discrimination rules. We will explore these in the upcoming chapters.

# SAFE HARBOR 401(K)

A safe harbor 401(k) allows HCEs to contribute the maximum, regardless of how much non-HCEs defer. It also reduces plan record-keeping costs.

A plan can qualify for safe harbor treatment in two ways.

1. The employer can make a fully-vested, non-elective contribution of 3 percent (of each eligible employee's compensation) into the plan.

2. The employer can agree to match every eligible employee's *contributions* into the plan. This match must be dollar for dollar, of up to 3 percent of each employee's compensation. The employer can choose to match an additional 50 cents on every dollar up to 5 percent of each employee's contribution. This brings the total maximum match to 4%.

To remain under the safe harbor provisions, employers must make either the matching contributions or the non-elective contributions every year.

The sponsor's plan document must specify which contributions will be made. This information must be provided to all eligible employees before the beginning of each year.

# Chapter Fifty-Eight
## HR
## Retirement Plans

## INTEGRATED PLANS

Retirement plan contributions can be "integrated" with Social Security.

Integration is based upon the concept that Social Security provides retirement benefits to all employees, but not all income. In 2012, the Social Security maximum taxable wage base is $110,100. Social Security ignores all income above the taxable age base.

With integrated contributions, employees earning less than the Social Security wage base receive a pro rata allocation into the retirement plan, based upon compensation. Those earning above the taxable wage base are eligible to receive an additional contribution, potentially as much as 5.7% of the excess compensation over the wage base.

The reason that integration is allowed is simple: Social Security does not pay benefits to retirees on earnings above the taxable wage base. To make up for this disparity, employers are allowed to make additional contributions into a plan under an integrated profit sharing formula.

Integration can be used to legally increase contributions to executives, as a method to make total retirement benefits more "equal" for all employees.

# Chapter Fifty-Nine
## HR
### Retirement Plans

## AGE WEIGHTED PROFIT SHARING PLANS

Businesses can make use of something known as "age weighting" in their profit sharing contributions.

In certain situations, age weighting allows far greater contributions to be made for a select group of employees.

## EQUALITY IS DEDUCTIBLE

One of the primary components of ERISA legislation was to limit the deductibility of company contributions into retirement plans. A main intent of the law was to create "equality" with regard to company contributions.

## ENTREPRENEURIAL REWARDS

Most small and mid-sized companies are privately held, and owned by one or a few individuals. These business entrepreneurs take enormous risks with their *personal* finances. They usually worked long hours and sacrificed for many years before they achieved their current financial success.

Private business owners pay competitive wages. They pay employees *before* they pay themselves. Many still endure sleepless nights wondering how to remain in business.

Once a business owner achieves financial success, the IRS demands a large portion of their profits for *taxes*.

Is it any wonder that most successful small business owner/executives would like to put as much into their retirement plans as possible?

Traditional profit sharing formulas don't allow companies to allocate a high percentage of contributions to the ownership/executive group. Under standard profit sharing, the executive group might receive only five or ten or twenty percent of company contributions into the plan, the same percentage that is received by all employees.

## WITH AGE WEIGHTING, EQUAL CAN BE MORE THAN "EQUAL."

Congress realized that equality does not always mean allocating the same percentage *contribution* into a plan for all employees. Equality can also mean making contributions to achieve the same *benefit* at retirement.

This concession by Congress can create significant retirement plan opportunities for many private businesses.

With age weighting, companies are often able to make profit sharing contributions in a manner that allocates a significant portion of contributions to the *management group*. With this technique it is not unusual for owner/executives to receive **50% - 90% of company contributions**.

## HOW AGE WEIGHTING WORKS

Traditional profit sharing contributions are made as a percentage of employee compensation. If the company decides upon a 10% contribution, everybody in the plan gets treated the same, with 10% of pay.

With age weighting, employees are also treated equally. In this case, "equal" may mean that one employee (someone young) receives a 1% contribution; while another (the older owner/executive) receives 25%. This is because age weighting adds an *age* feature to the "equality" equation.

- For a plan to retain favorable tax treatment there must be no discrimination against employees.

- Congress recognized that a similar percentage contribution to all employees can inadvertently *discriminate* against *older* employees. This is because older employees have far less time to see their investments grow before retirement.

### Focus on the *Future* Benefit

**Note:** The past decade has been perilous to retirement plan investments. The returns for both stocks and bonds have been significantly below their long-term averages. Over time however, stock and bond market returns historically revert to something approaching their long-term averages. From 1926 to 2010, the average annual rate of return for S&P 500 was 9.8%. Long-term U.S. Treasury Bonds returned an average of 5.4%. While there is no guarantee that we will see the same returns over the next 85 years, prudent managers normally plan with these rates in mind.

An employee's age relates directly to how long plan contributions can grow before retirement. For example: A $5,000 contribution might grow little in one year. With 8% annual growth, this same $5,000 will grow to more than $50,000 in thirty years.

Plan trustees (and their administrators) can use *time value* to tweak profit sharing contributions in favor of *older* employees.

### How it works.

With age-weighting, administrators assume a rate of return on investments from contribution date until retirement. (This rate of return must be within legal guidelines that are established by law.) Contribution are made for each employee, to give them all the *same percentage (of pay) benefit at retirement* — not today.

In our simplified example from above, a $5,000 contribution for someone thirty years from retirement (age 35) is essentially the *same* as a $50,000 contribution made for an employee retiring in a year (age 64).

**Example:** Let's compare the contributions for an employee who is age twenty-five versus contributions made for an employee who is age fifty-five. Our twenty-five-year-old will have forty years (assuming retirement at age 65) to grow a 10% profit sharing contribution, while an employee who is fifty-five will have only ten years.

If we assume an investment rate of return of 7.2%, our young employee will see this year's 10% plan contribution grow to 160% of current salary in forty years. Our older employee will see his/her 10% grow in the plan to just 20% of current salary in ten years.

In this case, to get the same 160% of current pay at retirement, our older employee would need to receive a profit sharing contribution of **80%** to receive the same *equal benefit as* **10%** under the age weighted concept. Conversely, the younger employee may receive a contribution of *1.25%* **versus** *10%* to receive *equal benefit* under the plan.

The following illustrates the benefit of age weighting in retirement plan design:

Assume we have a small company with an owner who is age 55 and two employees who are age 25. Our owner earns $100,000. Our two younger employees earn $50,000 each. This gives us a payroll of $200,000.

Under the traditional profit sharing concept, a 10% profit sharing contribution would lead to a total deposit into the plan of $20,000. Half goes to benefit the owner (10% of $100,000). Half benefits the employees (10% of $50,000 each).

Our owner now needs to make a choice. Should she make the profit sharing contribution? Let's do the math.

Assuming a 30% total owner tax bracket, our owner would keep $14,000, after paying taxes on the $20,000 profit.

Contributions into a profit sharing plan are tax deductible. In this example, our owner would pay no income taxes if she contributes the $20,000 profit into a retirement plan. Should she do this, our owner would have $10,000 in her personal profit sharing account, rather than $14,000 if she had just kept the money.

In this simplified example, our owner is $4,000 out-of-pocket if she contributes $20,000 to the profit sharing plan. Our owner will be tempted to keep her personal money and forget about funding for employees.

With age weighting our owner would be able to make the same $20,000 contribution. In this case, $16,000 would be contributed to the owner's account. $2,000 would be set aside for each employee.

With age-weighting our business owner will be far more inclined to make a profit sharing contribution. Everybody wins. Our owner is happy because she has saved for retirement. Our employees are happy, because they have received a nice profit sharing contribution. The taxing authorities will receive $6,000 less in owner income taxes.

Age-weighting can be a very attractive profit sharing feature for a private business with older executives.

**Note:** Calculations for age weighted plans are not quite so simple. Adjustments must be made for owners and highly compensated employees. There are limits to how much can be set aside for any single individual. Employees are often segregated into groups for other testing reasons, etc. Age weighted contributions can be made in different ways.

## Chapter Sixty
## HR
### Retirement Plans

## NEW COMPARABILITY/CROSS-TESTED PLANS

All businesses face financial challenges. Regulation is costly. Competition is fierce. Some companies compete against foreign operators with far less regulation and lower salary scales.

Private business owners and executives would like to set aside tax-favored funds while they can. This money can be used in retirement. It is not available to creditors in the event of a business failure.

In a perfect world, management groups would set aside as much as possible into retirement funds for all employees. Reality makes this a challenge.

Every dollar matters. Employers must carefully weigh making retirement plan contributions against all other options. Can extra funds be used for company expansion? Can they be used to hire new employees? Should they be used to increase pay for key individuals, or should they be set aside to weather future economic downturns? Should ownership take the money, pay the taxes and keep the balance?

### A Magnificent Option

Cross-testing is a hybrid plan design that can be used to direct a *much higher percentage* of employer contributions to the *management/owner group*.

Comparability designs can create a win-win for both employers and employees. Executive/owners are able to set aside a significant portion of contributions for themselves. Employees benefit from contributions they would not otherwise receive.

## HOW IT WORKS

Cross-tested plans allow the employer (trustees) to place eligible participants into various "tiers." Contributions are made on an *age-weighted* basis, using employees within these tiers for calculations, rather than each particular individual.

Tiers can be created based upon a variety of factors, such as, but not limited to:

- Company Position

- Compensation

- Longevity on the job

- Sales or Management Goals

Plan sponsors are also allowed to use a combination of traditional tier factors to create a unique tier that suits the company.

Individuals within each tier can receive differing amounts, yet still be treated "equally" under the law.

## WHY CREATE TIERS?

Tiers can be used to bring contributions within the acceptable limits to avoid discrimination. By using tiers, private businesses can create enormous flexibility with regard to retirement plan benefits and contributions. For example: If one individual opts to receive nothing, others may take the remaining allocation. **This allows certain employees to receive far larger contributions than under traditional plan designs.**

Here is a simple example of how it might work:

Let's say that contributions into a particular tier can average no more than 10%. We create a tier that has two members — the chairman of the board and his child, the CEO. Our chairman is semi-retired and has no need for retirement plan contributions. We set aside zero for our chairman. This allows us to set aside 20% for our CEO (averaging 10% for each) and avoid discrimination.

Here is another use:

A business owner is trying to recruit a new CEO from outside the company. By electing a zero contribution, our business owner is able to set aside 20% for the new CEO, creating a powerful (yet legal) tax-deductible perk to entice the new CEO.

There are dozens of favorable ways that comparability can be used to tailor contributions into retirement plans.

## Chapter Sixty-One
### _____HR_____
### Retirement Plans

# PLAN DESIGN: A COMPARATIVE EXAMPLE

The following is an example of how contributions can vary between different plan designs.

The original design featured a pension plan that was integrated with Social Security to allow for greater contributions to senior management.

The second plan design increased the integrated formula to allow for greater contributions for the management team. Contributions for key executives increase by $11,000. Unfortunately, it also increases total company contributions by $30,000.

The third plan utilized an age-weighted comparability design. This design allowed the employer to fund the *same* amount for key executives as the original design. It also allowed the company to *reduce total contributions into the plan by $130,000.*

The following pages illustrate the calculations:

**ABC, INC. Pension Plan**

**Pension Plan Specifications**

**2012 Plan Year**

| | |
|---|---|
| Effective Date: | 1/1/2012 |
| Valuation Date: | 12/31/2012 |

Eligibility:

| | |
|---|---|
| Minimum Age | 21 |
| Minimum Service | None |
| Entry Date | First day of the month following hire. |

Normal Retirement Age:          65

# ABC, INC. Pension Plan

## Total Contribution:
### Current Integrated Plan
$296,167, based on applying current Money Purchase Formula to total

### Alternative Integrated Plan
$324,864, based on increasing excess percentage over Taxable Wage Base from 2.8% to 5.7%.

### Comparability Plan
$165,494, based on giving Group 1 members same dollar contribution as they would receive under the Current Integrated Plan. Contributions for other groups were arbitrarily chosen and can be easily changed.

### Notes:
Under Comparability Plan:
>    Group 1 A,B,C,D
>    Group 2 E,F
>    Group 3 Others

Compensation used is total pay, including bonuses.

## SUMMARY OF RETIREMENT PROGRAMS: ABC, INC. Pension Plan

### For the Period 1/1/2012 through 12/31/2012

| Name | Age | Total Comp | Profit Sharing Contribution Current Comparability Plan | Alternative Integrated Plan | Integrated Plan |
|------|-----|-----------|------------------------------------------------------|-----------------------------|-----------------|
| **Group 1** | | | | | |
| A | 51 | 170,000 | 19,626 | 19,626 | 22,347 |
| B | 41 | 170,000 | 19,626 | 19,626 | 22,347 |
| C | 47 | 170,000 | 19,626 | 19,626 | 22,347 |
| D | 42 | 170,000 | 19,626 | 19,626 | 22,347 |
| **Total Group 1** | | **680,000** | **78,504** | **78,504** | **89,388** |
| **Group 2** | | | | | |
| E | 32 | 170,000 | 10,200 | 19,626 | 22,347 |
| F | 47 | 170,000 | 10,200 | 19,626 | 22,347 |
| **Total Group 2** | | **340,000** | **20,400** | **39,252** | **44,694** |
| **Group 3** | | | | | |
| G | 52 | 43,000 | 1,720 | 4,300 | 4,300 |
| H | 23 | 35,000 | 1,400 | 3,500 | 3,500 |
| I | 28 | 50,000 | 2,000 | 5,000 | 5,000 |
| J | 28 | 115,000 | 4,600 | 12,586 | 13,712 |
| K | 24 | 60,000 | 2,400 | 6,000 | 6,000 |
| L | 32 | 80,000 | 3,200 | 8,106 | 8,217 |
| M | 32 | 164,000 | 6,560 | 18,858 | 21,405 |
| N | 27 | 37,080 | 1,483 | 3,708 | 3,708 |
| O | 36 | 152,000 | 6,080 | 17,322 | 19,521 |
| P | 38 | 18,500 | 740 | 1,850 | 1,850 |
| Q | 28 | 52,000 | 2,080 | 5,200 | 5,200 |
| R | 56 | 85,104 | 3,404 | 8,760 | 9,018 |
| S | 48 | 75,833 | 3,033 | 7,583 | 7,583 |
| T | 41 | 170,000 | 6,800 | 19,626 | 22,347 |
| U | 35 | 113,000 | 4,520 | 12,330 | 13,398 |

| | | | | | |
|---|---|---|---|---|---|
| V | 29 | 65,000 | 2,600 | 6,500 | 6,500 |
| W | 24 | 40,000 | 1,600 | 4,000 | 4,000 |
| X | 42 | 79,250 | 3,170 | 8,010 | 8,099 |
| Y | 34 | 130,000 | 5,200 | 14,506 | 16,067 |
| Z | 37 | 100,000 | 4,000 | 10,666 | 11,357 |
| **Total Group 3** | | **1,664,768** | **66,590** | **178,411** | **190,782** |

**TOTAL: $2,684,768 Compensation**

| Comparability | Current Integrated | Alternate Integrated |
|:---:|:---:|:---:|
| **$165,494** | **$296,167** | **$324,864** |

**SUMMARY OF RETIREMENT PROGRAMS: ABC, INC. Pension Plan**

**For the Period**      **1/1/2012 through 12/31/2012**

|  |  |  | | Contribution as % Pay | |
| --- | --- | --- | --- | --- | --- |
| | **Total** | | **Comparability** | **Current Integrated** | **Alternative Integrated** |
| **Name** | **Age** | **Compensation** | **Plan** | **Plan** | **Plan** |
| **Group 1** | | | | | |
| A | 51 | 170,000 | 11.54% | 11.54% | 13.15% |
| B | 41 | 170,000 | 11.54% | 11.54% | 13.15% |
| C | 47 | 170,000 | 11.54% | 11.54% | 13.15% |
| D | 42 | 170,000 | 11.54% | 11.54% | 13.15% |
| **Total Group 1** | | **680,000** | **11.54%** | **11.54%** | **13.15%** |
| | | | | | |
| **Group 2** | | | | | |
| E | 32 | 170,000 | 6.00% | 11.54% | 13.15% |
| F | 47 | 170,000 | 6.00% | 11.54% | 13.15% |
| **Total Group 2** | | **340,000** | **6.00%** | **11.54%** | **13.15%** |
| | | | | | |
| **Group 3** | | | | | |
| G | 52 | 43,000 | 4.00% | 10.00% | 10.00% |
| H | 23 | 35,000 | 4.00% | 10.00% | 10.00% |
| I | 28 | 50,000 | 4.00% | 10.00% | 10.00% |
| J | 28 | 115,000 | 4.00% | 10.94% | 11.92% |
| K | 24 | 60,000 | 4.00% | 10.00% | 10.00% |
| L | 32 | 80,000 | 4.00% | 10.13% | 10.27% |
| M | 32 | 164,000 | 4.00% | 11.50% | 13.05% |
| N | 27 | 37,080 | 4.00% | 10.00% | 10.00% |
| O | 36 | 152,000 | 4.00% | 11.40% | 12.84% |
| P | 38 | 18,500 | 4.00% | 10.00% | 10.00% |
| Q | 28 | 52,000 | 4.00% | 10.00% | 10.00% |
| R | 56 | 85,104 | 4.00% | 10.29% | 10.60% |
| S | 48 | 75,833 | 4.00% | 10.00% | 10.00% |
| T | 41 | 170,000 | 4.00% | 11.54% | 13.15% |
| U | 35 | 113,000 | 4.00% | 10.91% | 11.86% |
| V | 29 | 65,000 | 4.00% | 10.00% | 10.00% |
| W | 24 | 40,000 | 4.00% | 10.00% | 10.00% |
| X | 42 | 79,250 | 4.00% | 10.11% | 10.22% |
| Y | 34 | 130,000 | 4.00% | 11.16% | 12.36% |
| Z | 37 | 100,000 | 4.00% | 10.67% | 11.36% |
| **Total Group 3** | | **1,664,768** | **4.00%** | **10.72%** | **11.46%** |
| | | | | | |
| **TOTAL** | | **2,684,768** | **6.16%** | **11.03%** | **12.10%** |

**\*\* This illustration assumes that each listed participant receives a contribution.**

**If this is not the case, the actual allocation of the total contribution may differ.**

As you can see, effective plan design can dramatically affect the amount of company contributions. If you work for an employer that would like to maximize company contributions in favor of the management/ownership group, you should review your plan design to make sure that it is as effective as possible.

The following chart summarizes our findings.

# Key Employees vs. Plan Costs

| □ Group 3 | □ Group 2 | ▣ Group 1 |

Contribution

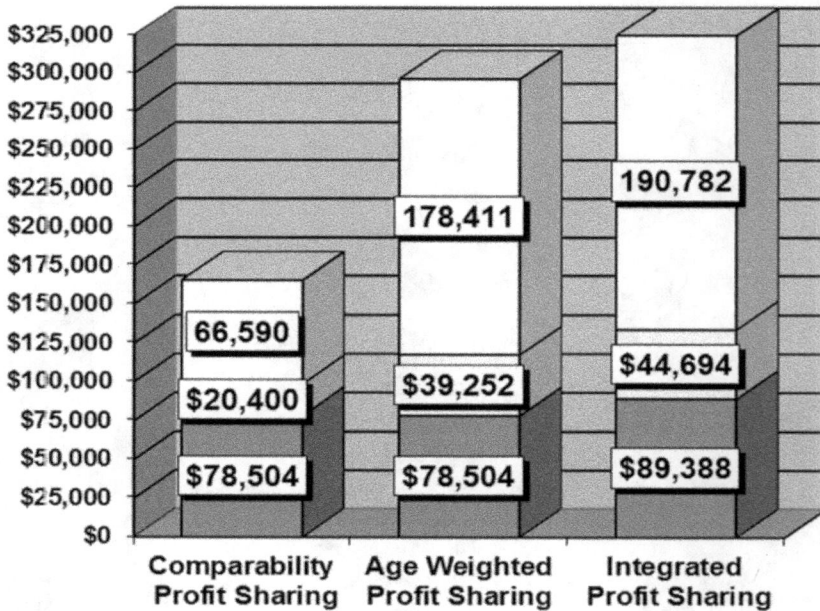

| | Comparability Profit Sharing | Age Weighted Profit Sharing | Integrated Profit Sharing |
|---|---|---|---|
| Group 3 | 66,590 | 178,411 | 190,782 |
| Group 2 | $20,400 | $39,252 | $44,694 |
| Group 1 | $78,504 | $78,504 | $89,388 |

**Plan Type**

# Chapter Sixty-Two
## _____HR_____
## Retirement Plans

### DEFINED BENEFIT PENSIONS FOR PRIVATE BUSINESSES

Defined benefit (DB) pension plans can be unusually attractive to private businesses, particularly those with older executives and owners.

In certain circumstances, DB plans can set aside 100% (or more) of an executive's pay into a plan each year. Contributions are tax deductible and grow tax deferred. The money is not accessible by creditors.

Here is a simple example:

Let's say that we have a business owner/executive who is age 55. He wants to retire at age 65. The owner needs a salary of $100,000 for living expenses. He is earning an additional $200,000 per year, all of it taxable.

We establish a pension plan that will pay our owner/exec 100% of salary at age 65. This gives us ten years to accumulate sufficient assets in the plan to pay our exec $100,000 per year for life.

Our actuaries run calculations. The calculations tell us that we will need $1,500,000 in ten years to provide our planned retirement benefit. How much must we set aside each year to achieve our $1.5 million?

With a zero rate of return, we would need to contribute $150,000 per year. Assuming a 6% return, an annual deposit of $110,000 would approach $1.5 million in ten years. Our executive is able to put $110,000 into the plan in year one.

Each year, our actuary will value the plan assets. He will combine this with an assumed future rate of return and life expectancy. This will determine our deposits in later years. If we earn less than our expected 6%, we can put more into the plan. If we earn more, our future deposits may be less.

If our business owner has employees, deposits must be made for them as well. If these employees are young, the deposits will be relatively small. If these employees leave the company, they will be due the present value of any vested benefits. As we have discussed, this may be a relatively small sum.

### Summary

With any small, consistently profitable company, a defined benefit pension plan can be highly attractive as a way to set aside large sums of money in a tax-friendly manner.

Law firms and CPA firms have been known to use this technique as a way to buy out senior management.

Aging owners have used it as a way to transition out of the business in favor of the next generation.

Businesses use it as a recruiting tool to attract highly skilled senior management from outside the company.

# Chapter Sixty-Three
## HR
## Retirement Plans

## 412(i)

A 412(i) is a defined pension plan that uses only life insurance and annuity contracts as the investment vehicle(s). A 412(i) allows for *much higher* contributions than traditional defined benefit plans. This is because actuaries are allowed to assume a very low rate of return, until and after retirement.

A 412(i) can be attractive for individuals who want *high deductions* and *low risk* investments for the plan. It is also attractive for individuals seeking assets that cannot be attached by creditors.

While a well-designed 412(i) is perfectly legal, care must be taken that this type of plan is the appropriate choice, and structured properly. 412(i) plans have been abused by uninformed insurance agents seeking high commissions. Designs that utilize life insurance as the only investment vehicle run counter to the original intent of IRS approval.

You should ask many questions and seek informed counsel before entering into this type of arrangement. If appropriate and structured properly, a 412(i) plan may be an attractive choice for a small profitable business.

# Chapter Sixty-Four
## _____HR_____
## Retirement Plans

## ESOPS

An Employee Stock Ownership Plan (ESOP) is a form of qualified plan that can be highly useful in certain situations. While many private business executives are not aware of ESOPs, they benefit more than 11 million workers in the United States.

ESOPs are extremely useful and flexible, but complicated. The following is a simple explanation. ESOPs can be used to:

- Purchase stock from company owners. If structured properly, sales proceeds may be tax free.

- Provide incentive to employees to maintain profitability.

- Retire company debt in a tax deductible manner.

- Give (most) benefits of corporate ownership to employees while maintaining voting control of the shares.

## HOW IT WORKS:

An ESOP is similar to a profit sharing plan, except that the ESOP invests in company stock, rather than other investments. All eligible employees must be part of the plan. The plan can have a vesting schedule. Vesting will either a three-year "cliff," or 20% per year.

Company stock can go into the plan in several different ways:

- The company may contribute company stock into the plan, in the same manner as cash into a profit sharing plan. Contributions are tax deductible to the company.

- The company may contribute cash, which is used to purchase stock from current owners.

- The plan may borrow money (typically from a bank), to make a single, larger purchase of stock. This money can be used to "cash out" an owner, often with little taxation.

  o The company then makes annual contributions into the plan, which ultimately retires the debt.

A good resource for understanding ESOPs is the National Center for Employee Ownership, which can be found at:

http://www.nceo.org.

# Chapter Sixty-Five
## HR
### Retirement Plans

## SOLO 401(K)

An Individual 401(k) works like a traditional 401(k), except that it is for owners (or partners) and their spouses only. There can be no other employees.

The plan can utilize pre-tax contributions, like a traditional 401(k). It can also be structured as a Roth 401(k), where contributions are made on an after-tax basis, but come out tax-free.

Solo 401(k)s are an ideal choice for professionals, such as doctors, writers, lawyers, consultants, accountants, tradesmen, and programmers. In today's shifting workplace, many employees are becoming independent contractors. This type of retirement plan works well for individuals who no longer work as traditional employees, but for themselves.

Here are the general rules for a Solo 401(k):

- Employer/owners may contribute up to $50,000, depending on their compensation, by making a combination of the following:
  - Salary deferrals of up to $17,000. This cannot exceed 100% of compensation.
  - Company contributions of up to 25% of compensation (or up to 20% of self-

employment income).
- Catch-up contributions, of up to $5,500, can be made annually for individuals over age 50, to a maximum total contribution of $55,500.
- Contributions can be made in the traditional, tax deductible 401(k) manner.
- Contributions can also be made with after-tax contributions by using a Roth feature.
  - A Roth 401(k) can ultimately be rolled into a Roth IRA.
- Other retirement plan assets can usually be rolled into a Solo 401(k) plan. Rollovers can be made from a SEP, SARSEP, SIMPLE IRA (after two years), traditional IRA, rollover IRA, Keogh, 401(k), 403(b) and 457 plans.
- Loans are allowable from most Solo 401(k) plans. This varies, according to the administrator of the plan.
- Withdrawals before the age of 59$_{1/2}$ are subject to a 10% penalty tax.

If your company is eligible for an Individual 401(k), you should take advantage. Solo 401(k)s are a low-cost, simple way to accumulate assets in a tax-favored manner.

# Chapter Sixty-Six
## _____HR_____
## Retirement Plans

## STOCK BONUS PLANS

A stock bonus plan is a qualified plan that allows for employer stock to be contributed to the plan in lieu of cash.

A stock bonus plan can be used by companies as an effective productivity tool. Employees will have an interest in seeing that the value of company stock increases, since an increase in stock value accrues to their accounts.

Stock bonus plans can help employers _increase_ current cash flow. When treasury stock is contributed to a qualified plan, the value of contributions is still a tax deductible expense to the company — even if the stock is privately held. This reduces taxable profits and preserves cash.

A profit sharing or 401(k) plan can utilize employer stock for company contributions and as an investment option. Large companies often use company stock for their 401(k) matching contributions.

Contributions to a stock bonus plan are usually discretionary. They can be made on a year-by-year basis, in the same way as traditional profit sharing payments. The same holds true when used as a 401(k) match. Companies may guarantee matching contributions at the beginning of each year, but rarely extend guarantees any further.

Earnings in a stock bonus plan accrue on a tax-deferred basis, as in any other qualified plan. Contributions and earnings become taxable to a participant when they are withdrawn from the participant's stock bonus account.

When distributions are made from a stock bonus plan, participants must have the right to demand that their employer stock be distributed from the plan. If employer securities are not publicly traded, employees must be given the right to receive cash for their shares, based upon a *fair value formula*. This value must be determined by independent, valuation professionals.

If employer shares are distributed, employees must be allowed to sell stock back to the employer for a period of 60 days. This is known as a "put" option. The employer must also open a 60 day purchase window at the end of each plan year. This window is available to holders who did not exercise their 60-day put option during the plan year.

### Summary:

A stock bonus plan can be a valuable and powerful tool in the HR toolbox. Stock bonuses give employees a powerful incentive to see that a company is profitable. Bonus plans can be implemented with a relatively small initial outlay. Care must be taken to manage future costs, particularly when employees begin to leave and demand cash. Regular company valuations must be conducted, and made available to employees, which may or may not be an issue with ownership.

# Chapter Sixty-Seven
## _____HR_____
## Retirement Plans

## 457 PLANS

Most state and local governments, as well as some non-governmental entities, are tax exempt under Section 501 of the Internal Revenue Code. This means that they pay no income taxes. These "non-profit" entities are allowed to establish tax-favored, _deferred compensation plans_ for their employees under Section 457 of the Internal Revenue Code.

The concept of deferred compensation is somewhat similar to that of a 401(k).

- Employees elect to defer a portion of their pay.

- Employees are not taxed on deferrals.

- Deferrals grow tax free.

- The benefits are taxed as income, when received by the employee.

- The employer may offer several different forms of investment choices.

- Employee deferrals may be placed into a pool, where they earn a common rate of return with all other deferrals.

- Deferrals may be placed into separate accounts, even placed into mutual funds, where they are directed by the employee.

  o In this arrangement, employees earn the net return of their investment portfolio.

- The employer may or may not choose to match deferrals.

In traditional deferred compensation, employee deferrals are retained as assets of the employer, and are offset by a liability to the employee. In the event of a default by the employer, employees can lose their deferrals to other creditors with more seniority. In governmental plans the risk of default is much lower, because of their taxing authority.

With the advent of separate accounts, an employee now has little or no chance of losing funds.

Under current (2012) law, employees in a 457 Plan are able to defer a maximum of $17,000.

**Special Note:** In many cases, teachers are allowed to participate in a 457 Plan *and* a 403(b) Plan concurrently. This includes catch-up contributions for both plans. (See next chapter.)

# Chapter Sixty-Eight
## HR
### Retirement Plans

## 403(B) PLANS

A 403(b) Plan is a retirement plan for certain employees of public schools, tax-exempt organizations and ministers.

Like a 401(k), employees can elect to defer a portion of their income into the plan. Employers can make non-elective contributions. There can be combination of deferrals and company contributions. Contributions into a 403(b) can also be made on an after-tax basis.

For many years, 403(b) retirement plans were required (by law) to be in the form of an annuity. It became known as "tax-sheltered annuities," or TSA plans.

In 2007, the 403(b) rules became very similar to those of 401(k) plans, particularly with regard to *fiduciary* responsibility. Many schools and charitable non-profits are now allowed to adopt 401(k)s in lieu of their 403(b)s.

403(b)s have one significant advantage over 401(k)s: There is no ADP (average deferral percentage) testing. Highly compensated executive (HCE) deferrals are not limited by the average deferral percentage of non-HCEs. Each HCE can defer the maximum, regardless of how much non-HCEs contribute to the plan.

Like a 401(k), 403(b) deferrals go into individual accounts for employees. Deferrals can be deposited into any of the following types of entities:

- An annuity contract. This is a contract provided through an insurance company.

- A custodial account. These are usually invested in mutual funds.

- A retirement income account set up for church employees. This type of account can invest in either annuities or mutual funds.

Employee deferrals are not subject to current federal or state income taxation. They are still taxed for Social Security and Medicare purposes. Annual contribution limits are the same as with a 401(k) plan.

# Chapter Sixty-Nine
## _____HR_____
## Retirement Plans

## ROTH 401(K)

A Roth 401(k) combines the features of a traditional 401(k) with those of the Roth IRA. We will discuss the Roth IRA provisions in chapter seventy-one. The primary difference between a traditional 401(k) and a Roth 401(k) is when monies are taxed.

With the traditional 401(k) monies are:

- Tax deductible when contributed.

- Tax deferred as they grow.

- Taxed when removed from the plan or a subsequent IRA.

With a Roth 401(k) monies are:

- Not tax deductible when contributed. All contributions are subject to normal income taxes in the year of deposit.

- Tax deferred as they grow.

- Tax free when removed from the plan or a subsequent Roth IRA. (Subject to certain limitations.)

The Roth retirement plan provisions were enacted as part of the Economic Growth and Tax Relief Reconciliation Act of 2001 (EGTRRA). Beginning in 2006, employers were allowed to amend existing 401(k) documents to allow employees to elect Roth IRA treatment of a portion or all of their 401(k) contributions.

Employers are allowed to make matching contributions to an employee's Roth contributions. However, employer contributions are treated in the same manner as traditional 401(k) matching contributions. They must be segregated into a *pre-tax* account.

### Who Wants a Roth?

Roth IRA contributions can be advantageous for younger workers who are in a low tax bracket today, but expect to earn more in the future. Paying a little tax today could save significant taxes in the future, as assets compound in growth.

A Roth can also be attractive to wealthy individuals who want to leave a *tax-free* legacy for their heirs.

## ROTH 403(B)

A Roth 403(b) has the same characteristics as a traditional 403(b), but with the unique Roth tax provisions.

# Chapter Seventy
## HR
## Retirement Plans

## IRAs

IRAs are individual retirement arrangements. IRAs were created so that individuals could have the same retirement advantages as employees covered under company qualified plans.

The major features of IRAs are as follows:

- An IRA is an Individual Retirement Arrangement/Account.

- IRAs are always owned and controlled by the individual, not by an employer.

- IRAs can be formed and funded by individuals for themselves.

- IRAs can also become part of an employer-sponsored retirement plan and funded by employers.

In most cases, individuals are able to take a tax deduction for funds that are contributed to an IRA. Contributions grow tax-deferred. They are taxed when they are withdrawn from the account.

As with anything having to do with favorable tax treatment, there are many rules and regulations regarding deductibility for income tax purposes. There may also be tax penalties for removing money before a certain age, or for not taking minimum distributions after a certain age.

We will not go into great depth regarding IRAs in this book, since my focus is how IRAs interface with qualified plans provided by employers.

### Deductibility

The deductibility of IRA deposits is affected by whether or not an employee is *participating* in a company-sponsored plan. Deductibility is also affected by a taxpayer's *adjusted gross income* for tax purposes. Adjusted gross income is the amount of income used by the IRS to determine tax liability.

## A BRIEF IRA HISTORY

IRAs are part of employee retirement planning, and an important part of your work in HR. Because of this, I thought it might be helpful for us to review the legislative history of IRAs.

IRAs were created with the enactment of the Employee Retirement Income Security Act (ERISA), in 1974.

In the beginning, individuals were allowed to contribute up to $1,500 per year into an IRA, provided they were not covered by another qualified retirement plan.

The Economic Recovery Tax Act of 1981 (ERTA) expanded the use of IRAs. This act removed the qualified plan restriction, allowing all taxpayers (under the age of 70½) to contribute to IRAs. ERTA raised the maximum annual contribution to $2,000, and allowed participants to contribute $250 for a nonworking spouse. At that time, all IRA contributions were tax deductible, and were taxable when withdrawn.

The Tax Reform Act of 1986 created phase out provisions for IRA contributions made by high-earning employees (or their spouses) that were covered by employment-based retirement plans.

The Small Business Job Protection Act of 1996 raised the limit for contributions on behalf of nonworking spouses from $250 to $2,000.

The Taxpayer Relief Act of 1997 created the *Roth IRA*.

- Roth IRA contributions are not deductible for income tax purposes.

- The growth of Roth IRA assets is tax free.

- Withdrawals from a Roth IRA are tax free.

Besides creating the Roth, the Taxpayer Relief Act of 1997 made other significant changes. This act increased the income threshold, above which deductible contributions were phased out. It also made adjustments to the accounts of taxpayers who were covered (and whose spouses were covered) by an employment-based plan.

The Economic Growth and Tax Relief Reconciliation Act of 2001 raised the limit on contributions beginning in 2002. It also allowed for catch-up contributions to be made by people ages 50 and above. The provisions of this act, (as well those of the Jobs and Growth Tax Relief Reconciliation Act of 2003) were extended until 2012.

As you can see, Congress has made many changes to IRAs over the years, and will continue to do so. Many of your employees may have personal or rollover IRAs. Others will have them when they retire. It is a good idea for you to understand how they integrate with company sponsored plans, and how they add to employee financial security.

## IRA DEDUCTIBILITY RULES

The deductibility of IRA contributions is affected by two factors:

- Participation (including spouses) in company-sponsored retirement plans.

- Adjusted gross income.

Complete details of the deductibility are available each year through IRS Publication 590:

http://www.irs.gov/pub/irs-pdf/p590.pdf

## 2012 COMBINED TRADITIONAL AND ROTH IRA CONTRIBUTION LIMITS:

**If you are under 50 years of age at the end of 2012**: The maximum contribution that can be made to a traditional or Roth IRA is the lesser of $5,000 or the amount of your taxable compensation for 2012. This limit can be split between a traditional IRA and a Roth IRA. Regardless of the split, the combined limit is always $5,000. The maximum deductible contribution to a traditional IRA, and the maximum contribution to a Roth IRA, may be *reduced* depending on your modified adjusted gross income. (See government tables.)

**If you are 50 years of age or older before the end of 2012**: The maximum contribution that can be made to a traditional or Roth IRA is the smaller of $6,000 or the amount of your taxable compensation for 2012. This limit can also be split between a traditional IRA and a Roth IRA. The combined limit is $6,000. The maximum deductible contribution to a traditional IRA and the maximum contribution to a Roth IRA may be *reduced* depending on your modified adjusted gross income.

These limits were not increased from the 2011 tax year.

See government tables: http://www.irs.gov/pub/irs-pdf/p590.pdf

# Chapter Seventy-One
## _____HR_____
## Retirement Plans

## ROTH IRA SUMMARY

The Taxpayer Relief Act of 1997 included a new twist to the IRA. Proposed by Senator William Roth of Delaware, the Roth IRA grants favorable tax treatment when money is withdrawn from an IRA, rather than when it is placed into the plan.

Contributions to a Roth IRA are _not_ tax deductible when made. However, contributions grow tax free, and are not subject to taxation when they are removed from the IRA.

Contributions can be made after the age of 70½, and individuals can leave them in the IRA as long as they live. This feature can act as a useful estate planning technique — leaving assets to heirs that will escape income taxation.

Certain individuals are allowed to convert traditional IRAs to a Roth, but must pay taxes as if the money were distributed.

The Roth feature would be particularly attractive to individuals in the highest tax brackets. However, Congress did _not_ make Roth IRAs available to the top income earners. Congress sets annual limits on who can benefit from a Roth. They are outlined at the following IRS location:

http://www.irs.gov/pub/irs-pdf/p590.pdf.

# Chapter Seventy-Two
## HR
## Retirement Plans

## SIMPLE IRA

A SIMPLE IRA (Savings Incentive Match Plan for Employees) can be established by businesses with less than 100 employees. This type of plan involves far less recordkeeping and administration than a traditional pension, profit sharing, or 401(k) plan.

Rather than contribute money into a centralized retirement plan, company contributions, employee deferrals, and company matches are made into employee IRAs. These IRAs are controlled by each employee, not by the plan sponsor. They are typically housed with a single mutual fund company.

**Salary reduction limits**. The amount an employee may contribute to a SIMPLE IRA cannot exceed $11,500 in 2012.

If an employee participates in another employer plan during the year, the total amount of the salary reduction contributions the employee can make to all the plans is limited to $17,000 for 2012.

- **Catch-up contributions**. If permitted by the SIMPLE IRA plan, participants who are age 50 or over, at the end of the calendar year, are allowed to make catch-up contributions. The catch-up contribution limit in 2012 is $2,500.

### Simplified Administration

In order to qualify for the simplified recordkeeping and administration, a number of requirements must be met:

- The company must make a contribution of 2% of pay for all employees, or match employee deferrals dollar for dollar up to a minimum of 3% of pay.

  - Company contributions are deductible to the company.

- All company contributions must be 100% vested, immediately.

- Annual notices must be provided to all employees.

- Contributions and employee withholdings grow on a tax deferred basis.

- Funds will be taxed when they come out of the employee IRAs.

You can learn more about SIMPLE plans at the following location:

http://www.dol.gov/ebsa/publications/simple.html

# Chapter Seventy-Three
## HR
## Retirement Plans

## SIMPLIFIED EMPLOYEE PENSIONS (SEPs)

A Simplified Employee Pension is available to any employer or sole proprietor. The primary advantage of a SEP is reduced administrative requirements and costs. Like in a SIMPLE plan, employer contributions are made to IRAs for the benefit of eligible employees. The primary features of a SEP are as follows:

- Discretionary contributions can be made up to 25% of pay, to a maximum of $50,000.

- Employees are not allowed to contribute to the plan.

- Vesting is immediate on 100% of plan contributions.

- Like any standard IRA, contributions grow on a tax deferred basis.

- Funds will be subject to taxation when removed from each individual's IRA.

## SARSEP

A SARSEP is a simplified employee pension that allows for salary deferrals. SAREPs are no longer available to companies. Plans put in place prior to 1997 can remain in force. New hires must be allowed to participate. You can learn more about SARSEPs here:
http://www.irs.gov/retirement/article/0,,id=112859,00.html

# Chapter Seventy-Four
## _____HR_____
## Retirement Plans

## THE DOL ON RETIREMENT PLANS – A SUMMARY

For your convenience, I have included the following DOL explanation detailing the main characteristics of pension and profit sharing plans:

**Defined Benefit Plan**     **Defined Contribution Plan**

**Employer Contributions and/or Matching Contributions**  Employer funded. Federal rules set amounts that employers must contribute to plans in an effort to ensure that plans have enough money to pay benefits when due. There are penalties for failing to meet these requirements. There is no requirement that the employer contribute, except in SIMPLE and safe harbor 401(k)s, money purchase plans, SIMPLE IRAs, and SEPs.

The employer may have to contribute in certain automatic enrollment 401(k) plans. The employer may choose to match a portion of the employee's contributions or to contribute without employee contributions. In some plans, employer contributions may be in the form of employer stock.

**Employee Contributions**  Generally, employees do not contribute to these plans. Many plans require the employee to contribute in order for an account to be established.

**Managing the Investment**  Plan officials manage the investment and the employer is responsible for ensuring that the amount it has put in the plan plus investment earnings will be enough to pay the promised benefit. The employee often is responsible for managing the investment of his or her account, choosing from investment options offered by the plan. In some plans, plan officials are responsible for investing all the plan's assets.

**Amount of Benefits Paid Upon Retirement**  A promised benefit is based on a formula in the plan, often using a combination of the employee's age, years worked for the employer, and/or salary. The benefit depends on contributions made by the employee and/or the employer, performance of the account's investments, and fees charged to the account.

**Type of Retirement Benefit Payments**   Traditionally, these plans pay the retiree monthly annuity payments that continue for life. Plans may offer other payment options.   The retiree may transfer the account balance into an individual retirement account (IRA) from which the retiree withdraws money, or may receive it as a lump sum payment. Some plans also offer monthly payments through an annuity.

**Guarantee of Benefits**   The Federal government, through the Pension Benefit Guaranty Corporation (PBGC), guarantees some amount of benefits. No Federal guarantee of benefits.

**Leaving the Company Before Retirement Age**   If an employee leaves after vesting in a benefit but before the plan's retirement age, the benefit generally stays with the plan until the employee files a claim for it at retirement. Some defined benefit plans offer early retirement options. The employee may transfer the account balance to an individual retirement account (IRA) or, in some cases, another employer plan, where it can continue to grow based on investment earnings. The employee also may take the balance out of the plan, but will owe taxes and possibly penalties, thus reducing retirement income. Plans may cash out small accounts.

The U.S. Department of Labor explains the various forms of retirement plans that are available to companies at the following Internet locations:

http://www.dol.gov/ebsa/faqs/faq_compliance_pension.html

http://www.dol.gov/ebsa/publications/wyskapr.html

# Chapter Seventy-Five
## _____HR_____
## Nonqualified Plans

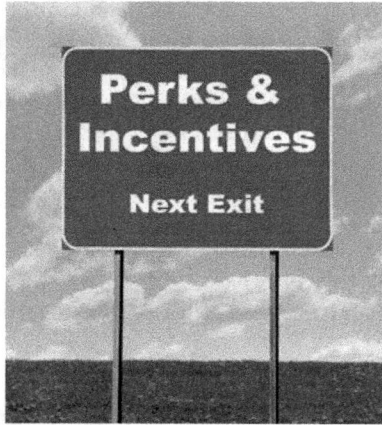

Nonqualified benefits can be highly useful to a private business, and may be used for many purposes.

Nonqualified plans do not qualify for special tax treatment under IRS laws. Nonqualified benefits come in different forms, each with advantages and disadvantages for both employers and employees.

# Types of Nonqualified Benefits

## Salary Continuation

Under a salary continuation agreement, an employer agrees to continue an executive's salary for a specified period of time. This can create a powerful incentive for key executives to remain with a private business.

- This type of plan is often used to supplement the **retirement income** of executives.

- It can also provide benefits in the event of **disability** or **death**.

Because the plan is nonqualified, the sponsoring company has expanded flexibility in plan design. Benefits can be 10% of salary or 200% of salary — for one year, five years, for life, or anything in between.

This type of agreement does *not* normally involve a reduction in current employee pay. It is provided by the employer *in addition* to all other benefits.

Important characteristics of salary continuation include:

- The amount of salary continuation is usually determined by a formula.

  o This formula is often a percentage of "salary."

  o Similar to a defined benefit pension, the salary used to determine benefits may be calculated using such measures as an average of the final three or five years' salary, or the average of the three or five years of highest earnings.

- Benefits often have a "years of service" or

target date component. For example, benefits may not be earned until an executive has accrued ten years of service.

- As with an integrated pension or profit sharing plan, benefits may be integrated with Social Security.

- Salary continuation may also be integrated with other company benefits.

## SALARY REDUCTION (Deferred Compensation)

Deferred compensation typically involves having an executive defer a portion of current pay until some future date. As we have discussed, this may be especially attractive if an executive expects to be in a lower tax bracket during retirement.

The employer can make additions to this deferral, in the form of a match or bonus. Matching contributions can help offset the financial risk an employee takes in the event of employer default.

## THE MECHANICS OF SALARY REDUCTION

Nonqualified salary reduction plans have many of the same features as qualified salary deferral plans. They also have features not seen in traditional qualified plans. Nonqualified plans usually have:

- A third party administrator who calculates benefits.

- Individual "accounts" with certain investment elements for participants.

    o These can be actual accounts, with segregated assets.

    o They can be shadow accounts, created with mere bookkeeping entries.

    o   Earnings can be real and accumulated.

- Earnings can be allocated to employee accounts based upon *hypothetical* performance of an assumed investment, such as an Investment Index.

- Earnings can be a guaranteed amount that is promised by the employer, such as 6% each year.

# SERP & EXCESS BENEFIT PLANS

The two most common types of salary continuation programs are:

- A Supplemental Executive Retirement Plan (SERP).

- An Excess Benefit Plan.

### SERP

SERPs typically provide executives a percentage of pay, as with a defined benefit plan. Benefits are normally paid in the event of:

- Retirement

- Death

- Disability.

### EXCESS BENEFIT PLAN

An Excess Benefit Plan (also known as a Top-Hat Plan) integrates with an executive's other benefits. This type of plan is normally used for highly compensated executives. In theory, an excess plan compensates for any benefits lost due to the limitations imposed on retirement plans by the Internal Revenue Code.

Excess benefit plans typically attempt to make up for contributions that would have been made for executives, were the qualified plan limitations not in place.

All unfunded excess benefit (Top-Hat) plans that are established for a "select group of management or highly compensated employees" are subject to minimal ERISA reporting requirements.

Unfunded Top-Hat plans must file a one-time statement about the arrangement with the Department of Labor. They must also be able to provide documentation upon request.

Virtually all nonqualified plans are limited to management and/or highly compensated employees and are informally funded. This is because formal funding creates negative income tax consequences for both the company and the executive.

## THE PAYMENT OF BENEFITS

Under nonqualified plans benefits become payable when certain milestones are achieved by the executive. An executive's account will have a calculated value at any given future date. How this value is paid will be determined by the agreement. Payments can take several forms. The most common methods of payment are:

- A lump sum

    o   This may be an agreed-upon figure.

    o   It may be an accumulated amount, based upon actual or theoretical investment returns.

    o   The present value future benefits, much like a lump-sum payment with your state's lottery.

- An annuity

    o   This may be paid in installments over time.

o   A lump sum may be used to purchase an actual annuity with an insurance company that assumes the payment liability.

# CONSTRUCTIVE RECEIPT

Income can be taxable, even if it is not actually received an executive. If income is "constructively received," it is considered paid. This is a problem that you would like to avoid.

Internal Revenue Code Section 1.451-2(a) outlines the constructive receipt doctrine. This doctrine states that income, even if not actually in a taxpayer's (employee's) possession, is "constructively received" if the taxpayer may draw upon it in any way. In other words, there must be a substantial *risk of forfeiture* for benefits earned under a plan to *avoid* current taxation.

Under IRS definition, assets are deemed received if "credited to the employees account, set aside, or otherwise made available." Taxation can result, even if an employee has received no distribution of cash, stock or property.

For example: If a company establishes an irrevocable trust to hold assets allocated to fund an agreement, this will be deemed as constructive receipt, as the risk of forfeiture has been removed.

Income is not constructively received if an employee's control is subject to substantial limitations or restrictions, such as a passage of time before benefits can be enjoyed. For example, if an amount is not payable for five years, termination, or retirement, the benefit will not be currently taxed.

### Risk of Forfeiture

*Lack of control* and imposed *restrictions*, along with company assets being *accessible to corporate creditors*, all help to create the risk of forfeiture needed to make any nonqualified plan work smoothly.

Another useful forfeiture provision is to require that an employee be available for consulting, after the separation of services, in order to receive the promised benefits.

Well drafted plans always avoid the constructive receipt of benefits, while still maintaining certain protections for the executive.

## DISTRIBUTIONS

Plan distributions must also be designed to avoid constructive receipt. For example, if an employee is allowed to accelerate payments, this will be considered receipt.

### Termination of Employment

Executives typically receive nonqualified benefits in the event of:

- Death

- Disability

- Retirement

### Vesting

Most companies use a vesting schedule. Vesting schedules are used for several purposes:

- The company imposes a vesting schedule to ensure that an employee fulfills the obligations under the agreement. Typically, benefits accrue the most as the executive approaches retirement.

- A vesting schedule can help avoid the constructive receipt of benefits.

   o This allows benefits to accrue without current taxation.

**Caution:**

When an executive becomes vested in benefits, and can demand these benefits, the benefits become *taxable*. You must always maintain a risk of forfeiture while an executive works for your company.

**Employee Protection**

You can build employee protection into your agreement in different ways. Most of these focus on vesting certain benefits upon specified events, such as:

- Retirement,

- Death

- Disability

**Employer Protection**

If you commit valuable resources to a nonqualified plan, you want to make sure that an executive doesn't walk away with your money — until the executive has fulfilled his or her part of the agreement. Your agreement should include termination provisions in the event that your executive defaults on his or her part of the bargain.

## FUNDING

Deferred compensation and SERP plans can be fully funded, partially funded, or not funded at all. Regardless of funding, the sponsoring company remains liable to fulfill the obligations of the agreement.

**Informally Funded**

If benefits are funded, and linked to the agreement, they become taxable whenever an employee becomes "substantially vested" under Code Section 83. Because of this, most nonqualified funding, within private businesses, is done on an informal, non-linked basis.

Informal means that the agreements do not mention specific

funding vehicles. The executive may not have direct control over funding vehicles. Nor, can the executive demand access to the funding vehicles under normal circumstances.

### Formal Funding

Formally funded plans usually become subject to ERISA vesting and fiduciary requirements. This causes significant problems for private businesses, making it an unattractive option for most companies.

## FINANCING

When productive employees are making long-term financial decisions, they want some measure of security and assurance that their employer's promises will be met.

## SINKING FUND

While most plans are not formally funded, most are financed with some sort of sinking fund. There are a number of ways to set aside assets to fulfill a company's obligation, each with advantages and disadvantages. In all cases, these funds must be accessible to the employer (with some limitations) and available to creditors.

## RESERVE ACCOUNTS WITH EMPLOYEE DIRECTION

Larger companies use deferred compensation plans that look and feel much like a 401(k). An employee elects to defer a portion of their current income. This money gets invested. The investments in these accounts must be far less specific than a 401(k). Employee choices are usually limited to generic choices, such as equity, bonds, fixed account or money market within a sponsoring mutual fund or insurance company plan.

Any ability to choose specific investments may lead to constructive receipt by employees, and immediate taxation.

# Corporate Owned Life Insurance

Most private-company nonqualified plans are "informally" funded with corporate owned life insurance. This holds true for both large and small companies.

Life insurance has a unique set of tax characteristics which gives it advantages over other funding vehicles. Life insurance can be used to:

- Provide salary continuation in the event of an executive's death.

- Fund payments in the event of an executive's disability.

- Accumulate assets in a predictable and tax-favored manner.

- Fund an executive's retirement income.

- Provide cost recovery to the employer for benefits paid to executives.

- Satisfy executive fears over security, through life insurance ownership in a "Rabbi Trust."

## Rabbi Trust

The first Rabbi Trust was created for a nonqualified plan that was established for an actual rabbi. The trust was established to hold property that was used to finance a deferred compensation plan. Under terms of the trust, the synagogue could not use the trust assets for its general purposes. The trust assets remained available to creditors in the event of financial insolvency.

Since that time, tens of thousands of similar trusts have been utilized by companies for the purpose of protecting assets for employees, without triggering constructive receipt of the property.

When drafted correctly, a Rabbi Trust meets with IRS approval, maintaining non-funding status, while protecting the executive against the unauthorized use of trust assets.

# TAXATION OF BENEFITS & COMPENSATION

### Employee Taxation

Employees that benefit from nonqualified deferred compensation will pay ordinary income tax on benefits in the year that the benefit is actually or constructively received.

Amounts that are deferred from pay are not subject to Social Security tax. When received, they are treated as compensation and will be subject to Social Security and income taxes at that time. This includes constructive receipt as well as actual receipt of assets.

### Employer Taxation

Employers receive a tax deduction in the tax year that benefits are actually or constructively received by the employee. Payments are deductible as long as they meet the "reasonable" standards that are outlined by law.

# Chapter Seventy-Six
## HR
### Nonqualified Plans

## NONQUALIFIED DEFERRED COMPENSATION

Nonqualified deferred compensation (deferred comp) is used by both public and private companies, particularly with senior management. For private businesses, deferred comp is a cost effective, selective benefit that can reward (and retain) key employees.

Because it is not "qualified," this type of plan has advantages and disadvantages when compared to plans that are qualified under ERISA.

Nonqualified deferred compensation is used for the following:

- For owners and senior executives in lieu of a qualified plan.

- To provide additional benefits beyond those provided by a company's qualified plans. There are many different types of benefits that can be provided.

- To give the benefits of company ownership without transferring actual ownership of a privately held company.

- To provide customized, tax-deferred benefits which are individually tailored to each person receiving them.

- When a company needs to provide additional incentives to:

    o   Recruit talented executives.

    o   Reward executives for outstanding service.

    o   Retain key personnel.

    o   Provide additional retirement benefits over and above company qualified plans.

## ADVANTAGES

## DEFERRED COMPENSATION

In order to maintain their tax-favored status, qualified plans must *restrict* the benefits given to senior management and selected individuals. While nonqualified deferred compensation plans do not enjoy the same favorable tax treatment, they have many significant advantages over qualified plans. Nonqualified deferred compensation can be provided for *anyone*, and can provide the following benefits:

- Nonqualified deferred compensation allows employers to select who receives benefits, without fear of discrimination.

- Benefits can be unlimited.

- Different benefits can be provided to each executive/employee.

- IRS and ERISA regulations are minimal.

- Fiduciary, reporting and disclosure requirements are minimal.

- Executives are not taxed on monies set aside to fund any benefits.

- It can be used to create "golden handcuffs," to keep key personnel from becoming competitors.

- It can be used to create a "golden parachute" of retirement benefits for executives and/or owners.

- Benefits may become payable when executives enjoy a lower tax bracket than at present.

- Executives may benefit from the compounding of tax deferrals.

- Performance incentives can be built into agreements.

  o Benefits can be tied to such things as profits and sales growth. They can also be linked to department or personal goals, or even the value of an employer's stock.

- Deferred comp can have any vesting schedule. Care must be taken to avoid the constructive receipt of benefits. As we have discussed, this can cause unfavorable tax treatment long before benefits are paid.

- Partial protection can be created for executives by the use of Rabbi Trusts.

- Assets that are set aside for executives remain on the company balance sheet as a corporate asset.

- There is no legal requirement that forces current assets to be set aside to fund nonqualified agreements. This can help with company cash flow.

## DISADVANTAGES

Nonqualified deferred compensation discriminates in favor of certain employees. As a result, a sponsoring company will not receive the same *current* favorable tax treatment as it would with a qualified plan — whether the company is making contributions, or simply promising benefits to employees.

While a company cannot take current deductions, as assets are set aside for executives, the company may deduct the cost of benefits as they are *paid* to the executive.

This disadvantage is not an issue for non-profit companies, as they already pay no income taxes.

**Note:** Companies that use accrual accounting may be able to expense the present value of future benefits, as they accrue to executives under a nonqualified plan. This is a discussion beyond the scope of this book. Discuss this with your benefit advisors.

Other disadvantages include:

- Benefits that are accrued under a nonqualified plan can only be secured by a company's promise to pay. Assets cannot be segregated for this purpose, and shielded from the claims of creditors.

  o   If a sponsoring company goes into receivership, any assets that had been set aside for executive benefits can be taken to satisfy the claims of senior creditors. If a company goes out of business, executives can lose any and all benefits they have accrued.

  o   A Rabbi trust does provide a measure of protection to the executive, as it prevents the sponsoring company from using such assets for general business purposes.

- Most companies that enter into nonqualified arrangements with executives must still report to the IRS. Although, the reporting can be minimal.

- S Corporations, LLCs, LLPs and Partnerships are less suited to nonqualified plans than traditional C corporations because they are taxed at the individual, not corporate level.

- Employee termination, whether voluntary or forced, may cause the forfeiture of benefits.

  o Executives may demand protection within their agreements against termination for unjust reasons.

As you can see, nonqualified deferred compensation has many benefits — for executives, and the companies that employ them. Care must be taken to structure and fund these agreements properly. When done so, employees have incentive to be productive, while companies have a cost-effective way to keep their most valued workers.

Our next chapter discusses the regulation of these plans in greater detail.

# Chapter Seventy-Seven
## HR
## Nonqualified Plans

## DEFERRED COMPENSATION & SECTION 409A

Nonqualified benefits are an important part of your employee benefit toolbox. They can be essential in attracting and retaining key employees.

Large companies use these agreements regularly. Look at the 8-K disclosure report of any public company and you will always find a section devoted to these benefits.

Private companies don't have the same resources as large companies. They can't afford to provide the same generous mix of insurance and qualified retirement benefits. However, they must often compete for the same executives.

Private companies can use nonqualified benefits to provide selective compensation to attract and retain the key employees that are essential to its success. Nonqualified benefits can allow smaller companies to compete effectively with their much larger competition.

The use of nonqualified plans has grown dramatically over the years. Regulation of these plans has become increasingly difficult. Because of this, Congress issued new legislation

As part of the American Jobs Creation Act of 2004, Section 409A was added to the Internal Revenue Code.

This section made significant changes to the rules regarding deferred compensation. Some of these changes were designed to protect employees against potential abuse by employers. Others were designed to tighten the rules regarding the taxation of benefits, particularly with regard to constructive receipt.

Section 409A expanded the definition of deferred compensation to include *any* agreement that allows an employee to defer compensation from one tax year to one in the future. Special rules were created for publicly traded companies (which I won't address). Examples of plans included under this regulation include:

- Elective deferral (traditional deferred compensation) plans.

- Split dollar life insurance plans.

- Severance plans.

- Nonqualified defined benefit plans.

- Expense reimbursement plans.

- Certain stock option and stock rights plans.

### 409A Changes

Section 409A created new regulations regarding:

- The timing of distributions.

- The timing of deferrals.

- The acceleration of benefits.

### Distributions

Under the new law, distributions from a nonqualified deferred compensation plan can now be made only under certain circumstances. Payments can be made:

- Based upon a fixed schedule or time outlined in the agreement.

- If an employee separates from service.

- If an employee becomes disabled.

- If an employee dies.

- If there is a change in company ownership or a change in effective control.

- If there is an unforeseen emergency.

### Deferrals

Section 409A made significant changes to the structure and timing of employee deferrals under any deferred compensation arrangement. The following is a brief summary of the provisions of this legislation.

### Initial Deferrals

Employees must elect to defer compensation in the year *before* the services (under the agreement) are to be performed. The deferral period must be at least five years if the deferred payments will be made upon:

- Separation from service.

- Change in company control.

- A specific payment schedule or payment date.

## PENALTIES

If the requirements of Section 409A are breached, employees may be subject to an acceleration of income taxes, plus an additional penalty tax of 20%.

## CONCLUSION

The regulations regarding deferred compensation are complicated, and must be followed precisely to avoid adverse taxation. When you enter into such agreements, you must make sure that you are using competent counsel.

If you want to learn more about Section 409A, the following resources will be helpful.

http://www.irs.gov/newsroom/article/0,,id=172883,00.html

http://www.principal.com/nqdc/referenceguide.pdf

# Chapter Seventy-Eight
## HR
### Nonqualified Plans

## SPLIT DOLLAR LIFE INSURANCE

Split dollar life insurance is a useful technique that companies use to provide nonqualified benefits to key employees.

Split dollar strategies offer many of the same benefits as traditional nonqualified plans, with far more simplicity. They are still covered under Section 409A, so care must be taken to implement this strategy properly.

As we discussed in our chapter on deferred compensation, life insurance offers advantages as a funding vehicle for executive benefits. It provides predictable, low risk cash accumulation, disability benefits and a lump sum payment in the event of death.

## SPLIT OWNERSHIP

With split dollar insurance, the payment, ownership and benefits of a life insurance policy become split between the sponsoring company and the employee. The splitting can occur in many different ways, depending upon the individual needs of the employer and the executive.

One of the primary reasons for the splitting of benefits is to allow the sponsoring company to provide most of the plan funding, without triggering a taxable event to the employee. Splitting can allow a company to recover its expenditures into the plan. It can also provide tangible benefits to an employee (such as a current death benefit) at a very low cost.

## ADVANTAGES OF SPLIT DOLLAR FOR THE EMPLOYER:

- It can provide benefits to selected employees.

- Benefits can be tailored to the individual needs of the company and executives.

- There is great flexibility regarding plan design.

- It can provide golden handcuffs or a golden parachute.

- It can provide predictable cash for promised benefits.

- Life insurance has tax advantages over most other investment vehicles.

- Cash values can provide a corporate emergency reserve.

- No formal IRS approval is needed.

- Minimal IRS and tax reporting is required.

- Recordkeeping costs are minimal.

## ADVANTAGES FOR THE EMPLOYEE:

- Split dollar plans can be used to supplement retirement income.

- Employees can accumulate cash in a tax favored manner.

- Plans can be designed to help the employee in the event of disability.

- Substantial tax free benefits can be available to the employee's family at death.

- A plan can be used to protect against future un-insurability.

- Executives can leverage personal outlays into a life insurance policy.

## HOW IT WORKS

All split dollar arrangements involve the purchase of a life insurance policy, with the executive being the insured. The payments (premiums) and benefits of the policy then become shared by the employer and the executive.

There are two broad types of split dollar arrangements.

### Endorsement Split Dollar:

- With endorsement split dollar, the employer owns the policy and pays the premiums.

- The employer retains an interest in the policy equal to the greater of cash values or the premiums paid.

- Through an endorsement in the policy, the remaining death benefit can be assigned to the employee's heirs.

- The executive may pay the annual imputed economic benefit (the PS-58 or the annual term rates). This keeps the life insurance benefits tax free to her heirs. Alternatively, the executive can pay the tax on the imputed benefit.

- When the executive retires, the policy may be

used to pay supplementary income under a nonqualified arrangement.

**Collateral Assignment:**

• With collateral assignment, the corporation enters into an agreement with the executive to assist with the payments of life insurance premiums.

• The executive purchases a life insurance policy on her life.

• The executive retains all ownership rights.

• The employer usually pays most or all of the premiums.

• The executive "collaterally assigns" a portion of the death benefit and cash values to the employer. This amount is generally equal to all or a portion of the employer's premiums.

• As in endorsement split dollar, the employee will pay (at least) the annual imputed economic benefit of the life insurance to maintain the tax free status in the event of death.

• In the event of death, the executive's heirs receive a tax-free lump sum distribution of their portion of the death benefit.

• At retirement, the executive terminates the agreement with the employer.

  ○ The employer may forgive any monies owed for its premium payments.

    ▪ This will be a taxable event. The employee may withdraw or borrow against policy values to pay any taxes due.

o   The employee can take loans or with-drawals from the policy to repay the employer for premiums it has made toward the policy.

## Summary

Split dollar plans can be a valuable, cost-effective tool when seeking ways to attract and retain key executives in a cost effective, simplified manner.

# Chapter Seventy-Nine
## _____HR_____
## Qualified & Nonqualified Plan Summary

# RETIREMENT BENEFITS SUMMARY:

## WHICH RETIREMENT PLAN IS RIGHT FOR YOUR BUSINESS?

We have discussed many types of retirement plans. Your job in HR is to decide which one(s) are most appropriate for your company. In order to help you with your decision, I have outlined the various plans below, along with the circumstances that might lead to their use by your company.

### DEFINED BENEFIT PENSION — BEST FOR:

- Companies with stable earnings and solid financials, particularly those who have already implemented other plans.

- Smaller companies with older executives who want to set aside large sums in a tax favored manner.

- Professional corporations who want to shelter income and protect assets.

### MONEY PURCHASE PENSION — BEST FOR:

- Companies with stable earnings and solid financials.

- Companies with bargaining units.

- Companies that want to provide greater retirement benefits beyond profit sharing and 401(k) plans.

## PROFIT SHARING — BEST FOR:

- Companies that want to create profit incentives for employees.

- Companies that have less predictable profits.

- Companies that want to set aside greater funds for key executives.

## INTEGRATED PENSION & PROFIT SHARING — BEST FOR:

- Companies that want to allocate a greater percentage of corporate contributions toward more highly compensated employees.

## AGE WEIGHTED PROFIT SHARING & NEW COMPARABILITY — BEST FOR:

- Companies that want to allocate more company contributions toward older and more highly compensated executives.

- Privately held companies that want to set aside qualified funds for the ownership and management groups.

## 401(K)

- With today's technology and pricing, **every** company, regardless of size, should offer a 401(k) plan to employees. A 401(k) is essential for any company that must compete for productive employees.

## SAFE HARBOR 401(K) — BEST FOR:

- Companies that want to make employee contributions.

- Companies with executives that want to maximize deferrals into the plan.

- Companies that want to reduce administrative costs and requirements.

## NONQUALIFIED DEFERRED COMPENSATION — BEST FOR:

- Companies that want to attract and retain key executives on a selective basis.

- Companies that want reward specific employees.

- Companies that want to allocate excess corporate resources toward a select group of executives.

## SPLIT DOLLAR LIFE INSURANCE — BEST FOR:

- Companies that want to attract and retain key executives on a selective basis.

- Companies that want reward specific employees.

- Companies that want to allocate excess corporate resources toward a select group of executives.

- Companies that want to minimize regulation.

- Companies that want to simplify recordkeeping.

- Companies that want predictable cash accumulation.

## Chapter Eighty
## HR
_____
## Business Owner Planning

# BUSINESS OWNER PLANNING

No book about human resources for private businesses would be complete without a section on planning for the owner(s).

If you work for a publicly traded company, with widely held stock, you can ignore this section and move on to the next.

If you work for one of the millions of privately held companies in America, then you are probably highly involved in the complex issues that involve the personal planning for the ownership group.

Your job, and your entire company, can be lost if certain events occur and proper planning has not been completed. Do not assume – not for a single moment – that all of this planning has been done. Make sure that it gets done.

# Chapter Eighty-One
## HR
## Business Owner Planning

## WILLS & TRUSTS

At a minimum, every business owner must have basic estate documents in place. This includes a *will*, a *living trust* and a *testamentary trust*.

**Will:**

A will does not need to be complicated. It can be a simple document that says who gets what.

**Living Trust:**

A living trust is a revocable document. It can be changed at any time. The person who sets up the trust is known as the "grantor." The grantor will also be the "trustee" and "beneficiary" of the trust.

The trustee controls the trust. The beneficiary gets to use and own the property. As trustee and beneficiary, our business owner has full use and control of the assets placed into the trust.

Virtually all non-retirement assets should be assigned to this trust. This means cars, bank accounts, investment accounts, and any personal effects of value.

In most cases, a business owner's personal real estate should be placed into revocable realty trusts. These trusts act in the same manner as living trusts, and can be changed at any time.

## TRUST MECHANICS

A living trust spells out who controls and owns the trust assets under any and all circumstances. It specifies the grantor's wishes in the event of incapacity, death or disability. It sets about for an orderly transition of trust assets in all circumstances.

This is important, because it avoids forcing others to petition the courts to make decisions, control and distribute assets when the grantor (business owner) can no longer do so.

By having trusts, if something happens to a business owner, his or her affairs (like running the company) can continue without interruption. This can be critical for any business.

# Chapter Eighty-Two
# _____HR_____
## Business Owner Planning

## TRANSITION STRATEGIES

Every business owner must give careful thought to what should happen in the event of the business owner's **death, disability** or **retirement**.

## DEATH

Most business owners never expect to die, at least not until a time that they choose. Perhaps there is an odd genetic mutation that affects business owners alone, one that shields & blinds them to the realities of death. More likely, the same single-minded determination that helps business owners succeed (against all odds) also makes them believe that they can't die while they are needed by the business.

### TRANSITION STRATEGY

Every business should have a transition strategy, a plan for what will happen in the event of a business owner's death.

- **Management continuity**. You need to know who is going to run the business if the owner dies.

- **Liquidity**. You need to make sure that there is enough liquidity in the business to maintain operations. Long established banking relationships will vanish with a business owner's death. You must be prepared for that, even if your bankers assure you it would never happen.

> o   Life insurance is often owned by the business, or heirs, with the intent of providing corporate liquidity in the event of a business owner's death.

- **Sell or keep**? If possible, a decision should be made, in advance, as to whether the business should be kept or sold. The business owner might wish that his spouse or family continue to receive his salary. This is often not feasible – for a number of reasons.

> o   The business may not have the resources.

> o   The IRS will look unkindly toward non-employees receiving compensation.

> o   Surviving shareholders may not want to pay others for "not working" in the business.

> o   If the business is to be sold to partners, employees, or family members, agreements should be in place to see that this is done in a fair and orderly fashion.

> o   If the business is to be sold to an outside party, sufficient liquidity should be in place to ensure that the business is sold as a vibrant, ongoing entity.

## BUY-SELL AGREEMENT

If the business is to be sold to known individuals, a buy-sell agreement should be in place that determines the conditions (mechanism, price, timing, funding, etc.) of the sale.

There are different types of buy-sell agreements, each with advantages and disadvantages.

- **Cross-purchase**. A cross purchase agreement typically involves an agreement between individuals. In the event of a shareholder's death, the other individual(s) purchase the deceased's shares. If there are more than a few shareholders, this is often done through a trustee, who is authorized to act for all.

  o   The major advantage of this arrangement is that purchasers get an increase in tax basis for their shares.

- **Entity purchase (Stock Redemption)**. This strategy involves the redemption of a stockholder's shares by the company. This is sometimes done because that's where the money is.

  o   The disadvantage of this arrangement is that the remaining shareholders will not increase the basis in their shares. This could lead to higher taxation in the event of a later sale.

# DISABILITY

In some ways, disability is like a living death. Disability can last a few months, a few years, or it may be permanent. In any given year, the chances of disability are greater than the chances of death.

There are several key issues that business owners should plan for in the event of disability:

- **Liquidity**. If a business owner becomes disabled for a short period of time, what strategies are in place to see that the business will be viable when she is ready to return?

- **Sale**. If the disability is long-term, how can the business be sold to maintain maximum value for the business owner and her family?

- **Disability Buy-Sell**. Many companies have a buy-sell agreement in place for the event of death. Many ignore the possibility of disability, even though this more likely to occur. The same sort of considerations should be made for disability buy-sell planning as in a death buy-sell.

## RETIREMENT

While many business owners plan to "die with their boots on," with full use of their faculties, experience shows that this is rarely the case.

Like the rest of us, business owners must plan for retirement. There is no guarantee that a business will be able to support an owner's retirement twenty years from now. There is no guarantee that there will be a competent management team to take the business helm when the owner retires, passes on, or can no longer sit in the executive chair.

Business owners must groom a successor years in advance. This may be a younger partner or a family member. It might involve convincing a key employee to remain with the company, by offering the benefits of ownership, or potential ownership itself.

If an owner expects to sell his business to finance retirement, he should have an accurate idea of what the business is actually worth. The actual market value of a business may be far different than the owner might think.

# Chapter Eighty-Three
## HR
## Business Owner Planning

## BUSINESS PROTECTION STRATEGIES

As an HR executive or business owner, you have heard many advisors and salespeople tell you what financial products you should own. Let's face it; you can't own everything without peering into the abyss of financial ruin.

There are a few products that every business owner should seriously consider. This is because they protect the value of the owner and the business itself. First, let's discuss the value that a business must protect.

### EXAMPLE:

Let's assume we have a business with 25 employees. Our owner draws a salary of $100,000. She receives additional benefits of $30,000 per year from health insurance and retirement plans. Company profits over the last five years have averaged $120,000 per year. This gives our owner $250,000 per year in total compensation from the business. What should we do to protect it, and how?

### What Is The Business Worth?

If our example business vanished, how much capital would it take to replace the lost income? $5,000,000 invested at 5% would replace the $250,000 per year in total compensation. $3,250,000, invested at 5% per year, and paying out $250,000 (without inflation), would fall to zero in twenty years.

Our example business will probably not have a multi-million dollar value on the open market. Its true market value will be much closer to $1,000,000 than to $5 million. It is the income power that has high intrinsic value to the ownership group. This is what our owners need to protect.

## ASK YOURSELF THIS QUESTION:

**What steps has your ownership group taken to preserve the value of the business in the event of death or disability?**

Death or disability can stop this income stream in a heartbeat. Even a short-term disability can render a vibrant business worthless in just a few months.

Protecting the business can be short money, when compared to the value that could be lost.

Some products you should consider are:

- **Key Person Life Insurance**. If a key person dies, owner or non-owner, your business may suffer financial losses that could cripple the business. Make sure that you can afford the loss of a key employee. If not, you should insure against their death.

  o Permanent key person insurance can be used for several purposes:

    ▪ The death benefit can be used to provide business liquidity in the event of death.

    ▪ Cash values can be used as an emergency source of business funds.

    ▪ The death benefit and cash values can be used to informally fund a selective compensation arrangement.

    ▪ Cash values can be used to help

fund payments to an executive in the event of disability.

○   Term insurance can be purchased at a very reasonable cost.

▪   Be cautious when utilizing term insurance for key person insurance. While the term end may be many years in the future, your needs may not end. Do not buy term insurance for a permanent need.

• **Disability Insurance**. A lifetime's worth of saving can be lost with just a few months of disability. If a key person becomes disabled, owner or non-owner, that individual could lose everything if their income is not continued. It is the rare business that can afford to lose a key employee and continue to pay their salary while they don't work.

○   By definition, a business that loses a "key" person must replace that employee immediately, especially an owner.

○   The business will need the disabled person's salary to pay to his replacement.

○   It is risky for a business owner to expect his business to replace a key person with a new employee while paying the disabled executive's salary as well. It is often impossible.

• **Disability Buy-Sell**. If a business has several owners, the long-term disability of one owner can cause the business to fail. The remaining owners will be forced to pay the replacement employee, while the disabled owner demands the continuation of salary.

• **Professional Overhead Insurance**. The disability of a small business owner does not mean that they can suddenly stop paying all of their bills. Business life goes on.

o   The office rent or mortgage will continue.

o   Salaries must be continued, to retain key employees.

o   Service and advertising contracts must be honored.

Without proper disability coverage, personal and business obligations can mount, sometimes leaving bankruptcy as the only answer. It is relatively inexpensive to purchase business overhead insurance, thereby protecting a far bigger asset than most business owners realize.

# Chapter Eighty-Four
# HR
## Business Owner Planning

### CHILDREN IN THE BUSINESS

Many business owners hope to pass the business to their children. They hire their offspring. They put them into positions of authority.

In many ways, the business becomes another family member. This can present many unique challenges to the HR manager.

Family issues can create complications within a private business, and dramatically impact the families that control them.

I have consulted with thousands of privately held companies. I have seen what works and what doesn't work. While there are exceptions to every rule, here are a few axioms that might help you manage family dynamics in the most efficient manner.

### • WHO'S THE BOSS?

> o Family owned businesses must establish clear lines of power and communication.

> o As the founder, or his descendants, begin to step away from the business, it is helpful to establish clear lines of authority.

o    Don't wait for fate to sort things out. Owners should take the time to talk things through with their children before it is too late, even if it is the hardest business decision they have ever had to face.

## • NO PLACE FOR NEPOTISM

o    There is an old saying that you "never give a pet away for free." If people don't pay for something, they won't appreciate it. The same holds true for the family business. Business owners should not give their business away for free. It should be paid for. Payment could be in the form of cash, or sweat equity that has been earned over the years.

o    There is a great temptation for business owners to make things easy for their kids. After all, one day, the business will be theirs. Owners often put their children into positions of too much responsibility before they are ready, or have earned the role on their own. Don't do this.

o    Business owners should not be afraid to make their children work hard, like other employees. If they are worthy, children will appreciate the challenge.

o    If children start out near the bottom, employees will respect them later, because they have "walked in their shoes."

o    If promotions are earned, not simply handed out, they are appreciated and respected.

## • EQUALIZE (OR NOT)

o   The family business often represents a significant portion of a family's wealth. Even so, not every child wants to follow in mom or dad's footsteps. While one son or daughter may want work in the business, other siblings may choose a different life.

o   If the child in the business earns his way over a long period of time, siblings may not resent the unequal sharing of wealth.

o   However, if the disparity is large, or if nepotism prevails, an unequal transfer of business shares may cause irreparable friction within a family.

### How to Equalize

Business owners can find ways to equalize family and business value between their children. Some of the ways may include:

▪   Cash payments, from children receiving the business, to their siblings.

▪   Cash or other assets (such as a building) given by the business-owner parent to certain children.

▪   Non-voting shares given to non-business children.

•   Those working in the business may receive fair salaries, while surplus profits may be shared according to a formula, or by ownership percentages.

- Life insurance can be used to equalize value at the death of a business owner. While one child receives a $5 million business, a second may receive life insurance proceeds instead.

## • TAKING CARE OF MOM OR DAD

o   When making any business plans, care should be taken to ensure that a business owner's spouse is protected.

o   Many small business owners expect that the business can simply continue a salary in the event of death. The IRS may have a different view of this, treating the continuation of salary as a business dividend. This can cause double taxation at a time when it is least affordable.

o   In your business owner planning, you should be aware of the income tax treatment in any plans that you make.

## • PLAN THE TRANSITION

o   As I mentioned above, business owners should plan their business transition long in advance. It can take many years to:

- Develop a business succession team.

- Build a company's value prior to sale.

- Equalize value among children in and out of the business.

It is worth the effort to plan ahead.

# Chapter Eighty-Five
## _____HR_____
## Compliance & Reporting

Every business must follow the government's rules and regula-tions. Failure to do so can lead to fines, lawsuits, jail time, or even the loss of a business. In the following pages, we'll review the major laws, their significance, and what they might mean to your business.

# COMPLIANCE AND REPORTING OUTLINE

## SECTION ONE — HEALTH AND WELFARE

- Form 5500
- Group Term Life Insurance Imputed Income
- Taxability Of Disability Benefits
- Domestic Partner / Same Sex Marriage (Income Tax Treatment)
- Fringe Benefits (IRS Publication 15-B)

- Health Care Reimbursement Accounts (HCRA) (IRS Section 125)
- Dependent Care Reimbursement Accounts (DCRA) (IRS Section 125)
- Section 125 Plan Grace Period
- Qualified Transportation Benefit Limits
- Health Reimbursement Arrangement
- HSA Limits For 2012
- Mileage Reimbursement
- Educational Assistance
- Medicare Prescription Drug Plans For 2006 And Beyond
- Medicare Secondary Payer Mandatory Insurance Reporting:
- HIPAA Privacy
- HIPAA Security
- HIPAA Portability Requirements
- Business Associate Agreements
- HITECH/ARRA (American Reinvestment & Recovery Act)
- Children's Health Insurance Program (CHIP)
- HIPAA Rules For Wellness Incentives
- Genetic Information Nondiscrimination Act (GINA)
- Mental Health Parity Act
- Michelle's Law To Extend Health Coverage For Students On Medical Leave

# SECTION TWO — STATE COMPLIANCE REQUIREMENTS (MASSACHUSETTS)

- Domestic Partner / Same Sex Marriage (Income Tax Treatment)
- MA Health Care Reform Act – Chapter 58
- Fair Share Contribution (FSC) Requirement
- Free Rider Surcharge
- Filing Schedule
- Documentation Requirements
- Health Insurance Responsibility Disclosure Form

- Cafeteria Plans
- Reporting On Form 1099-HC
- Dependent Coverage
- Dependent Eligibility
- Imputed Income
- Minimum Creditable Coverage
- Mental Health Parity
- Standards For The Protection Of Personal Information For Residents Of The Commonwealth

## SECTION THREE — RETIREMENT PLANS/DEFERRED COMPENSATION

- The Pension Protection Act Of 2006
- Corporate Owned Life Insurance
- Retirement Savings For Individuals
- Age 70 ½ Required Distributions
- Distributions To Terminated Participants With An Account Balance Less Than $5,000
- Taxable Income On Defaulted Loans
- Distribute A Summary Annual Report
- Annual Non-Discrimination Testing (ADP/ACP Testing)
- 401(k) Plan Safe Harbor Notice
- QDIA Annual Notice
- 2012 Retirement Contribution Limits
- Restatement For EGTRRA

## SECTION FOUR — MAJOR LAWS: DEPARTMENT OF LABOR

- The Age Discrimination In Employment Act Of 1967
- The Americans With Disabilities Act Of 1990
- The Civil Rights Act Of 1964 (1968 and 1991)
- Equal Employment Opportunity (EEO) Laws
- The Equal Pay Act Of 1963
- The Fair Credit Reporting ACT (FCRA)
- The Federal Fair Labor Standards Act Of 1938 (FLSA)

- The Women's Health & Cancer Rights Act (WHCRA)
- The Newborns' & Mothers' Health Protection Act
- The Uniformed Services Employment & Reemployment Rights Act
- The National Defense Authorization Act Of 2008
- Caregiver Leave
- The HEART Act Of 2008
- The Occupational Safety & Health Act (OSHA)
- Workers' Compensation Insurance
- The Employee Retirement Income Security Act (ERISA) Uniformed Services Employment & Reemployment Rights Act
- Insurance
- The Employee Benefit Security Organization (EBSA)
- Liability & Disclosure
- The Uniformed Services Employment & Reemployment Rights Act
- The Employee Polygraph Protection Act
- Garnishment Of Wages
- The Family & Medical Leave Act
- Plant Closings & Layoffs

# COMMON ACRONYMS AND DEFINITIONS

# Chapter Eighty-Six
## HR
## Compliance & Reporting

# SECTION 1 – HEALTH AND WELFARE COMPLIANCE REQUIREMENTS:

## Form 5500

If you sponsor benefit plans in your company, you should be aware of Form 5500. The Form 5500 Series was formed jointly by the Department of Labor, the Internal Revenue Service, and the Pension Benefit Guaranty Corporation. Its intent was to make sure that employee benefit plans were operated and managed in a manner that protects plan participants and beneficiaries.

Form 5500 provides the mechanism for companies to satisfy the annual reporting requirements of ERISA and the Internal Revenue Code.

The U.S Department of Labor uses Form 5500 for *disclosure*, *compliance* and *research* purposes.

- Form 5500 is a disclosure tool for the Department of Labor.
- It is a disclosure document for plan participants

and beneficiaries.

- It is a source of information and data that is used by various Federal agencies, Congress and the private sector.

- Form 5500 filings are used to help assess national employee benefit, tax, and economic trends.

## Form 5500 Reports

The following types of benefit plans must file Form 5500 Series returns/reports:

- Profit-sharing plans, stock bonus plans, money purchase plans, 401(k) plans, etc.
- Annuity arrangements under Code section 403(b)(1).
- Custodial accounts established under Code section 403(b)(7) for regulated investment company stock.
- Individual retirement accounts (IRAs) established by an employer under Code section 408(c).
- Church pension plans electing coverage under Code section 410(d).
- Pension benefit plans that cover residents of Puerto Rico, the U.S. Virgin Islands, Guam, Wake Island, or American Samoa. This includes plans that apply the ERISA provisions of section 1022(i)(2).
- Plans that satisfy the Actual Deferral Percentage requirements of Code section 01(k)(3)(A)(ii) by adopting the Simple provisions of section 401(k).

## Exceptions

All welfare benefit plans (medical, dental, life insurance, apprenticeship and training, scholarship funds, severance pay, disability, etc.) covered by ERISA are required to file a Form 5500 **except**:

- Welfare benefit plans that covered *fewer* than

100 participants, as of the beginning of a plan year, which are *unfunded*, *fully insured*, or a *combination* of insured and unfunded.

- Welfare benefit plans maintained outside the United States, primarily for persons substantially all of whom are nonresident aliens.
- Governmental plans.
- Unfunded or insured welfare benefit plans that are maintained for a select group of management or highly compensated employees, which also meet the requirements of 29 CFR 2520.104-24.
- Employee benefit plans that are maintained only to comply with disability insurance laws.
- Welfare benefit plans that participate in a group insurance arrangement that files a Form 5500 on behalf of the welfare benefit plan, as specified in 29 CFR 2520.103-2.
- Apprenticeship or training plans that meet all of the conditions specified in 29 CFR 2520.104-22.
- Unfunded dues-financed welfare benefit plans that are exempted by 29 CFR 2520.104-26.
- Church plans under ERISA section 3(33).
- Welfare benefit plans that are maintained solely for businesses owned by an individual, or an individual and his or her spouse.

Effective January 1, 2010, all of the following must be completed and filed electronically — by using EFAST2-approved third-party software, or by using iFile.

- All Form 5500 Annual Returns/Reports of Employee Benefit Plans.
- All Form 5500-SF Short Form Annual Returns/Reports of Small Employee Benefit Plans.
- Any required schedules and attachments.

# GROUP TERM LIFE INSURANCE — IMPUTED INCOME

Plan sponsors must determine the amount of *i*mputed income for all group term life plan participants. Employers must report this information to their payroll administrator, to ensure that the imputed income amount is reported on employees' W-2 forms.

Employers should include the imputed income in each employee's last paycheck of the year, since the imputed income is also subject to Social Security taxes.

- **Exclusion from wages**
    - Employers can generally exclude the cost of up to $50,000 of group-term life insurance from the wages of an insured employee.
    - Employers can exclude the same amount from the employee's wages when figuring Social Security and Medicare taxes.
    - In addition, employers do not have to withhold federal income tax or pay FUTA tax on any group-term life insurance provided to employees.
- **Coverage over the limit**
    - Employers must include the cost of group term life insurance that is more than the cost of $50,000 of coverage in employees' wages. This amount is subject to Social Security and Medicare taxes.
    - This taxable income should be reduced by the amount that any employee has paid toward the insurance.
    - This income should be reported as wages in boxes 1, 3, and 5 of an employee's Form W-2. It should also be included in box 12 with code C.

The monthly cost of the insurance to be included as wages can be determined by multiplying the number of thousands of dollars of insurance coverage over $50,000 (figured to the nearest $100) by the cost shown in the following table. Employers should use the employee's age on the last day of the tax year to determine this figure. Employers must prorate the cost from the table if less than a full month of coverage is involved.

## IRS Premium Table Rates

| Age | Cost per $1000 per month |
|---|---|
| Under 25 | $.05 |
| 25-29 | $.06 |
| 30-34 | $.08 |
| 35-39 | $.09 |
| 40-44 | $.10 |
| 45-49 | $.15 |
| 50-54 | $.23 |
| 55-59 | $.43 |
| 60-64 | $.66 |
| 65-69 | $1.27 |
| 70 and older | $2.06 |

## TAXABILITY OF DISABILITY BENEFITS

When group disability premiums are paid on behalf of employees, individual employees have the option of whether or not to include all, or a portion, of these premiums as taxable income.

If an employee pays current taxes on 100% of disability premiums, any disability benefits would be received tax free.

If an employee does not include disability premiums in their current taxable income, then any future disability benefits would be fully taxable as income.

Most insurers and third-party administrators withhold taxes on disability premiums and payments.

Employers must notify their insurer or administrator regarding each employee's *taxability ratio*. Employers must also notify insurers and administrators if there have been any changes in their disability tax ratios, due to contribution changes.

**Note**: I encourage you to recommend to employees that they include disability premiums as part of their current income. The tax that they pay on these premiums will be minimal. The tax savings (in the event of disability) could be quite great.

Some insurance carriers offer W-2 preparation on behalf of their clients. Others will only provide a "sick pay report," which contains the information needed for employee W-2s.

It is the employer's responsibility to obtain the necessary information from the insurance carrier, so that the appropriate information is reported to employees on their W-2s. Make sure you do this.

## DOMESTIC PARTNER / SAME SEX MARRIAGE (INCOME TAX TREATMENT)

Some employers are extending health care coverage to the domestic partners of their employees. This may include couples of the same sex and/or of the opposite sex.

Federal law does not treat domestic partners as spouses. Only health benefits provided to domestic partners who qualify as legal dependents or legal spouses can be excluded from taxable income.

Therefore, the "fair market value" of coverage provided by a health plan to a nondependent domestic partner (over the amount paid by the employee-participant for such coverage) is included in the income of the participant.

Benefits for non-spouses are viewed as wages for FICA, FUTA and income tax withholding purposes by the IRS. Additionally, an employee's contribution for the partner's coverage is subject to federal taxation.

Section 125 flexible benefits and spending accounts may not be provided to domestic partners. Employers are not required to offer COBRA coverage to domestic partners.

## FRINGE BENEFITS

As we discussed earlier, fringe benefits became popular as a way for companies to circumvent wage restrictions during the Second

World War. As the government limited salaries, creative companies found other, non-salary, ways to compensate certain selected employees.

Today, many companies use fringe benefits to supplement traditional compensation for selected employees. And the government makes sure to tax these benefits.

### Fringe Benefit Definition

Fringe benefits are any non-cash compensation to employees. Unless specifically excluded by law, they are taxed as earned income.

Fringe benefits are paid *selectively*, and not for specific business purposes. For example; a company car that is provided to a salesperson for making sales calls is not considered a fringe benefit. A company car issued to an employee for commuting would be considered a fringe benefit. This is because a car used for simple commuting is considered personal use, as all employees must commute.

Any fringe benefit (above certain allowable limits) is taxable and must be included in the recipient's pay. The income amount would be the "**fair market value**" of the benefit received, less any amount paid by the employee.

### W-2 Reporting

All fringe benefits paid to employees are subject to employment taxes. This income must be reported on the employee's Form W-2. Employers must withhold, deposit, and report the employment taxes according to special rules.

If the recipient of a taxable fringe benefit is not an employee, the benefit is not subject to employment taxes. The contractor must report this income themselves.

IRS Publication 15-B is a good source of information on this subject. Here is where you will find this document:

www.irs.gov/pub/irs-pdf/p15b.pdf

# HEALTH CARE REIMBURSEMENT ACCOUNTS (HCRA) (IRS SECTION 125)

Companies that sponsor Health Care Reimbursement Accounts must comply with something known as the Facts and Circumstances Test. (FACT)

FACT measures the extent to which health care plan(s) discriminate in favor of highly-compensated employees. Discrimination can be in the form of benefits and/or contributions.

Key Employees may not receive more than 25% of the total benefits enjoyed by all employees.

Different benefits can be provided to various groups, as long as the highly-compensated individuals don't receive an unfair advantage. The benefits tested include:

- Medical insurance plans
- Dental plans
- FSAs
- Any other benefits included under a Section 125 plan.

## DEPENDENT CARE REIMBURSEMENT ACCOUNTS (DCRA)

Many companies offer dependent care reimbursement as one of the benefits within their Section 125 Cafeteria Plan.

Sponsors of Dependent Care Reimbursement Accounts must notify all participants regarding all tax-free benefits they have received from the plan during any calendar year.

The total benefit must be reported on each individual's W-2 form. Therefore, most plan sponsors also use the W-2 to satisfy the notification requirement.

**Maximum Benefit**

With some limitations, the maximum tax free benefits which can be received are:

- $5,000 for an individual.
- $2,500 for married employees filing separate returns.

Dependent care assistance plans must also satisfy annual nondiscrimination requirements. These include (but are not limited) to the following:

- Five percent shareholders or owners cannot receive more than 25% of the total plan benefits.
- Average non-highly compensated benefits must

equal at least 55% of average highly compensated benefits.

# SECTION 125 PLAN GRACE PERIOD

Code Section 125 Cafeteria Plans can be amended (as a result of IRS Notice 2005-42) to provide for a 2 ½ month grace period following the end of each plan year.

A grace period can be a helpful tool for the management of health and dependent care flexible spending accounts. It is a way for employees to avoid forfeiting unused amounts in their accounts. Employers may adopt a grace period for their current plan year (and subsequent plan years) by amending their plan documents before the end of the plan year.

A grace period allows a participant who:

- Has unused benefits or contributions from the immediately preceding plan year, and
- Incurs expenses for the same qualified benefit during the grace period,
- To be paid or reimbursed for those expenses, as if the expenses had been incurred during the immediately preceding plan year.

# QUALIFIED TRANSPORTATION BENEFIT LIMITS

In most cases, transportation benefits provided to employees may be excluded from the employee's wages. There are limits to this exclusion. The limits for 2012 are:

- $230 per month for combined commuter highway vehicle transportation and transit passes.
- $230 per month for qualified parking.
- $20 per qualified bicycle commuting month.

If the value of a benefit for any month is more than its limit, employers must include the amount over the limit in the employee's wages. Employers must deduct any amount the employee paid for the benefit from this amount, taxing only the net excess benefit.

# HEALTH REIMBURSEMENT ARRANGEMENT

Health Reimbursement Arrangements (HRAs) are used by employers to reimburse employees for qualified medical expenses.

HRAs must be funded *solely by an employer*.

An HRA contribution may not be paid through a voluntary salary reduction agreement on the part of an employee.

Under an HRA, employees are reimbursed (tax free) for qualified medical expenses up to a maximum dollar amount for a coverage period. HRAs may be offered with other health plans, including flexible spending accounts, (FSAs). As companies move toward high deductible plans, this benefit is becoming more widely used.

The benefits of HRAs to employees are as follows:

- Contributions made by the employer are not included in an employee's gross income.
- Reimbursements are tax free, if paid for qualified medical expenses.
- Any unused amounts in the HRA can be carried forward for reimbursements in later years.

There is no limit on the amount that an employer can contribute to HRA accounts. The maximum reimbursement amount under an HRA may be increased or decreased by amounts not previously used.

In order to maintain favorable tax treatment, distributions from an HRA must reimburse qualified medical expenses only. Services for reimbursed expenses must have incurred on or after the date the enrollee was enrolled in the HRA.

**HRA Limitations**

As in all attractive benefits, certain limitations apply for highly compensated participants.

You can learn more about HRAs at the following Web address: http://www.irs.gov/publications/p969/ar02.html.

## HSA LIMITS FOR 2012

Earlier, we discussed HSAs and how they are used with high deductible health plans (HDHPs). HSAs have significant tax advantages to employees. Therefore, the government restricts their use.

### Allowable Limits

In order to avoid taxation, the government sets limits regarding the maximum contributions into HSAs. Congress has also set out-of-pocket spending limits for HDHPs. These amounts are indexed for cost-of-living adjustments. 2012 annual contribution levels are as follows:

- The maximum annual HSA contribution for an eligible individual with self-only coverage is $3,100.
- For family coverage, the maximum annual HSA contribution is $6,250.
- The maximum annual out-of-pocket amount for HDHP self-coverage is $6,050.
- The maximum annual out-of-pocket amount for HDHP family coverage is twice that amount, or $12,100.
- The minimum deductible for an HDHP is $1,200 for self-only coverage and $2,400 for family coverage.

## MILEAGE REIMBURSEMENT

The business mileage reimbursement rate is used to calculate the deductible costs of operating a car (also vans, panel or pickup trucks) for business purposes. At the end of 2011, the reimbursement rate was $.55.5/mile.

## EDUCATIONAL ASSISTANCE

Employers are allowed to provide tax-free educational assistance to employees.

The maximum annual amount of tax-free educational assistance that can be provided under an employee educational assistance program is $5,250.

In the absence of an educational assistance plan, employers can exclude the value of educational benefits from wages (even those exceeding $5,250) if they are a condition of employment, known as a "working condition benefit."

Payment of any property or service is considered a working condition benefit, if the amount paid would have been deductible to the employee as a business or depreciation expense.

## MEDICARE PRESCRIPTION DRUG PLANS

The Medicare Prescription Drug, Improvement, and Modernization Act of 2003 added a new prescription drug benefit for seniors.

Under this act, employers that provide prescription drug coverage to retirees have several options, including:

- They can keep existing coverage and apply for government subsidies.
- They can offer a wraparound plan and make Part D coverage primary.
- They can sponsor a Medicare Part D prescription drug plan.
- They can contract directly with a prescription drug plan to offer a private label plan.
- They can drop prescription drug coverage for retirees.
- They can continue their current funding arrangement without applying for a government subsidy.

If an employer provides prescription drug coverage to Medicare beneficiaries, they must provide a notification advising beneficiaries if the employer sponsored prescription drug program is "creditable coverage." Employers must provide this notification by November 15th each year.

Employers must log onto the Centers for Medicare & Medicaid Services (CMS) website (www.cms.hhs.gov/creditablecoverage) and complete an electronic verification of compliance. The deadline for this requirement is within 60 days after the beginning date of the plan year.

## MEDICARE SECONDARY PAYER
## MANDATORY INSURANCE REPORTING:

The Medicare Secondary Payer Mandatory Insurer Reporting

requirement was passed into law in 2008. This law seeks to identify when the Centers for Medicare and Medicaid Services (CMS) should be paying secondary to employer group coverage.

The goal of this law is to reduce the amount CMS spends as the primary insurer, when they should be paying as the secondary.

Group Health Plans must register as a CMS coordination OEM benefit contractor with CMS. Employers must report Medicare eligible individuals in group health plans (active, not retiree plans) using Social Security numbers for covered employees and family members as defined below:

- Individuals age 45 through 64 with coverage through their own or a family member's current employment status.
- Individuals age 65 and older with coverage through their own or a spouse's current employment status.
- Individuals with end-stage renal disease, regardless of their own or a family member's current employment status.
- Individuals under age 45 known to be covered by Medicare, who have group health plan coverage through their own or a family member's current employment status.

Note: If an employer has more than twenty employees, Medicare automatically becomes the secondary insurer for any Medicare-eligible employees.

## HIPAA PRIVACY

HIPAA requires health plans to establish written privacy policies and procedures. These requirements include:

- A definition of protected health information (PHI).
- Permitted uses and disclosures.
- Designation of a privacy official and privacy contact.

- Sanctions for violations.
- Privacy safeguards.
- A complaints procedure.
- Documentation and record retention.
- The establishment of business associate agreements.

Notice of Privacy practices must be distributed to new enrollees at the time of enrollment and once every three years thereafter.

## HIPAA SECURITY

Large health plans (those with $5 million or more in annual premiums or claims) that maintain or receive electronic protected health information were required to become compliant with the Health Insurance Portability and Accountability Act of 1996 (HIPAA) security requirements as of April 20, 2005.

Small health plans (with less than $5 million in premiums or claims) had until April 20, 2006.

Health plans must maintain their compliance by:

- Assessing risks.
- Implementing administrative, physical and technical safeguards.
- Training the health plan workforce.
- Preparing and updating various documents, such as plan amendments and business associate agreements.
- Creating internal policies and procedures.

Unlike the HIPAA privacy provisions, the HIPAA security rules require involvement by IT staff to review computer networks, workspaces and all electronic media.

## HIPAA PORTABILITY REQUIREMENTS

In addition to the privacy and security requirements under HIPAA, final regulations under HIPAA's portability rules require group health plans to:

- Offer special enrollment rights to individuals, by

allowing them to enroll in the plan upon the occurrence of certain events.

- Provide a notice of HIPAA special enrollment rights.
- Update and issue certificates of creditable coverage when an individual's coverage terminates.
- Eliminate hidden preexisting condition exclusions and provide certain notices.

## BUSINESS ASSOCIATE AGREEMENTS

Health plans/covered entities must obtain written statements from business associates, stating that the associates are appropriately using, disclosing, and safeguarding personal health information (PHI).

## HITECH/ARRA (AMERICAN REINVESTMENT AND RECOVERY ACT OF 2009)

ARRA made a significant change to HIPAA privacy and security rules. ARRA makes business associates directly responsible for complying with HIPAA privacy and security rules under Title XIII, the "Health Information Technology for Economic and Clinical Health."

Under the law, a business associate is a "person or entity that performs certain functions or activities that involve the use or disclosure of protected health information on behalf of, or provides services to, a covered entity. A member of the covered entity's workforce is not a business associate."

Business associates are now liable for privacy violations. They must follow certain security rules. They must:

- Perform a formal risk assessment.
- Appoint a security officer.
- Adopt written policies and procedures and train employees.

HITECH also dictates "breach notification" requirements and includes enhanced enforcement and steeper penalties for privacy and security violations.

Covered entities and business associates must provide notice of any breach of unsecured PHI, without unreasonable delay and within 60 days after the "discovery" of the breach. A breach is when the use or access of such PHI poses "a significant risk of financial, reputational, or other harm."

Notice must be made to the individual(s) affected, to HHS, and to media outlets within the employer's state or jurisdiction, provided the breach is believed to affect more than 500 residents of that state/jurisdiction.

## CHILDREN'S HEALTH INSURANCE PROGRAM (CHIP)

CHIP became effective on April 1, 2009. This law creates a new HIPAA special enrollment period, allowing employees and dependents to enroll in an employer group health plan if they lose Medicaid or CHIP eligibility. The enrollment period is also applicable when employees first become eligible for state premium assistance. Employees have 60 days from the qualifying event to enroll in the group plan.

The Children's Health Insurance Program Reauthorization Act of 2009 (CHIPRA) extends and expands CHIP. The following provisions of CHIPRA affect employer group health plans:

- **Premium Assistance Subsidy for Employer Coverage**. States may elect to offer a premium assistance subsidy to help CHIP and Medicaid eligible children obtain "qualified employer-sponsored coverage." The subsidy may be provided as a reimbursement directly to the employee or as a direct payment to the employer. Employers can opt-out of direct payments.

- **Notice of Premium Assistance Subsidy**. Employer group health plans, in states that provide Medicaid or CHIP premium assistance subsidies, must give notice to employees of the availability of the subsidy. The Department of Health and Human Services was required to develop model notices. The notices can be provided with open enrollment materials or with the summary plan description (SPD).

- **Disclosure to States**. Administrators of group health plans are required to disclose information about the plan to states upon request. Under the law, the Departments of Labor and Health and Human Services were required to develop a model disclosure form for plan administrators.

- **New Special Enrollment Rights**. In addition to existing special enrollment rights, group health plans must also allow employees, and dependents who are eligible but not enrolled for coverage, to enroll under certain circumstances:

  - If an employee or dependent loses eligibility for CHIP or Medicaid, enrollment must be requested within 60 days after the termination of the CHIP or Medicaid coverage. Note that the 60 day period is in contrast to other special enrollment rights which can be limited to 30 days.

  - If an employee or dependent becomes eligible for premium assistance, through Medicaid or CHIP, enrollment must be requested within 60 days after eligibility is determined.

# HIPAA Rules for Wellness Incentives

Companies are allowed to provide health and wellness incentives as part of their health plans. Incentives can reduce out-of-pocket premiums for healthy employees. However, HIPAA mandates that group health plans cannot discriminate based on health factors, unless they meet the "wellness program" rules. Wellness rules limit plan rewards. They also require:

- Annual and uniform availability.
- Alternatives for getting rewards.
- Communication to all employees.

**Health Factor:** The term, "health factor," is broadly defined. A plan's health factor definition can be expanded to include behavior related conditions, such as smoking, other addictions to nicotine, and obesity.

HIPAA rules apply when an employer's program gives a plan-related reward for achieving any health factor-related standard. An example of a health factor-related standard would be when an employer reduces an employee's monthly contribution by 10% for good cholesterol readings.

HIPAA rules don't apply if the reward isn't plan-related. Cash, gift certificates, or gym memberships are not appropriate incentives.

HIPAA rules also don't apply if health goals are not required to achieve rewards.

## GENETIC INFORMATION NONDISCRIMINATION ACT (GINA)

The Genetic Information Nondiscrimination Act of 2008 (GINA) was enacted in 2008.

Title I of GINA amended the Employee Retirement Income Security Act of 1974 (ERISA), the Public Health Service Act (PHS Act), the Internal Revenue Code of 1986 (Code), and the Social Security Act (SSA).

GINA prohibits discrimination in health coverage based on genetic information. It also builds upon existing protections added by HIPAA.

The HIPAA portability provisions already prohibit a group health plan or group health insurance issuer from imposing a preexisting condition exclusion based solely on genetic information. Title I of GINA prohibits group health plans, health insurance issuers offering group and individual insurance, and issuers of Medicare supplemental (Medigap) policies from discriminating based on genetic information.

Providers are also prohibited from collecting such information.

GINA required the U.S. Health and Human Services Department to revise the HIPAA privacy regulations to clarify that genetic information is "health information" under the rule. Under this rule, providers may not use or disclose genetic information for underwriting purposes.

**Genetic Information in Employment**

Title II of GINA prohibits discrimination in employment based on genetic information. It also limits the acquisition and disclosure of information by employers and other entities covered by GINA.

GINA also established rules that (generally) prohibit a group health plan and a health insurance issuer in the group market from:

- Increasing the group premium or contribution amounts based on genetic information.
- Requesting or requiring an individual or family member to undergo a genetic test.
- Requesting, requiring or purchasing genetic information prior to or in connection with enrollment, or at any time, for underwriting purposes.

# MENTAL HEALTH PARITY ACT

The Mental Health Parity and Addiction Equity Act became part of the Emergency Economic Stabilization Act in 2008.

Under this law, plans that offer mental health and/or substance abuse coverage must offer coverage equal to that offered for traditional medical conditions in terms of copayments, deductibles, and co-insurance.

Plans are prohibited from applying separate limitations to the number of visits or the number of inpatient days for mental health or substance abuse related expenses.

If out-of-network benefits are provided for medical conditions, then out-of-network benefits must also be provided for mental health and substance abuse expenses.

**Note:** Plans sponsored by employers with 50 or less employees are exempt.

## MICHELLE'S LAW TO EXTEND HEALTH COVERAGE FOR STUDENTS ON MEDICAL LEAVE

In 2008, ERISA was amended by HR 2851. The bill became known as Michelle's Law.

In order to remain on her parents' health insurance coverage, Michelle Morse was forced to remain a fulltime student, while fighting (and losing her battle with) cancer. HR 2851 prohibits a group or individual health plan from terminating the coverage of a dependent student while on a medically necessary leave of absence. The coverage must remain in place for up to a year, or until the coverage would terminate under the regular terms of the plan.

# Chapter Eighty-Seven
## _____HR_____
## Compliance & Reporting

## STATE-SPECIFIC COMPLIANCE REQUIREMENTS

Every state has its own set of laws that relate to HR issues.

My business is domiciled in Massachusetts, so I am knowledgeable regarding the Massachusetts requirements. I have included the important regulations here, so that you can see how dramatically states can affect your compliance duties. If you live outside Massachusetts, I encourage you to fully understand the particular requirements of your state.

# SECTION 2 - MASSACHUSETTS COMPLIANCE REQUIREMENTS

## DOMESTIC PARTNER / SAME SEX MARRIAGE (INCOME TAX TREATMENT)

In 2004, the Commonwealth of Massachusetts recognized marriage between same sex couples.

The status of marriage provides special legal rights, including the ability to apply benefits for a same-sex spouse in the same manner as a traditional spouse.

### Same-Sex Spousal Benefits Are Taxable

The Federal government does not recognize same-sex marriages for income tax purposes. While Massachusetts may allow a same-sex spouse to be included in benefit coverage, the IRS will still treat the fair market value of this benefit as a taxable event.

It is important that employers (and employees) are aware of the differences between state and federal policy. Employers are responsible for splitting out the cost of such benefits and adding this as taxable income for the employee.

## MA HEALTH CARE REFORM ACT

The Massachusetts Health Care Reform Act imposes health insurance mandates on both individuals and employers. There are five employer mandates. They are as follows:

- Fair Share Contribution Requirement.
- The Free Rider Surcharge.
- The "Health Insurance Responsibility Disclosure" (HIRD Form).
- The Cafeteria Plan Requirement.
- Reporting (Form 1099-HC).

## FAIR SHARE CONTRIBUTION (FSC) REQUIREMENT

Employers with 11 or more full-time equivalent (FTE) employees in Massachusetts must either:

- Make a "fair and reasonable premium contribution" to the health insurance of its employees; or
- Pay into the Commonwealth Care Trust Fund an "annual fair share employer contribution," not to exceed $295 per FTE.

### Contribution Test

In assessing whether an employer makes a "fair and reasonable premium contribution," a Fair Share Contribution Test must be completed. Here are the main parts of that test.

- **Threshold Coverage** – Does the employer have

11 or more FTEs for the relevant testing period?

- **Percentage Contribution Standard** – Does the employer offer a group health plan, to which the employer makes some contribution. Do 25% or more of the employers FTEs participate?
- **Premium Contribution Standard** – Does the employer offer to make premium contributions of at least 33% of the cost of individual coverage under the plan, no more than 90 days after the date of hire?
- **Calculation and Payment of the Annual Fair Share Employer Contribution** – If an employer passes the percentage and/or premium contribution tests above, then it has no obligations to make payments to the Commonwealth Care Trust Fund. Otherwise, it must make a per-employee fair share contribution not to exceed $295 per FTE based on a 2,000 hour year.

### Fair and Reasonable – Less Than 50 Employees

Firms with 50 or fewer full time employees will meet the "fair and reasonable" contribution standard if:

- 25% or more of their full-time employees are enrolled in their group health plan (percentage contribution test), or,
- They offered to contribute at least 33% towards the cost of health coverage for their full-time employees (premium contribution test).

### Over 50 Employees

In 2009, the rules were changed to require firms with 51 or more FTEs to pass:

- Both the percentage contribution test and the premium contribution test, or
- Have at least 75% participation in their group plan among their full-time employees.

## FILING SCHEDULE:

Employers may file annually if:
- They pass the FSC testing requirements in the first quarter, and,
- Receive notice from the DUA that they are not at risk of becoming liable for payment in future quarters.

Employers that are liable for payment in the first quarter (October 1 through December 31), or are at risk of becoming liable for payment in future quarters, must continue to file each quarter.

## DOCUMENTATION REQUIREMENTS:

Employers with 11 or more full time employees are required to maintain documentation about their group health plan and premium contributions. The requirements can be met through having the following:
- A fully executed plan document.
- Executed plan amendments.
- An executed group contract.
- Annual open enrollment materials.

Employers must also maintain the following:
- A written plan description, including:
  o A description of benefits.
  o Eligibility requirements.
  o The amount of the employer contribution.
- Evidence that the Plan was in place during the quarter.
- Copies of the employee handbook (or other written communications to employees) about the plan(s), detailing:
  o Plan benefits.
  o Eligibility requirements.
  o Employer contributions.

# Free Rider Surcharge

If an employer does not provide coverage to their employees, they must pay a charge equal to:

- A portion of the Commonwealth's cost of providing health benefits to the employer's uninsured employees if:
  - o Any one employee (or dependent of an employee) receives free care services four or more times in a single year or,
  - o The employer has five or more total instances in a single year among all its employees (or their dependents) receiving free care.

# Health Insurance Responsibility Disclosure Form (HIRD)

Employers with 11 or more full time employees must file the Employer HIRD form quarterly. This form contains the employer's:

- Legal name.
- DBA name.
- FEIN.
- Division of Unemployment Assistance Account Number.

Employers must disclose the following:

- Whether the employer adopts and/or maintains a Section 125 Cafeteria plan.
- Whether the employer collects Employee HIRD forms.
- What percentage the employer contributes to the premium cost of a group health plan for its employees.
- If the employer contributes to the premium cost, it must disclose the total monthly premium for the lowest priced health insurance that is offered.
- The timing of the plans open enrollment period.

- The employer's definition of a full-time employee.

Reporting employers must:
- Furnish an Employee HIRD Form to each employee who declines to enroll in an employer-sponsored group health plan.
- File a form for all ineligible employees.
- File a form for each employee that declines access to coverage (through the Connector) through the employer's Section 125 Cafeteria plan.

Model forms are available on the Connector website. The Connector can be found at the following Internet location:
https://www.mahealthconnector.org/

Employers must retain documentation for a period of three years. They must also provide signed documents to Division of Health Care Finance and Policy (DHCFP) on request.

## CAFETERIA PLANS

Cafeteria plans permit employees to make pre-tax contributions under employer-sponsored group health plans. Massachusetts has two cafeteria plan requirements:
- Employers with 11 or more full-time equivalent employees in the Commonwealth must adopt and maintain a cafeteria plan and file that plan with the Connector.
- Small groups that choose to designate the Connector as their group health plan must participate in a payroll deduction program. This benefits employees, as:
  o Payroll deduction facilitates the payment of health benefit plan premium payments by employees.
  o Cafeteria plan deductions are excluded from gross income.

# Reporting on Form 1099-HC

Employers and sponsors of group health plans are required to provide a report annually, on or before January 31st of each year. This report must be filed with the Department of Revenue, and must verify required information relating to the coverage of Massachusetts employees and residents.

Failure to comply will result in financial penalties. Employers and sponsors are allowed to hire insurance companies or third party administrators to provide these filings. This is usually a good option for employers.

# Dependent Coverage

Group health insurance policies that provide family coverage must maintain coverage for dependents up to:

- The earlier of age 26, or,
- 2 years following the loss of "dependent status" under the provisions of the Internal Revenue Code, as defined in Code § 152(c)(3) (terminating dependent status of a qualifying child at age 19 or age 24 for students).

All employees that include dependent children (between the ages of 19 and 26) on their health and/or dental coverage must complete the following forms annually:

- An annual Affidavit of Tax Dependent Status Form.
- Dependent Status Form.

These forms are used by Human Resources:

- To determine whether or not the dependent child is eligible for coverage and,
- Whether or not the cost of the coverage needs to be treated as imputed income to the employee.

# Dependent Eligibility

Dependent children may be covered under a parent's health coverage under the following circumstances:

- Full-time students and/or child federal tax until their 26th birthday.
- Children who lose tax dependent status on their 24th birthday, or who stop attending school on a full-time basis, are eligible for a two-year (tax year) coverage extension under the family policy.
- The two-year extension begins on January 1$^{st}$ of the year in which the dependent child loses tax dependent status or stops attending school on a full-time basis. It will last through the earlier of:
  - o  The end of two calendar years following the last year in which at least 50% of the dependent's support was provided by his/her parent(s), or,
  - o  The child's 26th birthday.

# Imputed Income

While Massachusetts allows employees to cover a grown child as a dependent on their insurance, it does not mean that the child can be considered a dependent for income tax purposes.

**Fringe Benefit**

Providing health care coverage for a child who is not a tax dependent is considered a fringe benefit by the U.S. Treasury Department. As with all fringe benefits, employers are to report the "fair market value" of such a benefit as taxable income to the employee.

Fair market value is considered to be the full cost of individual coverage for the plan in which the non-dependent child is covered. Imputed income applies to both medical and dental coverage.

# Minimum Creditable Coverage

All residents of Massachusetts, ages 18 and older, must obtain and maintain a minimum level of health insurance coverage. This is known as "creditable coverage."

Employers must understand the *minimum creditable coverage* requirements. The minimum requirements include the following:

- Coverage for a comprehensive set of services (e.g. doctor visits, hospital admissions, day surgery, emergency services, mental health and substance abuse, and prescription drug coverage).
- Doctor visits for preventive care, without a deductible.
- A cap on annual deductibles of $2,000 for an individual and $4,000 for a family.
- For plans with up-front deductibles or co-insurance on core services, an annual maximum for out-of pocket spending of (no more than) $5,000 for an individual and $10,000 for a family.
- No caps on total benefits for a particular illness, or for a single year.
- Policies may not cover only a fixed dollar amount per day or stay in the hospital, with the patient responsible for all other charges.
- For policies that have a separate prescription drug deductible, it cannot exceed $250 for an individual or $500 for a family.

## MENTAL HEALTH PARITY

House Bill 4423 amended Massachusetts's mental health parity laws by adding autism, substance abuse disorders, post-traumatic stress disorder and eating disorders to the list of diagnoses for which equal coverage must be provided in comparison to other medical disorders.

## STANDARDS FOR THE PROTECTION OF PERSONAL INFORMATION FOR RESIDENTS OF THE COMMONWEALTH (93H):

All entities in Massachusetts that own, license, store, or maintain personal information about a Massachusetts resident must:

- Complete a security risk assessment.
- Establish and maintain a written security program for the protection of personal information.
- Implement firewall protection.
- Encrypt data sent over the Internet or saved on a laptop.
- Provide training to employees.
- Notify the Office of Consumer Affairs and Business Regulation, the Attorney General's Office and the affected party when a security breach occurs.

Security breach provisions include data such as:

- Social Security number.
- Driver's license number or state-issued identification card number.
- Financial account number.
- Credit or debit card number, with or without any required security code, access code, personal identification number or password that would permit access to a resident's financial account.
- Information need not "reside" in Massachusetts.

Further information regarding these requirements can be found at the following locations:

- FAQs:

http://www.mass.gov/Eoca/docs/idtheft/201CMR17faqs.pdf

- Checklist:

http://www.mass.gov/Eoca/docs/idtheft/compliance_checklist.pdf

# Chapter Eighty-Eight
## _____HR_____
## Compliance & Reporting

# SECTION 3 – RETIREMENT PLANS/DEFERRED COMPENSATION

## THE PENSION PROTECTION ACT OF 2006 (PPA):

As we discussed earlier, defined benefit pension plans make long-term retirement guarantees to employees. A plan's trustees set aside funds to meet these promises. The amounts contributed are based upon an expected rate of return on those investments. If investments don't earn what was expected, a pension will have less in their investment accounts than it needs to fund their promises. This results in the pension becoming "underfunded."

It is no secret that many of the nation's defined benefit pension plans are severely underfunded. The anemic stock market of the last decade has not been kind to investment managers. Low bond yields made the problem worse. Mortgage backed securities looked like the perfect solutions for hungry pension investment managers. We know how that turned out.

There is significant pension underfunding across corporate America, particularly among companies with large union workforces. General Motors and Chrysler went into bankruptcy because they could no longer meet the financial promises they had made to current and former employees.

States, cities and towns made serious miscalculations as they lavished generous retirement benefits to their employees. Now, government pensions face a shortfall in the neighborhood of $1 trillion.

Throw this on top of our nation's debt, in excess of $15 trillion, and we've got major funding issues.

The Pension Protection Act of 2006 went into law before the most recent stock and mortgage securities collapse. It contained provisions designed to strengthen the funding rules for defined benefit pension plans. Employers offering traditional pension plans were required to fully fund them over a span of years. This started with a 92% funding requirement by 2008. Full funding was mandated by 2010. **Note:** In late 2011, a study conducted by Credit Suisse found that the unfunded pension gap was more than $380 billion, with assets funding only 77% of corporate pension liabilities.

In 2010, many employers were forced to file for relief under this act  Employers that elected relief are required to make additional contributions to their pension plans if they:

- Pay compensation to any employee in excess of $1 million.
- Pay extraordinary dividends.
- Engage in extraordinary stock buybacks during the first part of the relief period.

The PPA forced many public companies to fund their pensions more aggressively. It did little to solve the funding shortfalls in government pensions.

Relief from the PPA funding requirements has also been extended to plans sponsored by charitable organizations.

The PPA also encouraged the conversion of defined benefit pension plans to cash balance plans.

It liberalized payout and rollover rules.

It made a number of other changes relating to pension plans and their beneficiaries.

### Retirement Plan Rules Changes

If you oversee a retirement plan, here is what you should know about the PPA:

- With regard to pension funding, employers may rely on a "reasonable interpretation" of the funding rules in the statute.

- The act allows an exclusion from gross income of up to $100,000 per year for otherwise taxable distributions from an IRA that are donated to a charity. To qualify, an individual must be at least age 70½ on the date of the distribution. Any amount contributed from the IRA to the charity will not be taxable.
    - This provision has been extended several times.

- Section 529 College Savings Plans were made permanent.

- Catch-up contributions for employees over age 50 were made permanent.

- The act enabled individuals to direct part of their IRS tax refund as an IRA contribution.

- A non-spouse who is the beneficiary of an eligible retirement plan was given the same benefits that are available to a spouse who is a beneficiary.

- A non-spouse beneficiary was given the option of a tax-free rollover (to an IRA) of most inherited retirement distributions from eligible retirement plans.

# CORPORATE OWNED LIFE INSURANCE

The PPA limited the tax exemptions for proceeds received from corporate owned life insurance. Employers may receive all policy proceeds of COLI on a tax-free basis, provided certain conditions are met. They are as follows:
- The insured individual must have been a director or highly compensated employee at the time the policy was issued, or,

- Employed by the employer within the 12 months before his or her death.

- Before the policy was issued, the employer must have provided the deceased individual written notice of:

  - The employer's intent to insure the employee's life.

  - The maximum face amount of the policy at the time issued.

  - The fact that any proceeds paid on the employee's death will be paid to the employer.

  - The insured must have provided consent before the policy was issued.

  - Consent must specifically allow the employer to continue the coverage after termination of employment.

## Annual Reports

Under the PPA, employers are required to file annual reports that state:

- The number of employees at the end of the year.
- The number of employees insured by COLI at the end of the year.
- The total amount of COLI in effect at the end of the year.
- The name, address, taxpayer identification number, and type of business of the employer.
- That the employer has written consents from all insured employees.
- If any consents are missing, and how many are missing.

Employers are also required to maintain complete and accurate information.

# RETIREMENT SAVINGS FOR INDIVIDUALS

The PPA included a number of significant tax incentives to enhance retirement savings for individuals. Since we are focusing on HR issues, we won't review the changes for individuals. If you are interested, the full set of provisions for this act can be found here:

http://www.irs.gov/retirement/article/0,,id=165131,00.html

## AGE 70 ½ REQUIRED DISTRIBUTIONS

Retirement participants, who are age 70 ½ or over, are required by the IRS to take a minimum distribution from their accounts each year.

Plan Sponsors are required to make minimum annual distributions for those affected before April 1st of the year following the participant's attaining age 70 ½. The payments must be made by December 31st.

This means that in the year after a participant turns age 70 ½, two payments must be made – one by April 1st and another by December 31st.

If a participant is still employed at age 70 ½, they may defer their first distribution until the April following the year that they actually retire.

A 5% owner must start receiving distributions, no later than April 1st of the year following the calendar year the individual turns 70 ½, even if they are still working.

## DISTRIBUTIONS TO TERMINATED PARTICIPANTS WITH AN ACCOUNT BALANCE LESS THAN $5,000

Record-keeping for retirement plans can become expensive, particularly for employers who have many former employees with funds still in their plan(s).

In certain circumstances, employers are allowed to force the distribution of funds held by former employees. If an employee's balance is below $1,000, the employer can simply make a distribution.

Account balances greater than $1,000, but less than $5,000 can be rolled to IRAs for employees.

Employers may not force distributions for amounts held by former employees of more than $5,000.

By paying participants before the end of the year (for a December 31 plan year-end) an employer can reduce the number of participant records. In some cases, this may eliminate the need for a plan audit, as audits are not required for plans with less than *100 participants*.

Remember, payout rules are subject to terms of your particular plan(s). So, consult your plan document before processing any distributions.

## TAXABLE INCOME ON DEFAULTED LOANS

A participant loan typically goes into default after a participant has failed to make a quarterly scheduled payment on the outstanding plan loan. A default forces the loan to be treated as *income* to the employee, and causes taxation of the benefit.

You should explain this to plan participants with loans that are approaching default. If the scheduled payments are not made, the employee should receive a 1099-R the following January.

## DISTRIBUTE A SUMMARY ANNUAL REPORT

A Summary Annual Report (SAR) must be distributed to all participants and beneficiaries that are entitled to benefits under a plan. This must be received by participants no later than 2 months after the Form 5500 filing deadline.

A December 31st plan year end will typically have a July 31st due date. In this case, the SAR must be distributed by September 30th. If an extension is filed for the 5500 (October 15th), the SAR would need to be distributed by December 15th.

An SAR can be distributed either electronically or by paper.

# Annual Non-Discrimination Testing (ADP/ACP Testing)

Annual non-discrimination tests for retirement plans should be completed as soon as year-end records are compiled (preferably by January 31 for calendar year plans).

In order to remain "qualified," a plan may not discriminate in favor of highly compensated employees. If a plan fails its ADP/ACP tests, highly compensated participants must receive a distributions of the "excess contributions" made in the previous year, until the plan passes its tests.

If this has occurred with your retirement plan, you should examine your education practices. You may also wish to elect a negative election provision in your 401(k). This enrolls all new plan participants automatically. Participants must opt out of the plan if they don't want to participate, rather than having to elect in.

If your company has failed its ADP/ACP testing, you can find out how to resolve this issue at the following IRS Web location:

http://www.irs.gov/retirement/article/0,,id=154536,00.html

Caution: If excess contributions are returned to participants more than $2_{1/2}$ months following the plan year end, the employer must pay a 10% excise tax to the IRS. The excise tax is paid and reported to the IRS on Form 5330, which is due nine months after the plan year end.

To avoid plan disqualification, excess contributions and earnings must be refunded by the following plan-year-end.

# 401(k) Plan Safe Harbor Notice

Employers with a Safe Harbor 401(k) must annually notify eligible employees of their rights and obligations under the safe harbor arrangement. Your notification requirements are as follows:

- Written notice must be made within a reasonable period of time before the first day of each plan year. Reasonable is considered to be not less than 30 days, but not more than 90 days, after the plan year end.

- New employees must be provided with a Safe Harbor Notice (within a reasonable period of time) before the employee becomes eligible to participate in the plan.

Notifications may be completed via electronic medium, if reasonably accessible to employees, provided that:

- The electronic information is as understandable to employees as information received in written form.
- Employees are advised that, at any time, they may request and receive the Safe Harbor Notice in written form at no charge.

## QDIA ANNUAL NOTICE

### Automatic Enrollment

The PPA allowed employers to automatically enroll new employees into deferral retirement plans — typically a 401(k). This strategy can be critical in helping plans meet anti-discrimination testing requirements. This can be very important to senior management, (and you in your HR role). If you are not aware of this provision, you should talk to your retirement plan provider.

### Notice

Plans that comply with Qualified Default Investment Alternative (QDIA) regulations will receive fiduciary protection under ERISA 404(c)(5). In order to qualify for protection, participants must be given initial and annual notices.

The annual notice must be given at least 30 days, but not more than 90 days, before each following plan year. The notice must be given to:

- All active participants.
- Former employees with account balances.
- Beneficiaries who were defaulted into the QDIA, and who have not subsequently directed the investment of their account.

# 2012 RETIREMENT CONTRIBUTION LIMITS

Participants in a 401(k) or 403(b) plan are limited to maximum annual contributions. This amount is based upon a calendar year, regardless of the plan year.

Retirement plan sponsors should verify that no plan participant exceeds this maximum. The maximum is applied on a per participant basis

A summary of the most commonly used limit amounts for retirement plans is listed below:

The full list of 2012 contribution limits can be found at the IRS website:

http://www.irs.gov/newsroom/article/0,,id=248482,00.html

Here is a QUICK REFERENCE CHART

| | |
|---|---|
| Defined Contribution Annual 415 Limit | $50,000 |
| 401(k) Deferral Limit | $17,000 |
| 403(b)/457 Deferral Limit | $17,000 |
| Annual Compensation Limit | $250,000 |
| Catch up Contributions (for participants 50+) | $5,500 |
| Highly Compensated Employee (HCE) | $115,000 |
| Defined Benefit Plan Annual Benefit Limit | $205,000 |

Note: Many teachers are eligible for both 403(b) and 457 deferrals. This allows for a maximum deferral of $34,000, plus catch-up contributions, if appropriate.

# RESTATEMENT FOR EGTRRA

The Economic Growth and Tax Relief Reconciliation Act of 2001 (EGTRRA) became effective for all plan years beginning in 2002. All defined contribution plans must have been restated by April 30, 2010 to include the changes from EGTRRA. If you haven't done this, do it now.

# Chapter Eighty-Nine
## _____HR_____
## Compliance & Reporting

## SECTION 4 - THE MAJOR LAWS OF THE DEPARTMENT OF LABOR

The Department of Labor (DOL) administers and enforces more than 180 federal laws. These mandates, and the regulations that implement them, affect approximately 10 million employers and 125 million workers.

Following is a brief review of the DOL statutes that affect most private companies.

For authoritative information on these laws, you should always consult professionals, as well as the statutes and regulations themselves. For your convenience, I have included many of the key Web addresses, where you can find more detailed information.

## THE AGE DISCRIMINATION IN EMPLOYMENT ACT OF 1967

This act includes a broad ban against age discrimination and specifically prohibits:

- Statements regarding age in job notices.
- Advertisements of age preference and age limitations.
- Discrimination on the basis of age by apprenticeship programs, including joint labor-management apprenticeship programs.
- Denial of benefits to older employees.
  - Note: An employer may reduce benefits

based on age where the cost of providing the reduced benefits to older workers is the same as the cost of providing benefits to younger workers

An age limit may only be specified where age has been proven to be a bona fide occupational qualification (BFOQ).

The Older Worker's Benefit Protection Act of 1990 amended the age discrimination act to prevent age discrimination regarding benefits for older workers.

## THE AMERICANS WITH DISABILITIES ACT OF 1990

The U.S. Equal Employment Opportunity Commission states the following:

*"Title I of the Americans with Disabilities Act of 1990 prohibits private employers, state and local governments, employment agencies and labor unions from discriminating against qualified individuals with disabilities in job application procedures, hiring, firing, advancement, compensation, job training, and other terms, conditions, and privileges of employment.*

*"The ADA covers employers with 15 or more employees, including state and local governments. It also applies to employment agencies and to labor organizations.*

*"The ADA's nondiscrimination standards also apply to federal sector employees under section 501 of the Rehabilitation Act, as amended, and it's implementing rules.*

*An individual with a disability is a person who:*

- *Has a physical or mental impairment that substantially limits one or more major life activities:*
- *Has a record of such an impairment; or*
- *Is regarded as having such an impairment."*

### Protected Individuals

In your employment practices, you should be aware that the ADA protects disabled individuals from discrimination. You may not discriminate against current or potential employees who cannot perform major life activities — ones that an average person can perform with little or no difficulty, such as:

- Walking.

- Breathing.

- Seeing.

- Hearing.

- Speaking.

- Learning.

- Working.

### Who Is Qualified?

You may not discriminate against any disabled individual who is a qualified employment candidate. A qualified employee or applicant is someone who satisfies the requirements of:

- Skill,

- Experience,

- Education and,

- Other job-related requirements of the position held or desired who,

- With or without reasonable accommodation, can perform the essential functions of that position.

### Reasonable Accommodations

As an employer, you are required by law to provide reasonable accommodations to disabled individuals. Reasonable accommodations may include, but are not limited to:

- Making existing work facilities readily accessible to and usable by persons with disabilities.

- Job restructuring.

- Modification of work schedules.

- Providing additional unpaid leave.

- Reassignment to a vacant position.

- Acquiring or modifying equipment or devices.

- Adjusting or modifying examinations, training materials, or policies.

- Providing qualified readers or interpreters.

- Any reasonable accommodation that may be necessary to allow anyone with a disability to:

    o Apply for a job.

    o Perform job functions.

    o Enjoy the benefits and privileges of employment that are enjoyed by people without disabilities.

Employers are not required to lower production standards to make accommodations.

Employers are (generally) not obligated to provide personal use items, such as eyeglasses or hearing aids.

An employer is required to make a reasonable accommodation to a qualified individual with a disability, unless doing so would impose an undue hardship on the operation of the employer's business.

## Undue Hardship

Undue hardship means an action that involves significant difficulty or expense, when considered in relation to the following business factors:

- Size.

- Financial resources.

- The nature and structure of its operation.

## What You Can't Ask

Before making an offer of employment, an employer may not ask job applicants about the:

- Existence,

- Nature and,

- Severity of a disability.

## What You Can Ask

Applicants may be asked about their ability to perform job functions.

## Medical Examination

A job offer may be conditioned on the results of a medical examination, only if the examination is required for all entering employees in the same job category.

Medical examinations of employees must be job-related and consistent with business necessity.

## Drugs & Drug Tests

Employees and applicants taking illegal drugs are not protected by the ADA.

Tests for illegal use of drugs are not considered medical examinations. Therefore, they are not subject to the ADA's restrictions on medical examinations.

Employers may hold individuals who are illegally using drugs, and individuals with alcoholism, to the same standards of performance as other employees. You can learn more about this law at the following government website:

http://www.eeoc.gov/facts/fs-ada.html.

# THE CIVIL RIGHTS ACT OF 1964 (1968 AND 1991)

The Civil Rights Act of 1964 outlawed major forms of discrimination against blacks and women, including racial segregation.

This landmark decision created the foundation for the many anti-discrimination rules that employers face today.

The Pregnancy Discrimination Act of 1978 amended Title VII of the Civil Rights Act to prohibit sex discrimination on the basis of pregnancy.

# EQUAL EMPLOYMENT OPPORTUNITY (EEO) LAWS

### Discrimination

Under Title VII, the ADA, and the ADEA, it is illegal to discriminate in any aspect of employment. This includes, but is not limited to, the following:

- Hiring and firing.
- Compensation, assignment, or classification of employees.
- Transfer, promotion, layoff, or recall.
- Job advertisements.
- Recruitment.
- Testing.
- Use of company facilities.
- Training and apprenticeship programs.

- Fringe benefits.
- Pay, retirement plans, and disability leave.
- Any other terms and conditions of employment.

### Harassment

Harassment is considered a discriminatory practice under Civil Rights law. Employers are prohibited from harassing employees on the basis of:

- Race.
- Color.
- Religion.
- Sex.
- National origin.
- Disability.
- Age.

### Retaliation Prohibited

Employers may not retaliate against an individual for:

- Filing a charge of discrimination.
- Participating in an investigation.
- Opposing discriminatory practices.

### Stereotyping

It is against the law to make employment decisions based on stereotypes or assumptions about:

- The abilities,
- Traits and,
- The performance of individuals of a certain:
  - sex,
  - race,
  - age,
  - religion,
  - ethnic group or,
  - individuals with disabilities.

### Marriage Or Association

It is against the law to deny employment opportunities to a person because of marriage to, or association with, an individual of a particular:

- Race,
- Religion,
- National origin or,
- An individual with a disability.

Title VII also prohibits discrimination because of participation in schools or places of worship that are associated with a particular racial, ethnic, or religious group.

### Notices

Employers are required to post notices to all employees advising them of their rights under Civil Rights laws. Employees must also be informed that the EEOC enforces employee rights to freedom from retaliation.

Such notices must be accessible, as needed, to persons with visual or other disabilities that affect reading.

## THE EQUAL PAY ACT OF 1963

The Equal Pay Act of 1963 amended the Fair Labor Standards Act, with the intent of abolishing wage discrimination based on sex.

This has helped narrow the "gender gap," and break some of the glass ceilings that have existed in business for decades.

The spirit of this Act is to prevent (prohibit) employers from paying men more for same work as women. Do so at your own peril.

## THE FAIR CREDIT REPORTING ACT (FCRA)

The FCRA is designed to promote the accuracy, fairness, and privacy of information in the files of every consumer reporting agency (CRA).

Most CRAs are credit bureaus that gather and sell information about individuals to creditors, employers, landlords, and other businesses.

If an employer obtains personal information regarding their employees, they are required to protect this information.

If an employer (or potential employer) uses such information against an employee (or potential employee), that individual must be told.

Individuals must give their consent for an employer to obtain credit information. However, consent is generally not required in the trucking industry.

More information can be obtained at the following government website:

http://www.ftc.gov/bcp/menus/consumer/credit.shtm.

## THE FEDERAL FAIR LABOR STANDARDS ACT OF 1938 (FLSA) (29 USC §201 ET SEQ.; 29 CFR 510-794)

This law established federal standards for:
- Minimum wages.
- Overtime pay.
- Record-keeping.
- Child labor.

Amendments to the FLSA periodically set the Federal Minimum Wage. However, many states have their own minimum wage, which is often higher.

For example: In 2011, the Federal Minimum Wage was $7.25 per hour. In Massachusetts, this figure was $8.00 per hour. In Washington (the highest), the minimum wage was $8.67 per hour.

### Overtime

With few exceptions, overtime, time and one-half, must be paid for work of over forty hours a week.

### Working Age

The minimum working age for non-hazardous work is sixteen. Child labor regulations prohibit persons younger than eighteen years old from working in hazardous occupations.

Additional rules allow children under the age of sixteen to work in some jobs, such as certain types of farming.

# THE WOMEN'S HEALTH AND CANCER RIGHTS ACT (WHCRA)

WHCRA provides insurance protection for individuals who elect breast surgery, as well as reconstruction after a mastectomy.

WHCRA states that group health plans, insurance companies and health maintenance organizations (HMOs) that offer mastectomy coverage must also provide coverage for certain services relating to the mastectomy.

This requirement ensures that coverage includes all stages of reconstruction of the breast on which the mastectomy was performed. It also includes surgery and reconstruction of the other breast to produce a symmetrical appearance. The law also ensures that coverage is provided for prostheses and the treatment of physical complications arising from the mastectomy. This includes lymphedema.

Mastectomy benefits must be subject to the same deductibles and coinsurance as other medical and surgical benefits provided by the plan. Written notice about the availability of the mastectomy-related benefits must be provided to health plan participants upon enrollment, as well as each year thereafter.

# THE NEWBORNS' AND MOTHERS' HEALTH PROTECTION ACT

This act establishes minimum length of stays for health plans that provide benefits for hospital services related to childbirth. A covered hospital stay must be no less than 48 hours for vaginal delivery, and 96 hours for a cesarean section. Written notice should be provided in plan documents.

# THE UNIFORMED SERVICES EMPLOYMENT AND REEMPLOYMENT RIGHTS ACT (USERRA)

USERRA was enacted in 1994 to encourage non-career service

in the uniformed services. This act eliminated (or minimized) penalties and certain disadvantages to civilian employees of the uniformed services.

USERRA seeks to ensure that those who choose to serve their country can retain their civilian employment and benefits. It also guarantees that they can seek employment free from discrimination because of their service.

USERRA provides protection for disabled veterans, by requiring that employers make reasonable efforts to accommodate the disability.

Employers cannot discriminate in employment, or take any adverse employment action, against any person serving in the military.

USERRA gives employees the right to continue their existing, employer based health coverage, for up to 24 months while serving in the military.

The law can be read in greater detail at the Department of Labor website.

http://www.dol.gov/compliance/laws/comp-userra.htm

# THE NATIONAL DEFENSE AUTHORIZATION ACT OF 2008

The National Defense Authorization Act of 2008 (NDAA) expanded the Family and Medical Leave Act of 1993 (FMLA) to include active duty leave and caregiver leave:

## Active Duty Leave

- Employers with 50 or more employees (within 75 miles) are required to comply with NDAA. They must provide up to 12 weeks of unpaid leave to an immediate family member of someone who has been called to active duty as part of the National Guard or a military reserve unit.
  - Family member means spouse, son, daughter or parent.

Employees are entitled to take up to 12 weeks in any 12-month period for a qualifying exigency. The 12 weeks will be reduced by any other FMLA leave taken in same period.

Definitions of qualifying exigencies are as follows:

- Short-notice deployment.
- Military events and related activities.
- Childcare and school activities.
- Financial and legal arrangements.
- Counseling.
- Rest and recuperation.
- Post-deployment activities.

## Caregiver Leave

Employers with 50 or more employees (within 75 miles) must provide up to 26 weeks of unpaid leave within a single 12 month period for caregiver leave.

Eligible caregivers are the family members of someone who has suffered a serious illness or injury in the line of duty, while on active duty in the armed forces.

An eligible caregiver is defined as a service member's immediate family member — spouse, child, or parent, or the "nearest blood relative."

A service member who has suffered a serious illness or injury includes one who is:

- Undergoing medical treatment, recuperation or therapy.
- An outpatient.
- Disabled.

### How Leave Is Taken

Leave may be taken on an intermittent or reduced schedule basis. An employee may choose to substitute accrued paid leave during the unpaid leave period. An employer may require the employee to do the same.

An employee should provide "reasonable" and practicable" notice of his/her leave, especially if the leave is foreseeable. Employers may require the employee to submit certification regarding active duty service or health condition.

Additional information is available at:

http://www.ssa.gov/legislation/legis_bulletin_022108.html

# THE HEART ACT OF 2008

The Heroes Earnings Assistance and Relief Tax Act of 2008 (HEART) enacted many provisions affecting employee benefit plans. The main provisions of this law are as follows:

- Any U.S. military reservist that is called to active duty for a period of 180 days (or more) is entitled to a distribution of some or all of the funds in his/her health FSA.
- The Pension Protection Act permitted active duty reservists to receive a distribution (of elective deferrals) from a qualified retirement plan before December 31, 2007. HEART made this provision permanent. A reservist on active duty for 30 days or more is eligible for a distribution.
- Some employers choose to make up the difference in lost pay, while employees are serving their country. This differential pay is now treated as compensation for retirement plan purposes, rather than non-compensation. This allows active duty employees to make more elective deferrals to a retirement plan, and have this deducted from their pay.

## THE OCCUPATIONAL SAFETY AND HEALTH ACT (OSHA)

The Occupational Safety and Health Act is administered by the Occupational Safety and Health Administration (OSHA).

OSHA, or OSHA-approved state programs, are in place to oversee the safety and health conditions for most private and public employers.

Covered employers must comply with a complex set of regulations. These regulations vary by industry.

Basically, employers have a general duty to provide their employees with a workplace free from recognized, serious hazards. OSHA enforces the Act through workplace inspections and investigations.

Compliance assistance and cooperative programs are available on national and state levels. Employers can learn more about federal health and safety requirements at the following U.S. website address:

http://www.osha.gov/pls/oshaweb/owasrch.search_form?p_doc_type=standards&p_toc_level=0.

## WORKERS' COMPENSATION INSURANCE

Workers Compensation (known as workers comp) covers employees who become injured or sick during work activities.

### Administered By States

Workers comp is administered by the individual states. Each state requires employers to purchase an insurance policy to handle their statutory obligations to workers.

In Massachusetts, all covered employers, even those with just one employee, must purchase insurance. Larger employers may qualify to self-insure.

Cities and towns are not required to adhere to the Massachusetts Act (of 1911), although most do.

Employees in certain professions, such as railroad workers, seafarers, shipyard and harbor workers, police officers and firefighters are not covered under the Massachusetts law. Neither are independent contractors, or privately employed part-time individuals, such as babysitters and home yard workers.

U.S. government employees are also excluded from the law.

### Notice

A notice with the insurer's name must be prominently displayed in the workplace, or employers will be fined $100 per day. Employers who violate this requirement may also be subject to jail time, of up to one year.

Employees must be covered from their first day on the job, except for seasonal, part-time or temporary workers. Failure to carry workers' compensation insurance, or otherwise meet a state's regulations, will leave an employer exposed to paying for benefits out-of-pocket. There may be additional penalties levied by the state.

Benefits paid under workers compensation typically include:

- Medical expenses.
- Death benefits.
- Lost wages.
- Vocational rehabilitation.

Each state has information regarding their workers' compensation programs. You can learn more about Massachusetts program at the following location:

http://www.mass.gov/?pageID=elwdhomepage&L=1&L0=Home&sid=Elwd

## THE EMPLOYEE RETIREMENT INCOME SECURITY ACT (ERISA)

We discussed ERISA in our section on retirement plans. ERISA created a wide range of responsibilities for the sponsors of retirement plans. These provisions were put in place to protect the rights of employees. As we discussed, the most important features of this law are:

- Fiduciary requirements.
- Disclosure requirements.
- Reporting requirements.

### INSURANCE

Under Title IV, certain employers and plan fiduciaries must fund an insurance system to protect most qualified retirement benefits. Premiums must be paid to the federal government's Pension Benefit Guaranty Corporation (PBGC).

## THE EMPLOYEE BENEFIT SECURITY ORGANIZATION (EBSA)

The Employee Benefits Security Administration (EBSA) was created to help regulate, educate and assist the 150 million Americans covered by private retirement plans, health plans, and other welfare benefit plans.

EBSA's mandate is to balance proactive enforcement with compliance assistance. Part of its function is to provide assistance to plan fiduciaries, plan participants and beneficiaries. The EBSA helps educate plan sponsors, as well as other members of the employee benefits industry. Don't be afraid to contact the EBSA for free advice.

EBSA oversees the reporting requirements for the continuation of health-care provisions, as required under the Comprehensive Omnibus Budget Reconciliation Act of 1985 (COBRA). It also administers (and enforces) the requirements regarding health care portability created under the Health Insurance Portability and Accountability Act (HIPAA).

## LIABILITY & DISCLOSURE

Organizations like EBSA and the DOL understand that regulations are complicated. Honest mistakes happen, routinely. Never be afraid to contact these organizations if you discover that you have failed to comply with provisions of the law.

These organizations tend to be forgiving when honest, good faith mistakes have occurred. Government regulators are like the general public with sports figures or politicians. They are willing to forgive discretions when they are freely admitted and amends are made. The greatest problems occur when transgressions are denied and covered up. If you discover a problem, bring it up and get it fixed as soon as you can. Don't deny it and think it will go away.

You can learn more about EBSA at the following website address:

http://www.dol.gov/ebsa/

## EMPLOYEE POLYGRAPH PROTECTION ACT

Under EPPA, employers may not:
- Require,
- Request,
- Suggest, or,
- Cause an employee or prospective employee to

take or submit to any lie detector test.

Employers may not:
- Use,
- Accept,
- Refer to, or,
- Inquire about the results of any lie detector test

of an employee or prospective employee.

Employers may not:
- Discharge,
- Discipline,
- Discriminate against,
- Deny employment or promotion, or,
- Threaten to take any such action against and em-

ployee or prospective employee for the refusal to take
a test.

Employers also may not threaten to take any action against an
employee who files a complaint or testifies in any proceeding regarding the loss of rights afforded by the Act.

**Exemptions**

Federal, state and local governments are excluded.

Lie detector tests may be administered by the federal government to employees of federal contractors which are engaged in national security intelligence or counterintelligence functions.

The Act does include limited exemptions where polygraph tests
may be administered in the private sector. Polygraphs may be administered to employees who:
- Are reasonably suspected of involvement in a
  workplace incident that results in economic loss to
  the employer and,
  - Who had access to the property that is the
    subject of an investigation.
- To prospective employees of:
  - Armored car companies.

- o   Security alarm companies.
- o   Security guard firms who protect:
     - ▪   Facilities, materials or operations affecting health, safety, national security, or currency and other like instruments.
- o   Prospective employees of pharmaceutical and other firms authorized to:
     - ▪   Manufacture,
     - ▪   Distribute, or,
     - ▪   Dispense controlled substances.

This includes employers who will have direct access to controlled substances. It also includes current employees who had access to persons or property that are the subject of an ongoing investigation.

The EPPA is administered by the U.S. Wage and Hour Division.

## GARNISHMENT OF WAGES

Garnishment of employee wages by employers is regulated under the Consumer Credit Protection Act (CPCA), which is administered by the Wage and Hour Division.

## THE FAMILY AND MEDICAL LEAVE ACT

FMLA requires employers of 50 or more to give up to 12 weeks of unpaid, job-protected leave to eligible employees for:

- •   The birth and care of a newborn child within one year of birth.
- •   The placement (with the employee) of an adopted child.
- •   To care for a newly placed foster child within one year of placement.
- •   To care for an employee's spouse, child, or parent who has a serious health condition.
- •   A serious health condition that makes the employee unable to perform the essential functions of

his or her job.

- Any qualifying exigency which arises from an employee's spouse, son, daughter, or parent who is a covered military member on *covered active duty*.

Employees may take twenty-six weeks (during a single 12-month period) to care for a covered service member with a serious injury or illness. The service member must be a:

- o   Spouse.
- o   Son.
- o   Daughter.
- o   Parent.
- o   Next of kin to the employee (military caregiver leave).

This law is administered by the Wage and Hour Division. You can learn more about the act at:

http://www.dol.gov/whd/regs/statutes/fmla.htm.

# PLANT CLOSINGS & LAYOFFS

Plant closings and layoffs may be subject to the Worker Adjustment and Retraining Notification Act (WARN). WARN provides employees an early warning of impending layoffs or plant closings.

The Employment and Training Administration (ETA) provides information to the public on WARN. Neither the ETA nor the Department of Labor has administrative responsibility for the statute. It is enforced through private action in the federal courts.

# Chapter Ninety
## _____HR_____
## Compliance & Reporting

# COMMON ACRONYMS AND DEFINITIONS

The following are common acronyms and definitions that may be helpful in your work with HR.

AD&D Plan: Accidental Death and Dismemberment Plan
ADA: Americans with Disabilities Act
ADEA: Age Discrimination in Employment Act
ARRA: American Recovery and Reinvestment Act of 2009
ASO: Administrative Services Only
CDHC: Consumer-Driven Health Care
CFR: Code of Federal Regulations
CMS: Centers for Medicare and Medicaid Services – former Health Care Financing Administration
COBRA: Consolidated Omnibus Budget Reconciliation Act
DCAP: Dependent Care Assistance Program
DCTC: Dependent Care Tax Credit
DOL: Department of Labor
EAP: Employee Assistance Program
EBSA: Employee Benefits Security Administration – former Pension and Welfare Benefits Administration
EDI: Electronic Data Interchange
EFAST: ERISA Filing Acceptance System
EEOC: Equal Employment Opportunity Commission
EGTRRA: Economic Growth and Tax Relief Reconciliation Act
EOB: Explanation of Benefits

EOI: Evidence of Insurability
ERISA: Employee Retirement Income Security Act
FICA: Federal Insurance Contributions Act
FLSA: Fair Labor Standards Act
FMLA: Family and Medical Leave Act
FSA: Flexible Spending Arrangement
FUTA: Federal Unemployment Tax Act
GTL Insurance: Group Term Life Insurance
HCE: Highly Compensated Employee
HCFA: Health Care Financing Administration – now known as (CMS)
HCTC: Health Coverage Tax Credit
HDHC: High Deductible Health Coverage
HDHP: High Deductible Health Plan
Health FSA: Health Flexible Spending Arrangement
HEART Act: Heroes Earnings Assistance and Relief Tax Act of 2008
HHS: Department of Health and Human Services
HIPAA: Health Insurance Portability and Accountability Act
HIPAA SER: Health Insurance Portability and Accountability Act Special Enrollment Rights
HMO: Health Maintenance Organization
HRA: Health Reimbursement Arrangement
HAS: Health Savings Account
IRC: Internal Revenue Code
LTC: Long-term Care
LTD: Long-term Disability
MEWA: Multiple Employer Welfare Arrangement
MHPA: Mental Health Parity Act
MSP: Medicare Secondary Payer
MSA: Medical Savings Account (also known as an Archer MSA)
NAIC: National Association of Insurance Commissioners
NHCE: Non Highly Compensated Employee
NMHPA: Newborns' and Mothers' Health Protection Act
OCR: Office of Civil Rights
OTC: Over-the-counter Item or Drug
PCE: Preexisting Condition Exclusion

PEO: Professional Employer Organization
PHI: Protected Health Information
PPA: Pension Protection Act of 2006
POP: Premium Only Plan (Section 125 Cafeteria Plan)
PPO: Preferred Provider Organization
PWBA: Pension & Welfare Benefits Administration - now Employee Benefits Security Administration
QDRO: Qualified Domestic Relations Order
QMCSO: Qualified Medical Child Support Order
SAR: Summary Annual Report
SMM: Summary of Material Modifications
SPD: Summary Plan Description
STD: Short-term Disability
TPA: Third Party Administrator
USERRA: Uniformed Services Employment and Reemployment Rights Act
VEBA: Voluntary Employees' Beneficiary Association
VFC: Voluntary Fiduciary Correction Program
WHCRA: Women's Health and Cancer Rights Act

## Chapter Ninety-One
## _____HR_____
## Payroll Issues

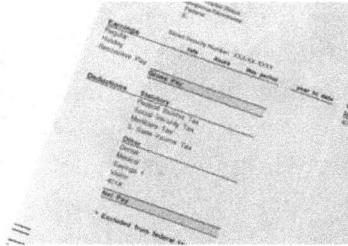

# PAYROLL PROCESSING

Every business should have a payroll system that maximizes its ability to stay on top of federal, state and local tax and withholding requirements. You also need a system to keep track of payments for health insurance and retirement plans.

The easiest and most efficient way to manage the payroll process is to outsource these functions to a reputable third party company. There are several national payroll companies. These can be a viable option for your business. Small payroll companies often have access to the same technology platforms as their larger competitors. Smaller companies may be able to deliver high quality services on a more personalized basis.

### HRIS

If you don't outsource, you might purchase software that will help you integrate your payroll with all of the other benefit and regulatory requirements of maintaining a business. The most advanced software will provide what is known as a Human Resource Information System (HRIS). HRIS software integrates human resource management and the information technology that is needed to run a business. An HRIS system will help you manage your basic HR activities. It will also help you manage the sophisticated data processing that is required for all but the smallest businesses.

Whether you use a payroll company or not, there are steps that every business must take in order to operate:

- All businesses must fill out IRS Form SS-4 to obtain an Employer Identification Number (EIN). You can apply for an EIN through the IRS website or contact the IRS directly. You will need to fill out IRS Form SS-4.

You can find Form SS-4 at the following location:

http://www.irs.gov/pub/irs-pdf/fss4.pdf

- Before hiring *employees* you must have your EIN. This becomes known as your Employer Tax ID.

- An EIN is necessary for the reporting of taxes and other documents to the IRS.

- And EIN is required for reporting information about your employees to state agencies.

- Obtain Local or State IDs and Permissions

  o You will need to pay an excise tax in the town or city where your business is located.

  o You may also need to obtain state and local licenses or ID numbers.

- Establish the difference between employee and independent contractor.

  o Independent contractors will be paid as

non-employees by your company.

o   For all full-time employees, you will need to withhold income taxes, Social Security and Medicare taxes. You must also pay unemployment taxes for all employees.

o   Remember to withhold taxes from any bonuses that you might pay.

o   You must send all taxes to the appropriate government entities.

- Form W-4.

o   Each employee must fill out Federal Income Tax Withholding Form W-4. This will help you determine the appropriate federal tax withholding. The IRS provides a withholding calculator on their website. Instructions are included on the form. You can locate this form at:

o   http://www.irs.gov/individuals/page/0,,id=14806,00.html

- Decide on a pay period.

o   Most states favor bi-monthly payments to employees.

- Determine when you must send withholdings to the IRS and to your state.

o   All employers must file Form 941, the Employer's Quarterly Federal Tax Return, along with the submission of employee withholdings. You can find the form here: http://www.irs.gov/pub/irs-pdf/f941.pdf

## RECORDKEEPING

The Federal Fair Labor Standards Act established employee

record keeping requirements for most businesses. If you have employees, you must set up an appropriate record keeping system to keep track of:

- Employee hours.

- Overtime.

- Exempt and non-exempt status of employees.

- Paid time off.

## SMALL BUSINESS TAXPAYERS

Employers who have an employment tax liability of $1,000 or less (for a year) may file Form 944, the Employer's Annual Federal Tax Return, instead of Form 941. The IRS will often notify eligible taxpayers by mail.

## COMBINED ANNUAL WAGE REPORTING (CAWR)

The U.S. government has a document matching program, entitled Combined Annual Wage Reporting (CAWR). This program compares the Employee Wage Information, which is reported to the Internal Revenue Service (IRS), with that reported to the Social Security Administration (SSA).

If the amounts that you report to the IRS do not match those from SSA, you may receive a notice requesting an explanation for the discrepancy.

The IRS may compute the additional taxes and/or penalties due and send you a bill. You may also receive notice CP253, or Letter 99C, regarding any missing Form W-2s. If the IRS determines that you have underreported employment taxes, they will issue notice CP251 or Letter 99C.

Pay attention to these notices. If you ignore them, you may be fined, or even (in extreme cases) spend time in jail.

# Chapter Ninety-Two
## HR
## Safety & Loss Control

# OSHA COMPLIANCE

In an earlier chapter, we discussed the Occupational Safety Act. OSHA is broad, sweeping legislation that affects every business in America.

Discussing the full extent of this law is beyond the scope of this book. However, in order to give you a useful snapshot of the major issues you must address with your business, this chapter will attempt to discuss the significant requirements of the legislation.

You can learn more about OSHA requirements at the following Web address:

http://www.osha.gov/dcsp/compliance_assistance/quickstarts/general_industry/gi_step1.html

If you have any questions, don't be afraid to call OSHA at 1-800-321-OSHA.

# OSHA Requirements — For Most (General Industry) Employers

## Hazard Communication Standard

If employees may be exposed to hazardous chemicals in the workplace, employers must prepare and implement a written Hazard Communication Program. They must also comply with other requirements of the standard.

## Emergency Action Plan Standard

When required by an OSHA standard, an emergency action plan must be in place. This plan should describe the actions employees should take to ensure their safety in a fire or other emergency situation.

## Fire Safety

When required by an OSHA standard, employers must have a fire prevention plan.

## Exit Routes

All employers must comply with OSHA's requirements for exit routes in the workplace.

## Walking/Working Surfaces

Slips, trips, and falls constitute the majority of general industry accidents. Therefore, OSHA is particularly vigilant regarding the safety of walking surfaces in the workplace.

The OSHA standards for walking and working surfaces apply to all permanent places of employment, except where only domestic, mining, or agricultural work is performed.

## Medical and First Aid

Employers must provide medical supplies and first-aid personnel which are commensurate with the hazards of the workplace.

The details of a workplace medical and first-aid program are dependent on the circumstances of each workplace and employer. If you have any hazards in your workplace, you should make sure that you have the appropriate materials and programs in place.

# Special Rules:

## Machinery

Employers with employees who operate heavy machinery, such as saws, slicers, shears, slitters & power presses may be subject to OSHA's Machine Guarding requirements.

Employers with employees who work with machines or equipment that could start up unexpectedly, or release hazardous energy, may be subject to OSHA's Lockout/Tagout requirements.

## Electrical

Electrical hazards are another area of major concern for OSHA. OSHA's electrical standards include both design requirements for electrical systems and safety-related work practices.

## Protective Gear

Employers must assess every operation in their workplace to determine if employees are required to wear personal protective equipment (PPE).

FYI: OSHA considers PPE to be the least desirable means of controlling employee exposure. OSHA prefers that companies use engineering changes and altered work practices to make safety improvements. If you can *reasonably* make your workplace safer, you are expected to do so.

## Respirators

If necessary to protect the health of employees, employers must provide appropriate respirators. Employers with poor air quality, or conditions which are hazardous to the lungs, must establish a Respiratory Protection program which meets the requirements of OSHA's Respiratory Protection standard.

## NOISE

If employees are exposed to excessive noise, defined as conditions that make normal conversation difficult, employers may be required to implement a Hearing Conservation Program.

## CONFINED SPACES

Employers are expected to evaluate their workplaces for the presence of confined spaces. A "confined space" has limited or restricted means for entry or exit, and is not designed for continuous employee occupancy.

Confined spaces include such areas as underground vaults, tanks, storage bins, manholes, pits, silos, process vessels, and pipelines.

Companies are expected to establish conditions which minimize employee use of such spaces.

## BODILY FLUIDS

OSHA has established a Bloodborne Pathogens Standard for employees who are exposed to blood or bodily fluids as part of their assigned duties. If your employees are exposed to bodily fluids, you must take the appropriate steps to protect them against the inadvertent transfer of harmful pathogens.

## POWERED INDUSTRIAL TRUCKS

If your company's employees operate forklifts, your company will be subject to OSHA's Powered Industrial Trucks standard.

## PUBLICATIONS

All companies are required to comply with OSHA laws. OSHA does not require that employers develop comprehensive safety and health training programs. However, the development and implementation of training programs is an effective way to prevent workplace injuries and illnesses, as well as comply with OSHA standards.

OSHA has produced a number of publications to help employers:

- Understand OSHA requirements and,

- Implement programs that comply with federal regulations.

The following publications may be particularly useful to you and your company.

**OSHA Small Business Handbook**
http://www.osha.gov/Publications/smallbusiness/small-business.html

**Hazard Awareness Advisor**
http://www.osha.gov/dts/osta/oshasoft/hazexp.html

**OSHA Training Resources**
http://www.osha.gov/dte/index.html

# RECORDKEEPING, REPORTING & POSTING

OSHA regulations vary — by industry and individual company. There are many variables that will determine the extent of OSHA's involvement in your business.

You should be aware of OSHA's requirements. The following pages highlight the major OSHA requirements regarding recordkeeping, reporting and posting.

A full list of all postings required by OSHA and the DOL can be found at the following Internet address:

http://www.dol.gov/oasam/programs/osdbu/sbrefa/poster/matrix.htm

## RECORDKEEPING

Employers in certain professions are required to keep records of workplace injuries and illnesses. Those in the most hazardous industries have the most stringent recordkeeping requirements.

Recordkeeping requirements are part of 29 CFR 1904. A full list of recordkeeping rules can be found at the following Web address:

http://www.osha.gov/pls/oshaweb/owasrch.search_form?p_doc_type=standards&p_toc_level=0

### Exempt Companies

Many companies are exempt from keeping OSHA injury and illness records (unless asked to do so in writing by OSHA or the Bureau of Labor Statistics). Companies in the following categories are not required to maintain such records:

- Companies with 10 or fewer employees during all of the previous calendar year.

- Certain low-hazard retail, service, finance, insurance, or real estate industries, as outlined in 29 CFR Part 1904, Subpart B, Appendix A.

If you do not qualify for these exemptions, you must comply with OSHA's recordkeeping requirements.

### Recordkeeping Handbook

If your company is affected by OSHA recordkeeping requirements, you should read OSHA's Recordkeeping Handbook to determine what your requirements might be.

The handbook can be found at the following website address:

http://www.osha.gov/recordkeeping/handbook/index.html

## REPORTING

All employers, regardless of size or industry, must report the work-related death of any employee, or the hospitalizations of three or more employees.

## OSHA POSTER

Every company must display an OSHA Poster (or their state's equivalent) in a prominent location in the workplace. Free posters can be ordered through the OSHA website, located at:

http://www.osha.gov/

## ACCESS TO EMPLOYEE EXPOSURE AND MEDICAL RECORDS

Under OSHA standards, employers must provide access to employee exposure and medical records to all:

- Employees.

- Designated employee representatives.

- OSHA.

Unless exempted, employers must maintain employee exposure records for 30 years. Employee medical records must be maintained for the duration of each employee's employment, plus 30 years.

## ADDITIONAL OSHA ASSISTANCE

Additional OSHA assistance can be found at the following website locations:

http://www.osha.gov/
http://www.osha.gov/dcsp/compliance_assistance/quickstarts/general_industry/gi_step7.html

# Chapter Ninety-Three
## HR
## Safety & Loss Control

# WORKPLACE VIOLENCE

Workplace violence is a serious safety and health issue. More than 10% of occupational deaths are the result of workplace homicide. Workplace violence is also a serious drain on business productivity and profitability.

OSHA has been charged with the regulatory management of workplace violence. While OSHA has committed significant time and resources toward its study, there are no specific regulatory standards for workplace violence.

### Environmental Conditions

OSHA has identified specific environmental conditions that are associated with workplace assaults. In order to help companies reduce the incidence of such violence, OSHA has developed:

- Control strategies,

- Guidelines, and,

- Recommendations.

### Be Vigilant

In your HR role, you must be continually watching for the signs of workplace violence. The signs can be subtle and hard to detect, even where the damage is emotionally and physically devastating.

**Four Major Categories**

Workplace violence falls into four major categories. They are as follows:

1   Criminal Intent

  • In this case, the perpetrator has no legitimate relationship to the business or its employee. This type of violence occurs in conjunction with a crime. Crimes include events such as robbery, shoplifting, trespassing, and terrorism. Eighty-five percent of workplace homicides fall into this category.

2   Customer/Client

  • In this case, the perpetrator has a legitimate relationship with the business.

  • The perpetrator becomes violent while being served by the business.

  • This includes customers, clients, patients, students, inmates, as well as any other group for which the business provides services.

  • A large portion of customer/client incidents occur in the health care industry. Common settings include nursing homes or psychiatric facilities. The victims may be patients or patient caregivers.

  • Police officers, prison staff, flight attendants, and teachers are professions which have a significant amount of workplace violence.

  • Customer/client workplace violence accounts for approximately 3% of all workplace homicides.

3   Worker-On-Worker

- In this instance, the perpetrator is an employee or former employee of the business.

- The perpetrator attacks or threatens current or past employee(s) in the workplace.

- Worker-on-worker fatalities account for approximately 7% of all workplace homicides.

4   Personal Relationship

- Here, the perpetrator does not have a relationship with the business.

- The perpetrator has a personal relationship with the intended victim.

- This category includes victims of domestic violence.

- Employees who are assaulted or threatened while at work account for about 5% of all workplace homicides.

Employees in the retail trades are most often affected by criminal intent violence.

Employees in the health care industry are normally affected by client, customer, or patient violence.

Worker-on-worker violence and personal relationship violence occur across all industry sectors.

**Violent Behaviors**

WPV, described by the U.S. government as "violent acts, including physical assaults and threats of assault, directed toward persons at work or on duty," encompasses many behaviors. Violent behaviors are not just physical assaults resulting in injury or death. These acts are everywhere, but they can be subtle, and not easily noticeable.

### Heavily Underreported

Workplace violence is heavily underreported. Threats, verbal abuse, hostility and harassment (including sexual) are not normally reported until the abuse reaches an employee's breaking point. Other forms, such as stalking, may not be reported until they reach the point of actual physical assault.

### Employer Resources

The following websites are effective resources for all employers, particularly those dealing with significant workplace violence issues.

http://www.osha.gov/SLTC/workplaceviolence/

http://www.cdc.gov/niosh/topics/violence/

# UNDERSTANDING WORKPLACE VIOLENCE

### Are You In Denial?

If you allow workplace violence to approach employee breaking points, you will create a poor work environment. This can lead to low productivity and high employee turnover. It can land you in court.

### Subtle Signs

Many HR managers are not aware of the prevalence of WPV in their companies. If you are not prone to violence yourself, it is often hard to conceive that others may act this way. The outward signs of WPV can be so subtle that large problems can exist deep beneath the surface, growing like a cancer in your business.

There are some effective strategies that you can use to reduce WPV in your workplace.

## STRATEGIES FOR TYPE I (CRIMINAL INTENT) PREVENTION

Industries in the retail trade, especially convenience and liquor stores, face higher than average risks for Type I WPV.

If you work in retail, there are specific environmental, behavioral, and administrative strategies that you can implement to reduce the risks of such violence. Such strategies include:

- **Environmental Interventions**

    o Keep excess cash in lock boxes where employees don't have access.

    o Provide adequate lighting control (indoor and outdoor).

    o Make sure that employees can see entrances (even if cameras must be used).

    o Control the access to exits.

    o Use adequate surveillance, such as mirrors and cameras, particularly closed-circuit cameras.

    o Provide adequate signage, including a warning that preventive measures have been taken against theft.

- **Behavioral Interventions**

    o Train your employees on appropriate robbery response.

    o Train employees on the use of safety equipment.

o   Train employees on how to deal with aggressive, drunk, or otherwise problem persons.

- **Administrative Interventions**

    o   Increase security during high risk hours of operations.

    o   Establish adequate precautions during opening and closing hours.

    o   Maintain a good working relationship with local police.

    o   Implement safety and security procedures for all employees.

# STRATEGIES FOR TYPE II (CUSTOMER/ CLIENT VIOLENCE) PREVENTION

No service business can eliminate customer complaints. Customers will gripe, even if your service is stellar.

Complaints are one thing. Violence is another.

You can reduce the incidence of client/customer violence by having enough well-trained staff members to effectively serve your client, customer, and/or patient needs. If your business is small, training and staffing may be a challenge, as financial resources can be tight.

There are some cost-effective steps that every service business can take to reduce the incidence and the risk of violence against employees. Here they are:

## RESPOND QUICKLY

Even if a problem cannot be fixed at once, your employees should still respond to the problem or need as quickly as possible.

For example: If you run a nursing home, patients will ring for a nurse if they need water, pain medication (usually before you can give it) or if they need a bedpan changed.

If your nurse cannot address your patient's issue immediately, your nurse should still *respond* to the call at once. Your nurse should not say, "I'll be right there," and not show up for half an hour. Your nurse should acknowledge the request and give a realistic time frame for response to the problem. An explanation can also be helpful.

If a patient or customer is given a realistic response, and a reason, they will not have unrealistic expectations and will be less prone toward a negative or violent response.

## NO ISOLATION

Social services or health care workers who work alone are much more vulnerable to physical assault. This is especially true in worker-client relationships, where the client has a criminal background, is mentally ill or emotionally disturbed.

Take whatever steps you can to reduce the unwarranted isolation of your employees. Have them work in pairs. When employees must visit remote locations of your facility, have them do so when others are around. Make sure that your parking facilities are well lighted, and that you encourage (and support) ways for employees to avoid walking to their cars alone or in isolation.

## TRAINING

Employees should be given training that helps them recognize the behavioral cues that precede violence. They should be taught violence de-escalation techniques, as well as interpersonal and communication skills that can help them diffuse violent situations.

In some jobs, employees should be trained in take-down and self-defense.

## PREVENTION STRATEGIES FOR TYPE III VIOLENCE (WORKER-ON-WORKER) PREVENTION

### Evaluate Prospective Workers

Preventing worker-on-worker violence begins during the hiring process. You should properly and thoroughly evaluate candidates, by using background checks and thoroughly verifying all candidate references.

### Training in Policies/Reporting

Employees should be trained on company workplace violence (WPV) definitions, policies, and procedures. They should be encouraged to report all prohibited behaviors between workers. This should include:

- Threats.

- Harassment.

- Bullying.

- Stalking.

- Sexual comments.

### Focus on Observable Behaviors

Perpetrators of worker-on-worker violence usually have intimate knowledge of their co-workers. They are well aware of company security measures, and may seek to avoid them. This means that a successful prevention strategy should provide procedures for reporting, and the addressing of observable behaviors that indicate a potential for violence. If an employee is "creepy," they could be a real creep.

# STRATEGIES FOR TYPE IV (PERSONAL RELATIONSHIP VIOLENCE) PREVENTION

### Abuse is Everywhere

Studies have shown that approximately 25% of relationships have some form of abuse.

Your company can help deal with the effects of this violence, even if it does not occur at your place of business. This can lead to a better work environment for all employees.

You can prevent personal relationship violence, and minimize its effects, by creating a supportive culture for the victims of abusive relationships. This includes assurances that no penalties exist for coming forward.

- Employees should know that complete confidentiality will be observed if they report abuse.

- Safety and security protocols should be implemented.

- Referrals to the appropriate community services should be provided as options to workers.

### Create Consequences

Companies should inform all workers about the consequences of interpersonal violence, or any other form of WPV.

Your company should communicate clearly, through policies and training, that violent behavior, however subtle, is inappropriate and will be dealt with severely.

## Chapter Ninety-Four
## HR
### HR Resources

# HR RESOURCES

There are many resources available to help you improve the HR functions at your company. Many of them are free, or come at a very low cost.

Before you hire high-priced HR consultants, or engage in a massive overhaul of your company practices, you should check these out.

### Associations & Organizations

Associations can be a highly useful source of industry specific information for the HR professional. Membership costs are usually quite reasonable and well worth the investment, for reasons far beyond HR issues.

The *Encyclopedia of Associations,* published by Gale Research Company, has a detailed list of most U.S. associations. This directory is available in most public libraries. You can visit a modified online version at the following address:

http://www.infoplease.com/ipa/A0004878.html

Another useful source for association information the Weddles Directory, which can be found online at:

http://www.weddles.com/associations/index.cfm.

**Websites**

There is an enormous amount of useful (and free) Human Resources information available over the Internet. The good news: If you run a Google search for "Human Resources," you will receive a list of nearly 400,000,000 websites. The bad news: Who's got time to sift through that morass of data?

I tried to narrow the list to a few dozen sites that will give you access to helpful information regarding a variety of useful HR topics. This list is not exhaustive, nor is it complete. It is, however, a good place to start if you are looking for quick answers to critical HR questions. Please let me know if you find other lists that are particularly useful.

## Top Websites:

American Society For Training and Development - http://www.astd.org/

Bureau of Labor Statistics - http://www.bls.gov/

Department of Labor ELAWS - http://www.dol.gov/elaws/

Department of Labor Index of Forms - http://webapps.dol.gov/libraryforms/FormsByTitle.asp/

Electric Library - http://www.elibrary.com/elibweb/elib/do/login

Employee Benefit Research Institute (EBRI) - http://www.ebri.org/

Equal Opportunity Commission - http://www.eeoc.gov/

Help Navigating DOL Laws and Regulations - http://www.dol.gov/compliance/

Human Resources Law Index - http://www.hrlawindex.com/

List of Laws - http://www.dol.gov/opa/aboutdol/lawsprog.htm

Occupational Safety and Health Administration - http://www.osha.gov/

Office of Workers' Compensation Programs (OWCP) - http://www.dol.gov/owcp/

Overview of the American Recovery and Reinvestment Act of 2009 (Recovery Act) - http://www.dol.gov/recovery/

Pension Benefit Guarantee Corp - http://www.pbgc.gov/

Society for Human Resources Management -

http://www.shrm.org/Pages/default.aspx

U.S. Equal Opportunity Commission - http://www.eeoc.gov/

Veterans Employment & Training Service (VETS) - http://www.dol.gov/vets/

Wage and Hour Division (WHD) – http://www.dol.gov/whd

Workforce Online - http://www.workforce.com/

## IRS:

http://www.irs.gov/

IRS Tax Topics  http://www.irs.gov/taxtopics/

## Retirement Plans (IRS)

http://www.irs.gov/retirement/sponsor/article/0,,id=155347,00.html

## Top Jobsites:

Career Builder  www.careerbuilder.com

Monster  www.monster.com

America's Job Bank  www.ajb.dni.us

NationJob Network  www.nationjob.com

## Publications

*HR Magazine* is the most widely read HR publication in the United States. This monthly magazine is a good source for topical information that may be helpful in your business. While much of it is tailored toward larger organizations, some of it translates to smaller, private companies.

There are many other good publications. If you are looking for books on the subject, I recommend that you visit Amazon or Barnes and Noble and read the reviews.

# Chapter Ninety-Five
## _____HR_____
## HR Summary

Managing the HR functions of a small business is a challenging and mundane task that never ends. Personnel must be hired, trained and fired. Ever-changing benefits must be reviewed and adjusted. Strangling regulations must be followed.

There is no manual that makes this easy. It will never be easy. It is a thankless task that receives too little notice by employees or management. Yet, HR is a vital organ of any business. Remove HR and a business dies.

I hope that this book will be of help as you push your own Sisyphean HR boulder.

Private business is the lifeblood of the American way. Press on. It matters greatly. I applaud you for your efforts and hope to be a small part in your continued success.

life insurance, 320–21
non-qualified deferred compensation,
  296
knowledge
areas of, 36
assessing, 72
desire for, 13
employee, 104
gap, 108–9
individual's cumulative, 74
of the industry, 66
product, 67, 108
sharing, 105
L
labor, child, 378
labor market, 109
labor standards. See also hiring process;
  job interview
  Bureau of Labor Statistics, 189, 401,
    413
  Child Labor Laws, 378
  Department of Labor, major laws of,
    370–89
  Department of Labor Index of
    Forms, 413
  Fair Labor Standards Act (FLSA),
    89, 121, 377–78
  Federal Fair Labor Standards Act
    (FLSA), 378
  U.S. Department of Labor (DOL),
    283, 370, 380, 388–89
labor statistics
  Bureau of Labor Statistics, 189, 401,
    413
labor unions, 371
language discrimination, 61, 63
laws. See regulatory compliance
lawsuits, 26, 327
layoffs, 388
learning environment, 115
leased employees, 98–99, 194–95

leave of absence. See also benefits
about, 141, 350
family leave, 101 (See also Family
  and Medical Leave Act (FMLA))
Family Medical Leave Act, 90, 330,
  387–88
medical leave, 328, 350 (See also
  Family and Medical Leave Act
  (FMLA))
military, 380–81, 388
military leave, 380–81, 388
pregnancy leave (See Family and
  Medical Leave Act (FMLA))
sick leave, 90
unpaid leave, 141, 373, 380–81
legal
conflict resolution, 170–72
conflicts, 166
dependents, 336
guidelines, 246
requirements, 229, 297
responsibilities, 226
rights, 351
tax deductions, 274, 294
trouble, 61
lie detector tests, 76. See also Employee
  Polygraph Protection Act (EPPA)
life insurance. See also experience
  rating; regulatory compliance
corporate owned, 293
Corporate Owned Life Insurance
  (COLI), 88, 293, 329, 363–64
group term life insurance, 334–35
key person, 320–21
policy, 304, 306–7
split dollar life insurance, 304–8, 311
LinkedIn, 70, 93, 101
living trust, 313
long-term care insurance, 217
long-term disability (LTD), 390
loyalty, 81, 94, 127, 138, 148, 219, 232

## About the Author

James McSweeney is a highly-skilled business innovator. He has built one of the country's most comprehensive, diversified national services organizations. James's companies include Comprehensive Insurance Providers, DaVinci Capital Management, DaVinci Advisory Group, Safe Hire Investigations, HR Solutions Group, Comprehensive Payroll, and CIP Real Estate.

James and his employees provide services to more than a thousand businesses throughout the country. As part of today's financial leading edge, James was asked to become a member of the National Financial Broker Dealer Advisory Board, the Massachusetts Health Connector Broker Advisory Committee, as well as the broker Advisory Boards of many nationally recognized health plans.

James has been recognized for his work in supporting charitable organizations. He lives in the Boston area with his wife and family. He can be reached through his company website at www.askcip.com.

YOU CAN ALWAYS FIND MORE DE-
TAILED INFORMATION, INCLUDING REG-
ULATORY UPDATES AT THE FOLLOWING
WEBSITE ADDRESS:

WWW.ASKCIP.COM